CW00348735

Copyright © 2020 by Rosemary King

All rights reserved. No part of this publication may be reproduced, distributed, or transmitted in any form or by any means, including photocopying, recording, or other electronic or mechanical methods, without the prior written permission of the publisher, except in the case of brief quotations embodied in critical reviews and certain other noncommercial uses permitted by copyright law.

Disclaimer: The information presented is purely to share my experience and for entertainment purposes. As always, check with a doctor before making any fitness or nutrition changes. The author disclaims liability for any damage, mishap, or injury that may occur from engaging in any activities or ideas from this site. All information posted is merely for educational and informational purposes. It is not intended as a substitute for professional advice. Should you decide to act upon any information in this book, you do so at your own risk. The content displayed in the book is the intellectual property of the author. You may not reuse, republish, or reprint such content without our written consent.

Contents

Introduction ·· **11**

Paleo Slow Cooker Breakfast Recipes ········· **13**

Cinnamon And Raisins Oatmeal ·········· 13

Chia And Strawberry Porridge ··············· 13

Chia Seeds Porridge ······················ 13

Delicious Breakfast Bowls ················· 14

Bacon And Leeks Breakfast Casserole ······· 14

Strawberries Breakfast Mix ················ 14

Hearty Breakfast Pork Mix ················· 15

Delicious Sausage and Eggs Casserole ······· 15

Special Breakfast Delight ················· 15

Easy Apple Porridge ······················ 16

Banana Oatmeal ························· 16

Cherries Oatmeal ························ 16

Butternut Squash Bowls ·················· 17

Delicious Mexican Breakfast ··············· 17

Special Egg Casserole ···················· 18

Easy Mushroom Scramble ················· 18

Simple Breakfast Meatloaf ················ 18

Breakfast Sweet Potatoes Casserole ········· 18

Easy Eggs and Chorizo Breakfast ·········· 19

Yam Breakfast Mix ······················· 19

Egg Casserole ·························· 19

Carrots And Zucchinis Bowls ·············· 19

Breakfast Apple Butter ··················· 20

Butternut Squash Breakfast Mix ············ 20

Sausage Casserole ······················ 21

Spinach And Tomato Casserole ············ 21

Veggie Omelet ·························· 21

Broccoli And Ham Mix ···················· 22

Delicious Frittata ······················· 22

Breakfast Apples and Sauce ··············· 22

Breakfast Meatloaf ······················ 23

Breakfast Yams ························· 23

Chorizo Mix Breakfast ···················· 23

Salsa Bowls ···························· 23

Breakfast Pulled Pork ···················· 24

Sweet Potato Breakfast Mix ··············· 24

Simple Breakfast Pie ····················· 24

Blueberries Coconut Oatmeal ············· 25

Almond Oatmeal ························ 25

Cranberry Mix ·························· 25

Herbed Breakfast Sweet Potatoes ··········· 26

Mexican Breakfast ······················· 26

Sausage and Eggs ······················ 27

Eggs and Bacon Casserole ················ 27

Spiced Fruits Mix ······················· 27

Eggs And Scallions ······················ 27

Jalapeno Eggs Mix ······················ 28

Tomato And Scallions Frittata ············· 28

Tasty Breakfast Meatloaf ················· 29

Breakfast Salad ························· 29

Delicious Veggie Omelet ·················· 29

Green Breakfast Mix ····················· 30

Eggs And Bacon Mix ····················· 30

Zucchini And Carrots Mix ················· 30

Thyme Eggs And Sweet Potatoes · · · · · · · · · · · 31

Chorizo Breakfast Casserole · · · · · · · · · · · · · 31

Eggs and Sweet Potato Pesto · · · · · · · · · · · · · 31

Delicious Pumpkin Butter · · · · · · · · · · · · · · · · 32

Squash And Cranberry Sauce · · · · · · · · · · · · · 32

Delicious Carrot Breakfast · · · · · · · · · · · · · · · · 32

Paleo Slow Cooker Side Dish Recipes · · · · · · · · · · · · · · · · · · **33**

Summer Veggies Surprise · · · · · · · · · · · · · · · 33

Simple Broccoli Mix · · · · · · · · · · · · · · · · · · · 33

Delicious Green Beans Mix · · · · · · · · · · · · · · · 33

Mushroom Cauliflower Rice · · · · · · · · · · · · · · · 33

Sausage Side Dish · 34

Parsley Sweet Potatoes · · · · · · · · · · · · · · · · · 34

Sweet Cabbage · 34

Delicious Sweet Potatoes and Bacon · · · · · · · · · 35

Flavored Carrots · 35

Tasty Mushroom Mix · · · · · · · · · · · · · · · · · · · 35

Spinach And Cauliflower Rice · · · · · · · · · · · · · 36

Delicious Glazed Carrots · · · · · · · · · · · · · · · · 36

Delicious Brussels Sprouts · · · · · · · · · · · · · · · 37

Shredded Sweet Potatoes · · · · · · · · · · · · · · · · 37

Orange And Sage Sweet Potatoes · · · · · · · · · · · 38

Cauliflower And Broccoli Mix · · · · · · · · · · · · · · 38

Simple Carrots And Parsnips · · · · · · · · · · · · · · 38

Special Acorn Squash and Cranberry Sauce · 39

Crazy Eggplant Delight · · · · · · · · · · · · · · · · · 39

Tasty Zucchini · 39

Zucchini, Squash And Mushrooms Mix · · · · · · · 40

Easy Brussels Sprouts · · · · · · · · · · · · · · · · · · 40

Pear And Sausage Mix · · · · · · · · · · · · · · · · · 40

Brussels Sprouts And Pine Nuts · · · · · · · · · · · 41

Scalloped Sweet Potatoes · · · · · · · · · · · · · · · · 41

Broccoli Side Dish · 41

Spinach And Carrots Mix · · · · · · · · · · · · · · · · 42

Simple Garlic Squash Mix · · · · · · · · · · · · · · · · 42

Brussels Sprouts And Apple Sauce · · · · · · · · · · 43

Celery And Beets · 43

Cauliflower Pilaf · 43

Sausage Side Dish · 44

Creamy Apples And Sweet Potatoes · · · · · · · · · 44

Creamy Carrots · 44

Zucchini And Squash Mix · · · · · · · · · · · · · · · · 45

Hot Cauliflower Mix · 45

Sweet Potatoes and Parsley · · · · · · · · · · · · · · 46

Glazed Carrots · 46

Green Beans And Tomatoes Mix · · · · · · · · · · · · 46

Chard Mix · 47

Celery, Bok Choy And Chestnuts · · · · · · · · · · · 47

Spicy Carrots · 47

Simple Tomato Mix · 47

Spicy Collard Greens · · · · · · · · · · · · · · · · · · 48

Fresh Butternut Squash Side Salad · · · · · · · · · · 48

Cauliflower Rice and Spinach · · · · · · · · · · · · · 48

Maple Sweet Potatoes Side Dish · · · · · · · · · · · 49

Creamy Spinach · 49

Beets And Cabbage Mix · · · · · · · · · · · · · · · · · 49

Chinese Brussels Sprouts · · · · · · · · · · · · · · · · 50

Balsamic Beets And Capers · · · · · · · · · · · · · · 50

Leeks And Fennel Mix · · · · · · · · · · · · · · · · · · 50

Sweet Potato Mash · 51

Kale Side Dish · 51

Incredible Veggie Mix · · · · · · · · · · · · · · · · · · 51

Cauliflower Mash · 52

Simple Scallions And Endives · · · · · · · · · · · · · · · · 52   Sweet Potatoes with Orange and Sage · · · · · · · 52

Paleo Slow Cooker Snack and Appetizer Recipes · · · · · · · · · · · · · · **53**

Simple Meatballs · 53   Meatballs Appetizer · 62

Chicken Spread · 53   Cauliflower and Jalapeno Dip · · · · · · · · · · · · · · 62

Tasty Chicken Wings · 53   Zucchini Bites · 63

Pepperoni Dip · 53   Coconut And Spinach Dip · · · · · · · · · · · · · · · · 63

Different Chicken Dip · 54   Cauliflower Bites · 64

Carrot Dip · 54   Special Mushrooms Appetizer · · · · · · · · · · · · · 64

Eggplant Spread · 54   Veggie Salsa · 65

Tasty Fish Sticks · 55   Squash Cubes · 65

Spicy Pecans · 55   Thyme Zucchini Snack · · · · · · · · · · · · · · · · · · 65

Tasty Sausage Appetizer · · · · · · · · · · · · · · · · · 55   Bacon Olives · 66

Asparagus Spread · 56   Mushroom Appetizer Salad · · · · · · · · · · · · · · · 66

Crab And Onion Dip · 56   Caramelized Onion Appetizer · · · · · · · · · · · · · · 67

Tomato And Artichoke Spread · · · · · · · · · · · · · 57   Sweet Potato Patties · · · · · · · · · · · · · · · · · · · 67

Amazing Eggplant Dip · · · · · · · · · · · · · · · · · · · 57   Tomato Salsa · 68

Incredible Spinach Dip · · · · · · · · · · · · · · · · · · · 58   Shrimp And Tomato Appetizer Bowls · · · · · · · · · 68

Coconut Meatballs · 58   Spicy Sausage Appetizer · · · · · · · · · · · · · · · · 69

Delicious Chicken Meatballs · · · · · · · · · · · · · · · 58   Zucchini Spread · 69

Apple Vinegar Cashew Dip · · · · · · · · · · · · · · · · 58   Cocktail Meatballs · 70

Smoked Cauliflower And Cashew Dip · · · · · · · · 59   Hot Dip · 70

Cauliflower, Tomatoes And Mushrooms Dip · · 59   Chicken Bites · 70

Cauliflower Hummus · 59   Seafood Salad · 70

Candied Pecans · 60   Apple Dip · 71

Chicken Wings · 60   Artichokes Salad · 71

Chicken Strips · 61   Chicken Dip · 71

Mussels Salad · 61   Radish Dip · 72

Olives Salad · 62   Tomato Dip · 72

Paleo Slow Cooker Main Dish Recipes · **73**

Flavored Tilapia · 73   Italian Beef Roast · 73

Special Seafood Chowder · · · · · · · · · · · · · · · · 73   Pork Shoulder Mix · 74

Easy Chicken Soup · 73   Pumpkin Soup · 74

Easy Slow Cooked Beef · 74

Cabbage Soup · 74

Great Veggie Mix · 75

Easy Beef Stew · 75

Simple Chili · 75

Dill Sea Bass · 75

Italian Chicken · 76

Elegant Salmon Dish · 76

Seafood Stew · 76

Divine Shrimp Scampi · 76

Steamed Pompano · 77

Special Poached Milkfish · 77

Great Catfish Dish · 77

Asian Style Salmon · 77

Lamb Stew · 78

Tasty Beef And Broccoli · 78

Pork Loin Mix · 78

Mexican Chicken Soup · 78

Easy Salsa Chicken · 79

Shredded Chicken Soup · 79

Easy Turkey Meatballs · 79

Garlicky Wings · 79

Chicken Curry · 80

Sweet Chicken Mix · 80

Chicken Stew · 80

Stylish Tuna Dish · 80

Wonderful Shrimp And Crawfish · · · · · · · · · · · · · 81

Tasty Braised Squid · 81

Seabass and Coconut Cream · · · · · · · · · · · · · · · 81

Jamaican Salmon · 82

Simple Clams · 82

Delicious Clam Chowder · 82

Easy Seafood Gumbo · 83

Coconut Curry Shrimp · 83

Lemon And Dill Trout · 83

Elegant Tilapia and Asparagus · · · · · · · · · · · · · · · 84

Seafood Chowder · 84

Tasty Seafood Stew · 84

Shrimp Mix · 84

Indian Chicken · 85

Turkey Breast And Figs Mix · · · · · · · · · · · · · · · 85

Simple Summer Soup · 85

Beef And Veggie Chili · 86

Apple Pork Loin · 86

Clam Chowder · 86

Slow Cooked Shrimp · 87

Fish Curry · 87

Italian Shrimp · 87

Asian Style Salmon · 88

Saffron Halibut Mix · 88

Cauliflower Cream · 89

Spring Cod And Sauce · 89

Cod With Tomatoes And Olives · · · · · · · · · · · · · 89

Tomato Shrimp · 90

Shrimp And Pineapple Sauce · · · · · · · · · · · · · · 90

Shrimp And Red Pepper Stew · · · · · · · · · · · · · · 91

Tomatoes And Mussels Soup · · · · · · · · · · · · · · 91

Italian Seafood Stew · 92

Salmon with Onions and Carrots · · · · · · · · · · · · 92

Slow Cooker Shrimp Dish · · · · · · · · · · · · · · · · 92

Indian Chicken Dish · 93

Delicious Turkey Breast · 93

American Roast · 93

Thai Chicken Soup · 94

Cod with Tomatoes and Olives · · · · · · · · · · · · · · 94

Unbelievable Turkey Chili · · · · · · · · · · · · · · · · · · 94

Salmon Fillets and Lemon Sauce · · · · · · · · · · · 94

Turkey Breast And Sweet Potatoes · · · · · · · · · 95

Mussels Stew · 95

Palestinian Chicken · 95

Cod Curry · 96

Salmon Dinner Mix · 96

Salmon, Carrots and Broccoli · · · · · · · · · · · · · · 96

Salmon and Special Sauce · · · · · · · · · · · · · · · · 96

Squid Stew · 97

Lemony Mackerel · 97

Delicious Pulled Chicken · · · · · · · · · · · · · · · · · · 97

Roasted Chicken · 98

Simple Italian Chicken · 98

Wonderful Salsa Chicken · · · · · · · · · · · · · · · · · 98

Superb Chicken Soup · 99

Divine Turkey Breast · 99

Cashew Chicken · 99

Sweet Chicken · 99

Chicken Stew · 100

Ginger Duck · 100

Chicken And Sausage Delight · · · · · · · · · · · · · 100

Savory Chicken · 100

Delicious Stuffed Chicken Breasts · · · · · · · · · · 101

Flavored Turkey Wings · · · · · · · · · · · · · · · · · · 101

Tasty Kimchi Chicken · · · · · · · · · · · · · · · · · · · 101

Wonderful Chicken · 101

Tasty Greek Chicken · 102

Mexican Chicken · 102

Chicken Chowder · 102

Flavored Chicken Soup · · · · · · · · · · · · · · · · · · 102

Chicken and Olives · 103

Italian Chicken · 103

Pineapple Chicken · 103

Lemon and Garlic Chicken · · · · · · · · · · · · · · · · 103

Creamy Chicken · 104

Chicken Breasts and Peach Sauce · · · · · · · · · · 104

Turkey Gumbo · 104

Turkey and Orange Sauce · · · · · · · · · · · · · · · · 104

Cinnamon Chicken · 105

Chicken and Celery · 105

French Chicken and Bacon · · · · · · · · · · · · · · · · 105

Creole Chicken, Sausage and Shrimp · · · · · · · 106

Chicken and Apricot Sauce · · · · · · · · · · · · · · · 106

Flavored Chicken Thighs · · · · · · · · · · · · · · · · · 106

Creamy Chicken and Broccoli · · · · · · · · · · · · · 107

Salsa Chicken Soup · 107

Hearty Pork Ribs · 107

Simple And Easy Roast · · · · · · · · · · · · · · · · · · 107

Mexican Pork Delight · 108

Hawaiian Pork · 108

Incredible Pork Tenderloin · · · · · · · · · · · · · · · · 108

Super Easy Pork Dinner · · · · · · · · · · · · · · · · · · 108

Simple Pork Stew · 109

Simple Beef Stew · 109

Lamb Stew · 109

Flavored Lamb Leg · 109

Exotic Lamb Curry · 110

Asian Style Ribs · 110

Tasty Lamb Shanks · 110

Greek Lamb · 110

Lamb And Bacon Stew · · · · · · · · · · · · · · · · · · · 111

French Lamb Chops · 111

Amazing Mediterranean Pork · · · · · · · · · · · · · · 111

Beef and Veggies · 111

Special Roast · 112

Delicious Beef And Pearl Onions · · · · · · · · · · · 112

Light And Flavored Beef · · · · · · · · · · · · · · · · · 112

Beef Brisket Delight · 112

Perfect Beef And Eggplants · · · · · · · · · · · · · · 113

Beef Cheeks · 113

Mediterranean Lamb · · · · · · · · · · · · · · · · · · · 113

Lamb and Mushrooms · · · · · · · · · · · · · · · · · · 113

Rich Lamb Delight · 114

Slow Cooked Sausages and Sauce · · · · · · · · 114

Pork Shoulder · 114

Flavored Beef · 114

Beef Chili · 115

Beef Stew · 115

Lamb Stew · 115

Beef Soup · 115

Tasty Ham Soup · 116

Beef and Dill · 116

Thai Pork Stew · 116

Beef Curry · 116

Creamy Beef · 117

Winter Beef and Mushrooms · · · · · · · · · · · · · 117

Tender Lamb Shanks · · · · · · · · · · · · · · · · · · · 117

Smoked Lamb Chops · · · · · · · · · · · · · · · · · · · 117

Ribs and Apple Sauce · · · · · · · · · · · · · · · · · · 118

Paleo Slow Cooker Dessert Recipes · **119**

Sweet Cookies · 119

Glazed Pecans · 119

Simple Poached Pears · · · · · · · · · · · · · · · · · · 119

Spiced Pears · 119

Simple Apples Stew · 120

Cinnamon Almonds Mix · · · · · · · · · · · · · · · · · 120

Lemony Apples · 120

Vanilla Apple Butter · 121

Raspberry Cake · 121

Chocolate Cake · 122

Pumpkin Cake · 122

Pear Dessert · 122

Orange Pudding · 123

Brownies · 123

Apple Crisp · 123

Lemon Cookies · 123

Berry Cobbler · 124

Berry Crumble · 124

Easy Apples Dessert · · · · · · · · · · · · · · · · · · · 124

Apple Bread · 124

Easy Peach Pie · 125

Banana Dessert · 125

Coffee Cookies · 125

Peanut Cake · 125

Blackberry Cake · 126

Special Dessert · 126

Apple Stew · 126

Strawberry Pudding · 126

Pumpkin Pudding Cake · · · · · · · · · · · · · · · · · 127

Coconut Lemon Jam · · · · · · · · · · · · · · · · · · · 127

Cherry Cream · 127

Strawberry Stew · 128

Carrot Pudding · 128

Apple Cauliflower Rice · · · · · · · · · · · · · · · · · · 129

Baby Carrots Bowls ························ 129

Dates Pudding ···························· 130

Almond Banana Cream ···················· 130

Papaya And Banana Dessert ··············· 131

Avocado Cake ···························· 131

Coconut And Green Tea Cream ············· 132

Rose Cauliflower Rice Pudding ············· 132

Cauliflower Rice Pudding ·················· 132

Pumpkin and Chia Pudding ················ 133

Apples and Sweet Sauce ·················· 133

Cherry Compote ························· 134

Plum Bowls ···························· 134

Almond Chia Pudding ····················· 135

Cinnamon Blueberries Cream ·············· 135

Cherry Bowls ··························· 136

Cashew Cake ··························· 136

Lemon Pudding ························· 137

Pumpkin Cake ·························· 137

Orange Pudding ························· 137

Fruits Mix ····························· 137

Plum Compote ·························· 138

Apple Cake ···························· 138

Conclusion ·································· **139**

Introduction

Slow cooker recipes belong to ultimately convenient homemade foods worth trying and worth cooking no matter how experienced you are. The simple idea of fixing a meal and letting it cook itself is a perfect one for working people, busy moms and those who prefer to cook as little as possible. The slow cooker is great because it prevents any kitchen from overheating, saves your time and cooks perfectly even the most common ingredients.

This cookbook will help you to combine the simplicity of slow cooker and healthy choices only the Paleo diet can provide. Enjoy your slow cooker meals without sacrificing your Paleo regime and have fun while cooking! This amazing slow cooker cookbook is stack-full of Paleo and Slow Cooker recipes for any taste and any experience level. The very first breakfasts will make you crave for more. Try your new Paleo desserts, rediscover classics of Paleo cooking with the cookbook you've always needed in your kitchen.

With this Paleo Slow Cooker cookbook, you will always be able to put a healthy Paleo meal on your table with no fuss after half an hour of preparations. Dump and go, let it cook the way it is supposed to. If you know very little about slow cooking, this cookbook will teach you. If you are an experienced cook, it will inspire you to try something completely new. Indulge in veggie and meat dishes, have fun while exploring Paleo desserts. Because health and taste are what Paleo cooking is all about.

Paleo Slow Cooker Breakfast Recipes

Cinnamon And Raisins Oatmeal

Preparation time: 10 minutes
Cooking time: 8 hours
Servings: 2

Ingredients:

¼ cup walnuts, chopped
1 tablespoon coconut flour
1 tablespoon flax meal
1 cup cashew milk
¼ teaspoon cinnamon powder
1 teaspoon chia seeds
2 tablespoons raisins
1 tablespoon stevia

Directions:

In your slow cooker, combine the walnuts with coconut flour, flax meal, cashew milk, cinnamon, chia seeds, raisins and stevia, toss, cover and cook on Low for 8 hours. Divide into bowls and serve. Enjoy!

Nutrition:

calories 201, fat 4, fiber 5, carbs 12, protein 8

Chia And Strawberry Porridge

Preparation time: 10 minutes
Cooking time: 6 hours
Servings: 2

Ingredients:

2 tablespoons chia seeds
¼ cup water
1 green apple, cored and grated
2 tablespoons coconut, desiccated
4 strawberries, halved
½ cup coconut milk
2 tablespoons hazelnuts

Directions:

In your slow cooker, combine the chia seeds with water, apple, coconut strawberries, coconut milk and hazelnuts, stir, cover, cook on Low for 6 hours, divide into 2 bowls and serve for breakfast. Enjoy!

Nutrition:

calories 200, fat 3, fiber 6, carbs 14, protein 9

Easy Porridge

Preparation time: 10 minutes
Cooking time: 6 hours
Servings: 3

Ingredients:

2 bananas, peeled and mashed
¾ cup almond meal
2 cups coconut milk
1 teaspoon cinnamon powder
¼ cup flax meal
½ teaspoon ginger, grated
A pinch of cloves, ground
A pinch of nutmeg, ground

Directions:

In your slow cooker, combine the bananas with the almond meal, coconut milk, cinnamon, flax meal, ginger, cloves and nutmeg, toss, cover, cook on Low for 6 hours, divide into bowls and serve. Enjoy!

Nutrition:

calories 210, fat 4, fiber 5, carbs 14, protein 7

Chia Seeds Porridge

Preparation time: 10 minutes
Cooking time: 7 hours
Servings: 3

Ingredients:

1 and ½ cups almond milk
2 tablespoons flaxseed
3 tablespoons chia seeds
3 tablespoons coconut, shredded and unsweetened
A handful almonds, chopped
1 teaspoon vanilla extract
1 tablespoon gelatin
1 mango, peeled and cubed

Directions:

In your slow cooker, combine the milk with flaxseed, chia seeds, coconut, almonds, vanilla and gelatin, toss, cover and cook on Low for 7 hours.
Divide into bowls, sprinkle mango pieces on top and serve. Enjoy!

Nutrition:

calories 210, fat 4, fiber 6, carbs 15, protein 6

Apple Butter

Preparation time: 10 minutes
Cooking time: 8 hours
Servings: 10

Ingredients:

Juice of 1 lemon
1 teaspoon allspice
1 teaspoon clove, ground
1 teaspoon ginger powder
3 pounds apples, peeled, cored and chopped
1 tablespoon cinnamon, ground
1 and ½ cups water
¼ teaspoon nutmeg, ground
1 cup maple syrup

Directions:

In your slow cooker, mix apples with water, lemon juice, allspice, clove, ginger powder, cinnamon, maple syrup and nutmeg.
Stir, cover and cook on Low for 8 hours.
Leave your mix to cool down for 10 minutes, blend using an immersion blender and pour into small jars.
Serve for breakfast!
Enjoy!

Nutrition:

calories 150, fat 3, fiber 1, carbs 4, protein 3

Delicious Breakfast Bowls

Preparation time: 10 minutes
Cooking time: 8 hours
Servings: 4

Ingredients:

½ cup almonds, soaked for 12 hours and drained
½ cup walnuts, soaked for 12 hours and drained
2 apples, peeled, cored and cubed
1 butternut squash, peeled and cubed
1 teaspoon cinnamon powder
1 tablespoon coconut sugar
½ teaspoon nutmeg, ground
1 cup coconut milk
Maple syrup for serving

Directions:

Put almonds and walnuts in your blender, add some of the soaking water, blend really well and transfer to your slow cooker.
Add apples, squash, cinnamon, coconut sugar, nutmeg and coconut milk, stir, cover and cook on Low for 8 hours.
Use a potato masher to mash the whole mix, divide into bowls and serve.
Enjoy!

Nutrition:

calories 140, fat 1, fiber 2, carbs 2, protein 5

Bacon And Leeks Breakfast Casserole

Preparation time: 10 minutes
Cooking time: 2 hours
Servings: 8

Ingredients:

2 leeks, sliced
5 bacon slices, cooked and chopped
A pinch of salt and black pepper
6 eggs, whisked
2 teaspoons thyme, chopped
2 cups coconut cream
1 cup coconut milk
1 tablespoon mustard
A pinch of nutmeg, ground
½ cup parsley, chopped
Cooking spray

Directions:

In a bowl, combine the eggs with thyme, salt, pepper coconut cream and milk, mustard, nutmeg and parsley and whisk well.
Grease your slow cooker with cooking spray, arrange bacon and leeks on the bottom, pour the eggs mix, spread, cover and cook on High for 2 hours.
Slice, divide between plates and serve for breakfast.
Enjoy!

Nutrition:

calories 200, fat 4, fiber 6, carbs 14, protein 8

Strawberries Breakfast Mix

Preparation time: 10 minutes
Cooking time: 8 hours
Servings: 8

Ingredients:

2 cups strawberries
2 cups almond milk
6 cups water
1 cup coconut flakes
1 teaspoon cinnamon powder
1 teaspoon vanilla extract

Directions:

In your slow cooker, combine the strawberries with almond milk, water, coconut, cinnamon and vanilla, toss, cover and cook on Low for 8 hours.
Divide into bowls and serve.
Enjoy!

Nutrition:

calories 200, fat 3, fiber 5, carbs 15, protein 11

Tasty Veggie Frittata

Preparation time: 10 minutes
Cooking time: 2 hours
Servings: 4

Ingredients:

Cooking spray	¼ cup spinach, chopped
6 eggs	
4 ounces mushrooms, chopped	2 green onions, chopped
1 teaspoon garlic powder	¼ cup cherry tomatoes, chopped
A pinch of black pepper	1 teaspoon olive oil

Directions:

Spray your slow cooker with cooking spray and leave aside for now.
Heat up a pan with the oil over medium heat; add onions, spinach, mushrooms and tomatoes, stir and sauté for a couple of minutes.
Transfer this to your slow cooker, add eggs, a pinch of pepper and garlic powder, stir gently, cover and cook on High for 2 hours.
Divide between plates and serve hot.
Enjoy!

Nutrition:

calories 140, fat 2, fiber 2, carbs 4, protein 4

Hearty Breakfast Pork Mix

Preparation time: 10 minutes
Cooking time: 8 hours
Servings: 4

Ingredients:

1 medium pork butt	2 onions, chopped
1 teaspoon coriander, ground	A pinch of black pepper
1 tablespoon oregano, dried	1 teaspoon lime juice
1 tablespoon cumin powder	4 eggs, already fried
2 tablespoons chili powder	2 avocados, peeled, pitted and sliced

Directions:

In a bowl, mix pork butt with coriander, oregano, cumin, chili powder, onions and a pinch of black pepper, rub well, transfer to your slow cooker and cook on Low for 8 hours.
Shred meat, divide between plates and serve with fried eggs and avocado slices on top and with lime juice all over.
Enjoy!

Nutrition:

calories 220, fat 2, fiber 2, carbs 6, protein 2

Delicious Sausage and Eggs Casserole

Preparation time: 10 minutes
Cooking time: 5 hours
Servings: 6

Ingredients:

1 broccoli head, florets separated	2 garlic cloves, minced
10 eggs, whisked	A pinch of sea salt
12 ounces sausages, cooked and sliced	Cooking spray
	Black pepper to the taste

Directions:

Spray your slow cooker with the cooking spray and layer half of the broccoli florets.
Add a layer of sausages, and then add half of the whisked eggs, a pinch of salt and some black pepper.
Add garlic, the rest of the broccoli, sausages and the rest of the eggs.
Cover and cook on Low for 5 hours.
Leave casserole to cool down, slice, divide between plates and serve.
Enjoy!

Nutrition:

calories 200, fat 3, fiber 3, carbs 6, protein 2

Special Breakfast Delight

Preparation time: 10 minutes
Cooking time: 6 hours and 10 minutes
Servings: 4

Ingredients:

1 and 1/3 cups leek, chopped	8 eggs
2 tablespoons coconut oil	2/3 cup sweet potato, grated
1 cup kale, chopped	1 and ½ cups beef sausage, casings removed and chopped
2 teaspoons garlic, minced	

Directions:

Heat up a pan with the oil over medium high heat, add leek, stir and cook for 1 minute.
Add garlic, sweet potatoes and kale, stir, cook for 2 minutes more and transfer to your slow cooker.
Add eggs and sausage meat, stir everything, cover and cook on Low for 6 hours.
Leave this tasty mix to cool down before slicing and serving it for breakfast.
Enjoy!

Nutrition:

calories 190, fat 2, fiber 2, carbs 6, protein 10

Easy Apple Porridge

Preparation time: 10 minutes
Cooking time: 3 hours
Servings: 2

Ingredients:

1 cup almond milk
3 tablespoons chia seeds
3 tablespoons almond butter
4 dates, chopped
2 tablespoons coconut sugar
1 teaspoon apple pie spice
2 apples, cored, peeled and chopped
½ teaspoon cinnamon powder

Directions:

In your slow cooker, combine the almond milk with chia seeds, almond butter, dates, sugar, pie spice, cinnamon and apples, toss, cover and cook on High for 3 hours.
Divide into bowls and serve.
Enjoy!

Nutrition:

calories 182, fat 4, fiber 6, carbs 15, protein 8

Banana Oatmeal

Preparation time: 10 minutes
Cooking time: 6 hours
Servings: 2

Ingredients:

1 banana, peeled and mashed
¼ cup almond meal
2 eggs, whisked
¼ cup almond milk
1 tablespoons flax seeds
1 tablespoons blueberries

Directions:

In your slow cooker, combine the banana with almond meal, eggs, almond milk, flaxseed and blueberries, toss, cover, cook on Low for 6 hours, divide into bowls and serve.
Enjoy!

Nutrition:

calories 198, fat 4, fiber 7, carbs 15, protein 7

Tapioca Porridge

Preparation time: 10 minutes
Cooking time: 6 hours
Servings: 4

Ingredients:

¼ cup tapioca pearls
6 ounces water
14 ounces coconut milk
1 teaspoon vanilla extract
1 tablespoon maple syrup

Directions:

In your slow cooker, combine the tapioca with water, milk, vanilla and maple syrup, toss, cover, cook on Low for 6 hours, divide into bowls and serve for breakfast.
Enjoy!

Nutrition:

calories 201, fat 4, fiber 6, carbs 14, protein 7

Cherries Oatmeal

Preparation time: 10 minutes
Cooking time: 6 hours
Servings: 2

Ingredients:

½ cup almond milk
1 banana, peeled and chopped
½ cup cashew meal
½ teaspoon cinnamon powder
¼ cup coconut, shredded
1 tablespoons flax seed
2 tablespoons cherries

Directions:

In your slow cooker, combine the almond milk with the banana, cashew meal, cinnamon, coconut, flaxseed and cherries, toss, cover, cook on Low for 6 hours, divide into bowls and serve.
Enjoy!

Nutrition:

calories 201, fat 4, fiber 4, carbs 14, protein 6

Pear Breakfast Mix

Preparation time: 10 minutes
Cooking time: 8 hours
Servings: 4

Ingredients:

6 pears, cored, peeled and chopped
2 tablespoons coconut oil, melted
6 ounces coconut milk
2/3 cup coconut butter
1 tablespoon vanilla extract
3 cups coconut, shredded
½ teaspoon cinnamon powder

Directions:

In your slow cooker, combine the pears with the coconut oil, milk, coconut butter, vanilla, coconut and cinnamon, toss, cover and cook on Low for 8 hours.
Divide into bowls and serve for breakfast.
Enjoy!

Nutrition:

calories 199, fat 4, fiber 4, carbs 15, protein 6

Butternut Squash Bowls

Preparation time: 10 minutes
Cooking time: 6 hours
Servings: 3

Ingredients:

1 banana, peeled and chopped
1 teaspoon cinnamon powder
1 cup coconut, shredded
½ cup butternut squash puree
½ cup coconut milk

Directions:

In your slow cooker, combine the banana with the cinnamon, coconut, squash puree and coconut milk, toss, cover and cook on Low for 6 hours.
Divide into bowls and serve for breakfast.
Enjoy!

Nutrition:

calories 210, fat 8, fiber 6, carbs 15, protein 6

Coconut Breakfast Mix

Preparation time: 10 minutes
Cooking time: 8 hours
Servings: 4

Ingredients:

1 cup coconut flakes granola
2 cups water
1 cup coconut milk
2 tablespoons maple syrup
2 tablespoons walnuts, chopped
½ cup strawberries
¼ cup blueberries

Directions:

In your slow cooker, combine the coconut flakes with the water, coconut milk, maple syrup, walnuts, strawberries and blueberries, toss, cover and cook on Low for 8 hours.
Divide into bowls and serve for breakfast.
Enjoy!

Nutrition:

calories 196, fat 4, fiber 8, carbs 15, protein 7

Delicious Mexican Breakfast

Preparation time: 10 minutes
Cooking time: 8 hours and 5 minutes
Servings: 4

Ingredients:

1 sweet potato, grated
½ cup bacon, chopped
8 eggs, whisked
1 red bell pepper, chopped
1 yellow onion, chopped
8 ounces mushrooms, chopped
A pinch of cumin, ground
A pinch of black pepper

Directions:

Heat up a pan over medium high heat, add bacon, fry until it's crispy, transfer to paper towels, drain and leave aside for now.
Heat up the same pan over medium high heat, add onion, stir and cook for 3 minutes.
Transfer this to your slow cooker; also add fried bacon, sweet potato, mushrooms, bell pepper and eggs.
Whisk gently, season with black pepper and cumin, cover and cook on Low for 8 hours.
Leave this Mexican casserole to cool down, slice and serve it.
Enjoy!

Nutrition:

calories 200, fat 4, fiber 2, carbs 7, protein 5

Special Egg Casserole

Preparation time: 10 minutes
Cooking time: 8 hours and 10 minutes
Servings: 4

Ingredients:

1 red onion, chopped
1 pound bacon, cooked and chopped
1 red bell pepper, chopped
2 medium sweet potatoes, grated
12 eggs
2 garlic cloves, minced
1 tablespoon coconut oil
1 teaspoon dill, chopped
1 cup coconut milk
A pinch of red pepper, crushed
Black pepper to the taste
A pinch of sea salt

Directions:

Heat up a pan with the coconut oil over medium high heat, add garlic, bell pepper and onion, stir and cook for 5 minutes.
Add grated sweet potato, red pepper, black pepper and a pinch of salt, stir and cook for 2 minutes more.
Transfer half of this to your slow cooker and spread on the bottom.
In a bowl, mix eggs with coconut milk and whisk well.
Pour half of the eggs over the veggies, add bacon, then add another veggie layer and top with the rest of the eggs.
Sprinkle dill all over, cover and cook on Low for 8 hours.
Leave this tasty casserole to cool down before serving for breakfast.
Enjoy!

Nutrition:

calories 240, fat 2, fiber 3, carbs 6, protein 8

Easy Mushroom Scramble

Preparation time: 10 minutes
Cooking time: 5 hours
Servings: 4

Ingredients:

6 eggs, whisked
1 pound white mushrooms, sliced
1 cup green onions, chopped
1 tablespoon olive oil
A pinch of salt and black pepper
1 zucchini, chopped
¼ cup coconut aminos

Directions:

Grease your slow cooker with the oil, add mushrooms, green onions, salt, pepper, zucchini, aminos and whisked eggs, toss, cover and cook on Low for 5 hours.
Divide between plates and serve.
Enjoy!

Nutrition:

calories 212, fat 5, fiber 8, carbs 12, protein 7

Simple Breakfast Meatloaf

Preparation time: 10 minutes
Cooking time: 3 hours and 10 minutes
Servings: 4

Ingredients:

1 onion, chopped
2 pounds pork, minced
1 teaspoon red pepper flakes
1 teaspoon coconut oil
3 garlic cloves, minced
¼ cup almond flour
1 teaspoon oregano, chopped
1 tablespoon sage, minced
A pinch of sea salt
1 tablespoon paprika
1 teaspoon marjoram, dried
2 eggs

Directions:

Heat up a pan with the oil over medium high heat, add onion, stir and cook for 2 minutes.
Add garlic, stir, cook for 2 minutes more, take off heat and leave aside to cool down.
In a bowl, mix pork with a pinch of salt, pepper flakes, flour, oregano, sage, paprika, marjoram and eggs and whisk everything.
Add garlic and onion and stir again.
Shape your meatloaf, transfer to your slow cooker, cover and cook on Low for 3 hours.
Leave aside to cool down, slice and serve.
Enjoy!

Nutrition:

calories 200, fat 3, fiber 2, carbs 7, protein 10

Breakfast Sweet Potatoes Casserole

Preparation time: 10 minutes
Cooking time: 3 hours and 10 minutes
Servings: 6

Ingredients:

3 tablespoons olive oil
¼ cup mushrooms, sliced
¼ cup yellow onion, chopped
¼ teaspoon garlic powder
1 cup coconut milk
½ cup coconut cream
2o ounces sweet potatoes, peeled and grated
A pinch of salt and black pepper

Directions:

Heat up a pan with the oil over medium-high heat, add onion, mushrooms, garlic powder, salt and black pepper, toss, cook for 10 minutes and transfer to your slow cooker.
Add sweet potatoes, coconut milk and coconut cream, cover the pot and cook on High for 3 hours.
Slice, divide between plates and serve.
Enjoy!

Nutrition:

calories 231, fat 5, fiber 7, carbs 14, protein 8

Easy Eggs and Chorizo Breakfast

Preparation time: 10 minutes
Cooking time: 6 hours and 10 minutes
Servings: 4

Ingredients:

4 garlic cloves, minced
1 yellow onion, chopped
1 pound chorizo, casings removed and chopped
12 eggs
1 cup coconut milk
1 butternut squash, peeled and cubed
2 tablespoons coconut oil

Directions:

Heat up a pan with half of the oil over medium high heat; add onion and garlic, stir and sauté for 5 minutes.
Add chorizo, stir, cook for 3 minutes more and take off heat.
In a bowl, mix eggs with coconut milk and stir well.
Grease your slow cooker with the rest of the oil and add butternut squash on the bottom.
Add onions mix and spread as well.
Add eggs at the end cover and cook on Low for 6 hours.
Leave aside to cool down, slice and serve for breakfast.
Enjoy!

Nutrition:

calories 189, fat 5, fiber 3, carbs 6, protein 7

Yam Breakfast Mix

Preparation time: 10 minutes
Cooking time: 5 hours
Servings: 4

Ingredients:

3 yams, peeled and cubed
1 green bell pepper, chopped
1 red bell pepper, chopped
1 yellow onion, chopped
12 ounces chicken sausage, sliced
1 cup coconut cream
¼ teaspoon basil, dried
¼ teaspoon oregano, dried
2 tablespoons parsley, chopped

Directions:

In your slow cooker, combine the yams with the green bell pepper, red bell pepper, onion, sausage, basil, oregano and cream, toss a bit, cover and cook on Low for 5 hours.
Divide between plates, sprinkle the parsley on top and serve for breakfast.
Enjoy!

Nutrition:

calories 214, fat 4, fiber 6, carbs 15, protein 9

Egg Casserole

Preparation time: 10 minutes
Cooking time: 3 hours
Servings: 8

Ingredients:

20 ounces cauliflower rice
8 bacon slices, cooked and chopped
6 green onions, chopped
12 eggs, whisked
½ cup coconut milk
A pinch of salt and black pepper
Cooking spray

Directions:

Grease a slow cooker with the cooking spray, spread cauliflower on the bottom, add bacon, green onions, eggs mixed with coconut milk, sprinkle salt and pepper at the end, cover and cook on High for 3 hours.
Slice, divide between plates and serve.
Enjoy!

Nutrition:

calories 213, fat 4, fiber 5, carbs 15, protein 7

Carrots And Zucchinis Bowls

Preparation time: 10 minutes
Cooking time: 8 hours
Servings: 4

Ingredients:

½ cup coconut flakes granola
1 and ½ cups coconut milk
1 carrot, grated
1 zucchini, grated
A pinch of nutmeg, ground
A pinch of cloves, ground
½ teaspoon cinnamon powder
2 tablespoons maple syrup

Directions:

In your slow cooker, combine the coconut granola with milk, carrots, zucchini, nutmeg, cloves, cinnamon and maple syrup, cover and cook on Low for 8 hours.
Divide into bowls and serve for breakfast.
Enjoy!

Nutrition:

calories 204, fat 4, fiber 6, carbs 15, protein 7

Turkey Sausage Breakfast

Preparation time: 10 minutes
Cooking time: 3 hours
Servings: 4

Ingredients:

32 ounces cauliflower florets
1 pound turkey sausage, ground
6 eggs, whisked
2 tablespoons coconut cream
½ teaspoon thyme, dried
Cooking spray
½ teaspoon garlic powder
A pinch of salt and black pepper

Directions:

Grease your slow cooker with the cooking spray, add cauliflower florets on the bottom, add turkey sausage, eggs, cream, thyme, garlic powder, salt and black pepper, toss, cover, cook on High for 3 hours, divide between plates and serve.
Enjoy!

Nutrition:

calories 231, fat 4, fiber 7, carbs 16, protein 8

Breakfast Apple Butter

Preparation time: 10 minutes
Cooking time: 8 hours
Servings: 8

Ingredients:

8 cups apples, peeled, cored and chopped
1 teaspoon allspice, ground
1 teaspoon clove, ground
1 teaspoon ginger powder
Juice from 1 lemon
1 tablespoon cinnamon powder
¼ teaspoon nutmeg, ground
1 and ½ cups water
1 cup maple syrup

Directions:

In your slow cooker, mix apples with allspice, clove, ginger, cinnamon, nutmeg, maple syrup, water and lemon juice, stir, cover and cook on Low for 8 hours.
Leave your apple butter mix to cool down, blend using an immersion blender, divide into jars and serve for breakfast.
Enjoy!

Nutrition:

calories 212, fat 4, fiber 6, carbs 12, protein 3

Great Veggie Breakfast Frittata

Preparation time: 10 minutes
Cooking time: 2 hours
Servings: 4

Ingredients:

6 eggs, whisked
4 ounces mushrooms, sliced
¼ cup spinach, chopped
2 green onions, chopped
1 teaspoon ghee
¼ cup cherry tomatoes, sliced
2 teaspoons Italian seasoning

Directions:

Heat up a pan with the ghee over medium high heat, add mushrooms, onions, spinach, green onions and tomatoes, stir and cook for 2-3 minutes.
Transfer this mix to your slow cooker, add whisked eggs, season with Italian seasoning, stir a bit, cover and cook on High for 2 hours.
Leave your frittata to cool down a bit, slice and serve.
Enjoy!

Nutrition:

calories 200, fat 4, fiber 6, carbs 12, protein 3

Butternut Squash Breakfast Mix

Preparation time: 10 minutes
Cooking time: 8 hours
Servings: 4

Ingredients:

2 apples, peeled, cored and cubed
½ cup walnuts, soaked for 12 hours and drained
½ cup almonds
1 butternut squash, peeled and cubed
1 teaspoon cinnamon powder
½ teaspoon nutmeg, ground
1 tablespoon coconut sugar
1 cup coconut milk

Directions:

In your slow cooker, mix walnuts with almonds, squash cubes, apples, cinnamon, nutmeg, coconut sugar and milk, stir a bit, cover and cook on Low for 8 hours.
Mash using a potato masher, divide into bowls and serve for breakfast.
Enjoy!

Nutrition:

calories 182, fat 3, fiber 7, carbs 14, protein 2

Sausage Casserole

Preparation time: 10 minutes
Cooking time: 8 hours
Servings: 8

Ingredients:

1 broccoli head, florets separated and chopped
3 tablespoons olive oil
1 pound pork sausage, sliced
12 eggs, whisked
6 green onions, chopped
6 ounces coconut cream

Directions:

Grease your slow cooker with the oil, add broccoli on the bottom, also add sausage, eggs, onions and cream, toss, cover and cook on Low for 8 hours.
Divide between plates and serve for breakfast.
Enjoy!

Nutrition:

calories 217, fat 5, fiber 8, carbs 15, protein 9

Spinach And Tomato Casserole

Preparation time: 10 minutes
Cooking time: 8 hours
Servings: 4

Ingredients:

1 pound spinach, chopped
1 punnet tomatoes, chopped
4 spring onions, chopped
3 eggs, whisked
6 ounces coconut cream
1/3 cup coconut milk
A pinch of salt and black pepper
½ teaspoon smoked paprika
Cooking spray

Directions:

Grease your slow cooker with the spray, add spinach, tomatoes onions, salt, pepper and toss.
Add eggs mixed with cream and coconut milk, cover and cook on Low for 8 hours.
Slice, divide between plates and serve.
Enjoy!

Nutrition:

calories 241, fat 4, fiber 6, carbs 15, protein 8

Mexican Casserole

Preparation time: 10 minutes
Cooking time: 5 hours
Servings: 8

Ingredients:

12 ounces pork sausage, chopped
½ teaspoon garlic powder
½ teaspoon coriander, ground
1 teaspoon cumin, ground
1 teaspoon chili powder
A pinch of salt and black pepper
1 cup chunky salsa
1 cup coconut milk
1 avocado, peeled, cored and cubed
Cooking spray

Directions:

Grease your slow cooker with cooking spray, add pork sausage, garlic powder, coriander, cumin, chili powder, salt, pepper, salsa and milk, toss, cover and cook on Low for 5 hours.
Divide between plates, top with avocado and serve for breakfast.
Enjoy!

Nutrition:

calories 300, fat 12, fiber 1, carbs 6, protein 12

Veggie Omelet

Preparation time: 10 minutes
Cooking time: 2 hours
Servings: 4

Ingredients:

½ cup coconut milk
A pinch of salt and black pepper
A pinch of garlic powder
A pinch of chili powder
6 eggs, whisked
Cooking spray
1 cup broccoli florets
1 red bell pepper, chopped
1 yellow onion, chopped
1 garlic clove, minced

Directions:

In a large bowl, combine the eggs with coconut milk, salt, pepper, garlic powder, chili powder, broccoli, bell pepper, onion and garlic and stir.
Grease the slow cooker with the cooking spray, add eggs mixture, cover and cook on High for 3 hours.
Slice, divide between plates and serve.
Enjoy!

Nutrition:

calories 251, fat 4, fiber 6, carbs 15, protein 8

Broccoli And Ham Mix

Preparation time: 10 minutes
Cooking time: 2 hours and 30 minutes
Servings: 8

Ingredients:

3 cups broccoli florets, chopped
1 teaspoon olive oil
7 ounces ham, chopped
1 teaspoon Italian seasoning
A pinch of salt and black pepper
12 eggs, whisked
1 tablespoon green onions, chopped

Directions:

Grease your slow cooker with the oil, add broccoli, ham, Italian seasoning, salt, pepper, onions and eggs, toss, cover and cook on Low for 2 hours and 30 minutes.
Slice, divide between plates and serve for breakfast.
Enjoy!

Nutrition:

calories 223, fat 4, fiber 6, carbs 15, protein 8

Delicious Frittata

Preparation time: 10 minutes
Cooking time: 3 hours
Servings: 6

Ingredients:

2 teaspoons olive oil
5 ounces baby kale
6 ounces roasted red peppers, chopped
¼ cup green onions, chopped
8 eggs, whisked
A pinch of salt and black pepper

Directions:

Grease your slow cooker with the oil, add baby kale, roasted peppers, onions, eggs, salt and pepper, toss a bit, cover and cook on Low for 3 hours.
Slice, divide between plates and serve for breakfast.
Enjoy!

Nutrition:

calories 255, fat 5, fiber 8, carbs 15, protein 8

Breakfast Stuffed Apples

Preparation time: 10 minutes
Cooking time: 1 hour and 30 minutes
Servings: 4

Ingredients:

½ cup maple syrup
¼ cup figs, dried
1 teaspoon coconut sugar
¼ cup pecans, chopped
1 teaspoon lemon zest, grated
½ teaspoon orange zest, grated
1 teaspoon cinnamon powder
¼ teaspoon nutmeg, ground
1 tablespoon lemon juice
1 tablespoon coconut oil
½ cup water
4 apples, cored and tops cut off

Directions:

In a bowl, mix maple syrup with figs, coconut sugar, pecans, lemon zest, orange zest, ½ teaspoon cinnamon, nutmeg, lemon juice and coconut oil, whisk really well and stuff apples with this mix.
Add the water to your slow cooker, add ½ teaspoon cinnamon as well, stir, add apples inside, cover and cook on High for 1 hour and 30 minutes.
Divide apples between plates and serve them for breakfast.
Enjoy!

Nutrition:

calories 189, fat 4, fiber 7, carbs 19, protein 2

Breakfast Apples and Sauce

Preparation time: 10 minutes
Cooking time: 4 hours
Servings: 4

Ingredients:

1/3 cup coconut oil, melted
1 tablespoon lemon juice
¼ cup cane juice, evaporated
½ teaspoon cinnamon powder
1 teaspoon vanilla extract
5 apples, cored, peeled and cubed

Directions:

In your instant pot mix, coconut oil with cane juice, lemon juice, cinnamon and vanilla and whisk well.
Add apple cubes, toss well, cover and cook on High for 4 hours.
Divide into bowls and serve for breakfast.
Enjoy!

Nutrition:

calories 200, fat 4, fiber 6, carbs 16, protein 3

Breakfast Meatloaf

Preparation time: 10 minutes
Cooking time: 3 hours
Servings: 4

Ingredients:

1 yellow onion, chopped
2 pounds pork meat, ground
3 garlic cloves, minced
1 tablespoon coconut oil, melted
1 teaspoon red pepper flakes, crushed
¼ cup almond flour
1 teaspoon oregano, dried
1 tablespoon sage, chopped
A pinch of salt and black pepper
1 tablespoon smoked paprika
1 teaspoon marjoram, dried
Cooking spray
2 eggs

Directions:

Heat up a pan with the oil over medium-high heat, add garlic and onions, stir, cook for 4 minutes, take off heat, cool down, transfer to a bowl and mix with pork, pepper flakes, almond flour, oregano, sage, salt, pepper, paprika, marjoram and eggs and stir really well.
Grease your slow cooker with cooking spray, shape a meatloaf out of the pork mix, add it to the cooker, cover and cook on Low for 3 hours.
Slice, divide between plates and serve for breakfast.
Enjoy!

Nutrition:

calories 261, fat 5, fiber 7, carbs 15, protein 8

Breakfast Yams

Preparation time: 10 minutes
Cooking time: 2 hours
Servings: 2

Ingredients:

2 yams, peeled and cut into chunks
2/3 cup walnuts, chopped
2 cups basil, chopped
1 garlic clove, minced
½ cup olive oil
Juice of ½ lemon
A pinch of salt and black pepper

Directions:

In your blender, combine the walnuts with basil, garlic, oil, lemon juice, salt and pepper and pulse well.
Put the yams in your slow cooker, add the walnuts pesto, toss, cover, cook on Low for 2 hours, divide into bowls and serve for breakfast.
Enjoy!

Nutrition:

calories 221, fat 4, fiber 6, carbs 17, protein 8

Chorizo Mix Breakfast

Preparation time: 10 minutes
Cooking time: 8 hours
Servings: 4

Ingredients:

1 yellow onion, chopped
1 pound chorizo sausage, casings removed and chopped
4 garlic cloves, minced
12 eggs, whisked
1 cup coconut milk
1 butternut squash, peeled and cubed
1 teaspoon coconut oil, melted

Directions:

Grease your slow cooker with the oil, add onion, garlic, squash and chorizo.
Also add eggs mixed with the milk, cover and cook on Low for 8 hours.
Divide between plates and serve.
Enjoy!

Nutrition:

calories 261, fat 6, fiber 8, carbs 9, protein 12

Salsa Bowls

Preparation time: 10 minutes
Cooking time: 6 hours
Servings: 8

Ingredients:

16 ounces pork meat, ground
1 green bell pepper, chopped
¼ cup scallions, chopped
15 ounces canned tomatoes, chopped
1 cup chunky salsa
¼ teaspoon cumin, ground
½ teaspoon turmeric powder
½ teaspoon smoked paprika
A pinch of salt and black pepper
¼ teaspoon chili powder
3 cups baby kale, chopped

Directions:

In your slow cooker, combine the meat with bell pepper, scallions, tomatoes, salsa, cumin, turmeric, paprika, salt, pepper, chili powder and kale, toss, cover and cook on Low for 6 hours.
Divide into bowls and serve for breakfast.
Enjoy!

Nutrition:

calories 231, fat 4, fiber 7, carbs 14, protein 7

Pork Casserole

Preparation time: 10 minutes
Cooking time: 6 hours
Servings: 4

Ingredients:

1 teaspoon lemon zest, grated
1 pound pork, ground
1 tablespoon lemon juice
1 tablespoon white vinegar
2 garlic cloves, minced
10 ounces spinach, torn
½ cup yellow onion, chopped
½ teaspoon basil, dried
8 ounces mushrooms, sliced
Salt and black pepper to the taste
¼ teaspoon red pepper flakes
Cooking spray

Directions:

Spray your slow cooker with some cooking spray, add pork, lemon zest, lemon juice, vinegar, garlic, spinach, onion, basil, mushrooms, salt, pepper and pepper flakes, toss, cover and cook on Low for 6 hours.
Divide between plates and serve.
Enjoy!

Nutrition:

calories 221, fat 6, fiber 8, carbs 12, protein 4

Breakfast Pulled Pork

Preparation time: 10 minutes
Cooking time: 10 hours
Servings: 4

Ingredients:

4 pounds pork butt roast
1 tablespoon cumin powder
2 tablespoons chili powder
1 teaspoon coriander, ground
1 tablespoon oregano, dried
2 yellow onions, sliced
2 avocados, peeled, pitted and sliced

Directions:

In your slow cooker, mix pork butt with chili, cumin, oregano and coriander and rub well.
Add onions, cover and cook on Low for 10 hours.
Shred meat using 2 forks, divide between plates, top each with avocado slices and serve for breakfast.
Enjoy!

Nutrition:

calories 300, fat 4, fiber 10, carbs 24, protein 5

Sweet Potato Breakfast Mix

Preparation time: 10 minutes
Cooking time: 2 hours and 30 minutes
Servings: 2

Ingredients:

1 yellow bell pepper, roughly chopped
1 orange bell pepper, roughly chopped
3 ounces butternut squash, peeled and cubed
3 ounces sweet potatoes, peeled and cubed
2 tablespoons coconut oil
1 teaspoon thyme, dried
1 teaspoon garlic, minced
2 tomatoes, chopped
1 teaspoon mustard powder

Directions:

In your slow cooker, mix orange bell pepper with yellow one, butternut squash, sweet potatoes, oil, thyme, garlic, mustard powder and tomatoes, toss a bit, cover and cook on High for 2 hours and 30 minutes.
Divide between plates and serve for breakfast.
Enjoy!

Nutrition:

calories 182, fat 4, fiber 7, carbs 12, protein 3

Simple Breakfast Pie

Preparation time: 10 minutes
Cooking time: 8 hours
Servings: 4

Ingredients:

1 sweet potato, shredded
8 eggs, whisked
2 teaspoons coconut oil, melted
1 pound pork sausage, crumbled
1 tablespoon garlic powder
1 yellow onion, chopped
2 teaspoons basil, dried
2 red bell peppers, chopped
A pinch of sea salt and black pepper

Directions:

Grease your slow cooker with the coconut oil and add sweet potatoes.
Also add sausage, garlic powder, bell pepper, onion, basil, salt and pepper.
Add whisked eggs, toss, cover and cook on Low for 8 hours.
Divide between plates and serve warm.
Enjoy!

Nutrition:

calories 254, fat 7, fiber 8, carbs 14, protein 6

Blueberries Coconut Oatmeal

Preparation time: 10 minutes
Cooking time: 8 hours
Servings: 4

Ingredients:

1 cup blueberries
1 cup coconut flakes
1 cup coconut milk
2 tablespoons coconut sugar
½ teaspoon vanilla extract
Cooking spray

Directions:

Grease your slow cooker with cooking spray, add blueberries, coconut flakes, milk, sugar and vanilla extract, toss, cover and cook on Low for 8 hours.
Divide into bowls and serve.
Enjoy!

Nutrition:

calories 182, fat 6, fiber 8, carbs 11, protein 7

Almond Oatmeal

Preparation time: 10 minutes
Cooking time: 8 hours
Servings: 2

Ingredients:

½ cup coconut flakes
½ cup almond milk
1 teaspoon vanilla extract
1 cup water
2 tablespoons coconut sugar
4 tablespoons almond butter

Directions:

In your slow cooker, combine the coconut flakes with milk, vanilla extract, water, sugar and almond butter, whisk well, cover, cook on Low for 8 hours, divide into bowls and serve.
Enjoy!

Nutrition:
calories 202, fat 3, fiber 7, carbs 11, protein 7

Mediterranean Frittata

Preparation time: 10 minutes
Cooking time: 6 hours
Servings: 4

Ingredients:

1 tablespoon olive oil
6 eggs, whisked
1 yellow onion, chopped
¼ teaspoon turmeric powder
3 tablespoons garlic, minced
A pinch of salt and black pepper
1 red bell pepper, chopped
1 cup kalamata olives, pitted and halved
1 teaspoon oregano, dried
1 tablespoon lemon juice

Directions:

Grease your slow cooker with the oil, add onion, garlic, turmeric, salt, pepper, red bell pepper, olives, oregano and lemon juice and toss.
Add the eggs, toss, cover and cook on Low for 6 hours.
Slice, divide between plates and serve for breakfast.
Enjoy!

Nutrition:

calories 271, fat 4, fiber 7, carbs 20, protein 6

Cranberry Mix

Preparation time: 10 minutes
Cooking time: 2 hours
Servings: 4

Ingredients:

1 cup coconut flakes granola
3 cups almond milk
1 teaspoon vanilla extract
3 teaspoons coconut sugar
¼ cup cranberries, dried
1/8 cup almonds, chopped

Directions:

In your slow cooker, combine the coconut flakes with the almond milk, vanilla, sugar, cranberries and almonds, toss, cover and cook on High for 2 hours.
Divide into bowls and serve for breakfast.
Enjoy!

Nutrition:

calories 196, fat 5, fiber 5, carbs 10, protein 6

Simple Sweet Potatoes

Preparation time: 10 minutes
Cooking time: 4 hours
Servings: 4

Ingredients:

Cooking spray	8 ounces coconut milk
4 sweet potatoes, cut into wedges	A pinch of salt and black pepper
1 yellow onion, cut into wedges	1 tablespoons parsley, chopped

Directions:

Grease your slow cooker with the cooking spray, add sweet potatoes, onion, salt, pepper and coconut milk, toss, cover, cook on Low for 4 hours, divide between plates and serve for breakfast.
Enjoy!

Nutrition:

calories 206, fat 6, fiber 4, carbs 10, protein 12

Herbed Breakfast Sweet Potatoes

Preparation time: 10 minutes
Cooking time: 3 hours
Servings: 10

Ingredients:

4 pounds sweet potatoes, sliced	½ teaspoon thyme, dried
3 tablespoons coconut sugar	½ teaspoon sage, dried
½ cup orange juice	2 tablespoons olive oil
A pinch of salt and black pepper	

Directions:

In a bowl, mix orange juice with salt, pepper, sugar, thyme, sage and oil, whisk well and add to your slow cooker.
Add sweet potato slices, toss a bit, cover, cook on High for 3 hours, divide into bowls and serve.
Enjoy!

Nutrition:

calories 189, fat 4, fiber 4, carbs 16, protein 4

Breakfast Sausage Casserole

Preparation time: 10 minutes
Cooking time: 4 hours
Servings: 4

Ingredients:

1 and 1/3 cups leek, chopped	1 cup kale, chopped
2 tablespoons coconut oil, melted	8 eggs, whisked
2 teaspoons garlic, minced	1 and ½ cups beef sausage, chopped
	2/3 cup sweet potatoes, grated

Directions:

Heat up a pan with the oil over medium high heat, add garlic, leek and kale, stir and cook for a couple of minutes.
In a bowl, mix eggs with sausage and sweet potato and stir well.
Add sautéed veggies, stir, pour everything into your slow cooker, cover and cook on Low for 4 hours.
Divide this mix into plates and serve for breakfast.
Enjoy!

Nutrition:

calories 232, fat 4, fiber 8, carbs 12, protein 4

Mexican Breakfast

Preparation time: 10 minutes
Cooking time: 6 hours
Servings: 5

Ingredients:

8 eggs, whisked	8 ounces mushrooms, chopped
1 sweet potato, cubed	1 red bell pepper, chopped
1 yellow onion, chopped	Guacamole for serving
½ pound turkey bacon, cooked and crumbled	Salsa for serving

Directions:

In your slow cooker, mix eggs with sweet potato, onion, bacon, mushrooms and red bell pepper, stir a bit, cover and cook on Low for 6 hours.
Divide between plates, top with guacamole and salsa and serve for breakfast.
Enjoy!

Nutrition:

calories 213, fat 4, fiber 6, carbs 12, protein 4

Sausage and Eggs

Preparation time: 10 minutes
Cooking time: 3 hours
Servings: 6

Ingredients:

1 broccoli head, florets separated and chopped
12 ounces pork sausage, cooked and sliced
2 garlic cloves, minced
10 eggs, whisked
A pinch of salt and black pepper

Directions:

In a bowl, mix eggs with salt, pepper, garlic, sausage slices and broccoli and whisk well.
Transfer this to your slow cooker, cover and cook on High for 3 hours.
Slice, divide between plates and serve.
Enjoy!

Nutrition:

calories 261, fat 4, fiber 7, carbs 10, protein 3

Eggs and Bacon Casserole

Preparation time: 10 minutes
Cooking time: 8 hours
Servings: 6

Ingredients:

1 red onion, chopped
1 pound bacon, cooked and chopped
1 red bell pepper, chopped
2 garlic cloves, minced
1 teaspoon ghee
2 sweet potatoes, grated
12 eggs, whisked
1 cup coconut milk
1 teaspoon dill, chopped
A pinch of red pepper, crushed
A pinch of sea salt and black pepper

Directions:

In a bowl, mix eggs with onion, bacon, garlic, bell pepper, sweet potatoes, coconut milk, dill, salt, pepper and red pepper and whisk everything.
Grease your slow cooker with the ghee, add eggs and bacon mix, cover and cook on Low for 8 hours.
Slice eggs casserole, divide between plates and serve.
Enjoy!

Nutrition:

calories 261, fat 6, fiber 6, carbs 12, protein 4

Spiced Fruits Mix

Preparation time: 10 minutes
Cooking time: 6 hours
Servings: 6

Ingredients:

4 apples, cored, peeled and cut into medium chunks
1 teaspoon lemon juice
4 pears, cored, peeled and cut into medium chunks
5 teaspoons coconut sugar
1 teaspoon cinnamon powder
½ teaspoon ginger, ground
½ teaspoon cloves, ground
½ teaspoon cardamom, ground

Directions:

In your slow cooker, mix apples, pears, lemon juice, sugar, cinnamon, ginger, cloves and cardamom, stir, cover, cook on Low for 6 hours, divide between plates and serve for breakfast.
Enjoy!

Nutrition:

calories 191, fat 3, fiber 7, carbs 14, protein 6

Eggs And Scallions

Preparation time: 10 minutes
Cooking time: 2 hours and 30 minutes
Servings: 4

Ingredients:

4 eggs
A pinch of garlic powder
A pinch of salt and black pepper
A pinch of sesame seeds
1 tablespoons scallions, chopped
Cooking spray

Directions:

In a bowl, combine the eggs with the garlic powder, salt, pepper, sesame seeds and scallions and whisk.
Grease your slow cooker with the cooking spray, add eggs and scallions mix, cover, cook on Low for 2 hours and 30 minutes, stir a bit, divide between plates and serve for breakfast.
Enjoy!

Nutrition:

calories 190, fat 5, fiber 2, carbs 12, protein 6

Eggs And Kale Mix

Preparation time: 10 minutes
Cooking time: 3 hours
Servings: 6

Ingredients:

1 yellow onion, chopped
6 eggs
1 cup bacon, cooked and crumbled
1 cup kale, chopped
1 teaspoon Italian seasoning
A pinch of salt and black pepper
Cooking spray

Directions:

In a bowl, mix eggs with onion, kale, bacon, salt, pepper and Italian seasoning and whisk well.
Grease the slow cooker with the cooking spray, add the eggs mix, spread, cover and cook on Low for 3 hours.
Divide between plates and serve for breakfast. Enjoy!

Nutrition:

calories 212, fat 5, fiber 4, carbs 12, protein 7

Jalapeno Eggs Mix

Preparation time: 10 minutes
Cooking time: 3 hours
Servings: 4

Ingredients:

2 tablespoons olive oil
1 cup sweet potatoes, cubed
4 eggs, whisked
2 jalapeno peppers, chopped
½ cup yellow onion, chopped
1 tablespoon cilantro, chopped
A pinch of salt and black pepper

Directions:

Add the oil to your slow cooker, arrange the sweet potatoes on the bottom and top with onion and jalapenos.
Add whisked eggs, salt, pepper and cilantro, toss a bit, cover, cook on Low for 3 hours, divide between plates and serve. Enjoy!

Nutrition:

calories 212, fat 5, fiber 5, carbs 13, protein 6

Ham And Sausage Mix

Preparation time: 10 minutes
Cooking time: 3 hours
Servings: 4

Ingredients:

6 eggs, whisked
A pinch of salt and black pepper
½ cup coconut milk
1 cup sausage, cooked and ground
½ cup ham, chopped
2 green onions, chopped

Directions:

In a bowl, combine the eggs with salt, pepper and coconut milk and whisk.
Add this to your slow cooker, top with sausage, ham and green onions, cover and cook on Low for 3 hours.
Divide this mix between plates and serve for breakfast.
Enjoy!

Nutrition:

calories 213, fat 4, fiber 5, carbs 14, protein 8

Tomato And Scallions Frittata

Preparation time: 10 minutes
Cooking time: 3 hours
Servings: 4

Ingredients:

4 ounces sweet potatoes, cubed
6 eggs, whisked
A pinch of salt and black pepper
1 tablespoon olive oil
¼ cup scallions, chopped
1 garlic clove, minced
¼ cup coconut milk
1 teaspoon tomato sauce
Cooking spray

Directions:

In a bowl, combine the eggs with the sweet potatoes, salt, pepper, scallions, garlic, coconut milk and tomato sauce and whisk well.
Grease your slow cooker with the oil, add eggs mix, spread into the pot, cover and cook on Low for 3 hours.
Divide between plates and serve for breakfast. Enjoy!

Nutrition:

calories 203, fat 7, fiber 2, carbs 10, protein 7

Delicious Sweet Potatoes and Pork Casserole

Preparation time: 10 minutes
Cooking time: 6 hours
Servings: 4

Ingredients:

2 red onions, chopped
7 eggs, whisked
2 sweet potatoes, grated
2 tablespoons smoked paprika
1 pound pork, ground
2 teaspoons coconut oil, melted

Directions:

In a bowl, mix eggs with onions, sweet potatoes, paprika and minced meat and whisk well.
Grease your slow cooker with coconut oil, add eggs and meat mix, cover and cook on Low for 6 hours.
Slice, divide between plates and serve warm for breakfast.
Enjoy!

Nutrition:

calories 261, fat 6, fiber 4, carbs 12, protein 3

Tasty Breakfast Meatloaf

Preparation time: 10 minutes
Cooking time: 3 hours and 10 minutes
Servings: 4

Ingredients:

3 garlic cloves, minced
1 yellow onion, chopped
2 pounds pork, ground
1 tablespoon coconut oil
¼ cup almond flour
1 teaspoon red pepper flakes, crushed
1 teaspoon oregano, dried
1 tablespoon sage, chopped
1 teaspoon marjoram, dried
2 eggs
1 tablespoon smoked paprika

Directions:

Heat up a pan with the oil over medium high heat, add onion, stir and sauté for 3 minutes.
Add garlic, stir and cook for 3 minutes more.
In a bowl, mix sautéed onions and garlic with pork, almond flour, pepper flakes, oregano, sage, marjoram, paprika and eggs and stir really well.
Shape your meatloaf using your wet hands, put it in your slow cooker, cover and cook on Low for 3 hours.
Leave meatloaf to cool down, slice and serve it for breakfast.
Enjoy!

Nutrition:

calories 273, fat 4, fiber 7, carbs 14, protein 5

Breakfast Salad

Preparation time: 10 minutes
Cooking time: 10 hours
Servings: 4

Ingredients:

1 yellow onion, chopped
3 pounds pork shoulder
1 tablespoon cumin, ground
2 tablespoon smoked paprika
1 tablespoon chili powder
1 tablespoon garlic powder
2 teaspoons oregano, dried
1 teaspoon allspice, ground
1 teaspoon cinnamon powder
A pinch of salt and black pepper
Juice from 1 lemon
1 romaine lettuce head, leaves torn

Directions:

In your slow cooker, mix pork with onion, cumin, paprika, chili, garlic powder, oregano, allspice, cinnamon, salt, pepper and lemon juice, rub well, cover and cook on Low for 10 hours.
Transfer pork shoulder to a cutting board, cool it down, shred using 2 forks and transfer to a bowl.
Add lettuce leaves, add some of the cooking liquid from the pot, toss and serve right away.
Enjoy!

Nutrition:

calories 261, fat 4, fiber 6, carbs 13, protein 3

Delicious Veggie Omelet

Preparation time: 10 minutes
Cooking time: 2 hours
Servings: 4

Ingredients:

½ cup coconut milk
6 eggs, whisked
A pinch of salt and black pepper
A pinch of garlic powder
A pinch of chili powder
1 red bell pepper, chopped
1 cup cauliflower florets
1 garlic clove, minced
1 yellow onion, chopped
2 tomatoes, chopped
1 tablespoon parsley, chopped
Cooking spray

Directions:

In a bowl, mix eggs with coconut milk, salt, pepper, garlic powder, chili powder, bell pepper, cauliflower, garlic and onion and whisk well.
Grease your slow cooker with cooking spray, add eggs mix, spread, cover and cook on High for 2 hours.
Slice omelet, divide between plates and serve with chopped tomatoes and parsley on top.
Enjoy!

Nutrition:

calories 142, fat 3, fiber 4, carbs 7, protein 4

Green Breakfast Mix

Preparation time: 10 minutes
Cooking time: 2 hours
Servings: 4

Ingredients:

2 pounds mustard leaves
1 tablespoons olive oil
1 teaspoon ginger, grated
2 yellow onions, chopped

4 garlic cloves, minced
1 teaspoon cumin, ground
½ teaspoon turmeric powder
A pinch of salt and black pepper

Directions:

Grease your slow cooker with the oil, add ginger, onions, garlic, cumin, turmeric, salt and pepper and toss.
Add mustard leaves, toss, cover the pot, cook on Low for 2 hours, divide into bowls and serve for breakfast.
Enjoy!

Nutrition:

calories 210, fat 3, fiber 2, carbs 8, protein 7

Eggs And Bacon Mix

Preparation time: 10 minutes
Cooking time: 3 hours
Servings: 4

Ingredients:

2 green onion, chopped
4 eggs
¼ teaspoon lemon pepper

4 bacon slices, cooked and crumbled
Cooking spray

Directions:

Grease your slow cooker with the cooking spray, add eggs, green onions, lemon pepper and bacon, toss, cover, cook on Low for 3 hours, divide between plates and serve for breakfast.
Enjoy!

Nutrition:

calories 212, fat 4, fiber 5, carbs 12, protein 7

Cherry Tomatoes Breakfast Mix

Preparation time: 10 minutes
Cooking time: 2 hours and 30 minutes
Servings: 4

Ingredients:

1 tablespoon olive oil
2 yellow onions, chopped
6 zucchinis, chopped
1 pound cherry tomatoes, halved

2 garlic cloves, minced
A pinch of salt and black pepper
1 tablespoon parsley, chopped

Directions:

Grease your slow cooker with the oil, add onions, zucchinis, tomatoes, garlic, salt, pepper and parsley, toss, cover, cook on Low for 2 hours and 30 minutes, divide into bowls and serve for breakfast.
Enjoy!

Nutrition:

calories 170, fat 2, fiber 4, carbs 8, protein 6

Zucchini And Carrots Mix

Preparation time: 20 minutes
Cooking time: 2 hours
Servings: 4

Ingredients:

2 tablespoons olive oil
3 pounds zucchinis, peeled and roughly chopped
2 yellow onions, chopped

4 carrots, chopped
½ cup tomatoes, crushed
A pinch of salt and black pepper

Directions:

Grease your slow cooker with the oil, add zucchinis, onions, carrots, tomatoes, salt and pepper, toss, cover, cook on Low for 2 hours, divide into bowls and serve cold for breakfast.
Enjoy!

Nutrition:

calories 170, fat 3, fiber 4, carbs 14, protein 7

Okra Breakfast Mix

Preparation time: 10 minutes
Cooking time: 2 hours
Servings: 4

Ingredients:

1 cup red onion, roughly chopped
1 cup cherry tomatoes, halved
3 cups okra, sliced
1 cup mushrooms, sliced
A pinch of salt and black pepper
2 tablespoons basil, chopped
½ cup olive oil
½ cup balsamic vinegar

Directions:

In your slow cooker, mix the onion with cherry tomatoes, okra, mushrooms, salt, pepper and the basil and toss.
In a bowl, combine the oil with the vinegar, whisk, add over the okra mix, cover the pot, cook on Low for 2 hours, divide into bowls and serve.
Enjoy!

Nutrition:

calories 181, fat 2, fiber 2, carbs 7, protein 6

Thyme Eggs And Sweet Potatoes

Preparation time: 10 minutes
Cooking time: 3 hours
Servings: 4

Ingredients:

4 bacon slices, cooked and crumbled
4 sweet potatoes, peeled and shredded
1 tablespoon thyme, chopped
4 eggs, whisked
A pinch of salt and black pepper
2 tablespoons olive oil

Directions:

In a bowl, combine the bacon with the sweet potatoes, thyme, eggs, salt and pepper and whisk well.
Add the oil to your slow cooker, add eggs and sweet potatoes mix, spread, cover and cook on Low for 3 hours.
Divide between plates and serve for breakfast.
Enjoy!

Nutrition:

calories 189, fat 6, fiber 4, carbs 12, protein 6

Chorizo Breakfast Casserole

Preparation time: 10 minutes
Cooking time: 10 hours
Servings: 8

Ingredients:

1 pound chorizo, casings removed and chopped
12 eggs, whisked
1 yellow onion, chopped
1 cup coconut milk
1 butternut squash, peeled and cubed
1 teaspoon ghee

Directions:

Heat up a pan over medium high heat, add chorizo, stir and cook for a few minutes.
Add onion, stir, cook for a couple more minutes and take off heat.
In a bowl, mix eggs with chorizo, onion, coconut milk and squash and whisk.
Grease your slow cooker with the ghee, pour eggs and chorizo mix, cover and cook on Low for 10 hours.
Slice chorizo casserole, divide between plates and serve for breakfast.
Enjoy!

Nutrition:

calories 246, fat 4, fiber 6, carbs 8, protein 5

Eggs and Sweet Potato Pesto

Preparation time: 10 minutes
Cooking time: 4 hours
Servings: 4

Ingredients:

4 sweet potatoes, pricked with a fork
4 eggs, fried
2/3 cup walnuts, soaked for 12 hours and drained
1 garlic clove
1 and ½ cups basil leaves
½ cup olive oil
Juice from ½ lemon
A pinch of salt and black pepper

Directions:

Wrap sweet potatoes in tin foil, add them to your slow cooker, cover and cook on High for 4hours.
Transfer sweet potatoes to a cutting board, unwrap, cool them down, peel and mash them with a fork.
In your food processor, mix walnuts with garlic, basil, oil, salt, pepper and lemon juice and pulse really well.
Mix sweet potato mash with basil pesto and stir well.
Divide fried eggs between plates, top each with sweet potato pesto and serve for breakfast.
Enjoy!

Nutrition:

calories 163, fat 5, fiber 6, carbs 13, protein 4

Delicious Pumpkin Butter

Preparation time: 10 minutes
Cooking time: 4 hours
Servings: 8

Ingredients:

30 ounces pumpkin puree
½ cup apple cider
1 cup coconut sugar
1 teaspoon vanilla extract
1 teaspoon cinnamon, ground
1 teaspoon nutmeg, ground
2 teaspoon lemon juice
1 teaspoon ginger, grated
¼ teaspoon cloves, ground
¼ teaspoon allspice, ground

Directions:

In your slow cooker, mix pumpkin puree with apple cider, coconut sugar, vanilla extract, cinnamon, nutmeg, lemon juice, ginger, cloves and allspice, stir, cover and cook on Low for 4 hours.
Blend using an immersion blender, cool down and serve for breakfast.
Enjoy!

Nutrition:

calories 222, fat 3, fiber 3, carbs 6, protein 3

Squash And Cranberry Sauce

Preparation time: 10 minutes
Cooking time: 5 hours
Servings: 4

Ingredients:

¼ teaspoon cinnamon powder
14 ounces cranberry sauce, unsweetened
2 acorn squash, peeled and cut into medium chunks

Directions:

In your slow cooker, combine the squash chunks with cranberry sauce and cinnamon powder, cover, cook on Low for 5 hours, divide into bowls and serve for breakfast.
Enjoy!

Nutrition:

calories 210, fat 3, fiber 2, carbs 12, protein 5

Veggies And Chorizo Mix

Preparation time: 10 minutes
Cooking time: 6 hours
Servings: 2

Ingredients:

1 pound chorizo, chopped
2 poblano peppers, chopped
1 cup kale, chopped
8 mushrooms, chopped
½ yellow onion, chopped
3 garlic cloves, minced
½ cup parsley, chopped
4 eggs, whisked
Cooking spray

Directions:

Grease your slow cooker with the cooking spray, add chorizo, peppers, kale, mushrooms, onion, garlic and parsley and toss.
Add the eggs, toss everything a bit, cover, cook on Low for 6 hours, divide between plates and serve for breakfast.
Enjoy!

Nutrition:

calories 200, fat 5, fiber 5, carbs 12, protein 6

Delicious Carrot Breakfast

Preparation time: 10 minutes
Cooking time: 6 hours
Servings: 10

Ingredients:

1 cup raisins
6 cups water
23 ounces applesauce, unsweetened
1/3 cup splenda
2 tablespoons cinnamon powder
14 ounces carrots, shredded
8 ounces canned pineapple, crushed
1 tablespoon pumpkin pie spice

Directions:

In your slow cooker, mix carrots with applesauce, raisins, splenda, cinnamon, pineapple and pumpkin pie spice, stir, cover and cook on Low for 6 hours.
Divide into bowls and serve for breakfast.
Enjoy!

Nutrition:

calories 139, fat 2, fiber 3, carbs 20, protein 4

Paleo Slow Cooker Side Dish Recipes

Summer Veggies Surprise

Preparation time: 10 minutes
Cooking time: 3 hours
Servings: 4

Ingredients:

1 and ½ cups red onion, cut into medium chunks
1 cup cherry tomatoes, halved
2 cups okra, sliced
2 and ½ cups zucchini, sliced
2 cups yellow bell pepper, chopped
1 cup mushrooms, sliced
2 tablespoons basil, chopped
1 tablespoon thyme, chopped
½ cup olive oil
½ cup balsamic vinegar

Directions:

In a large bowl, mix onion chunks with tomatoes, okra, zucchini, bell pepper, mushrooms, basil and thyme.
Add oil and vinegar and toss to coat everything.
Transfer to your slow cooker, cover and cook on High for 3 hours.
Divide between plates and serve as a side dish.
Enjoy!

Nutrition:

calories 150, fat 2, fiber 2, carbs 6, protein 5

Simple Broccoli Mix

Preparation time: 10 minutes
Cooking time: 2 hours and 30 minutes
Servings: 10

Ingredients:

10 ounces coconut cream
6 cups broccoli florets
¼ cup yellow onion, chopped
A pinch of salt and black pepper

Directions:

In your slow cooker, combine the broccoli with the cream, onion, salt and pepper, cover and cook on High for 2 hours and 30 minutes.
Divide between plates and serve as a side dish.
Enjoy!

Nutrition:

calories 160, fat 6, fiber 2, carbs 11, protein 6

Delicious Green Beans Mix

Preparation time: 10 minutes
Cooking time: 2 hours
Servings: 12

Ingredients:

16 cups green beans
½ cup coconut sugar
½ cup olive oil
1 teaspoon coconut aminos
1 teaspoon garlic powder

Directions:

Put the oil in your slow cooker, add green beans, sugar, aminos and garlic powder, toss, cover and cook on Low for 2 hours.
Divide between plates and serve as a side dish.
Enjoy!

Nutrition:

calories 162, fat 7, fiber 3, carbs 12, protein 3

Mushroom Cauliflower Rice

Preparation time: 10 minutes
Cooking time: 3 hours
Servings: 6

Ingredients:

1 cup cauliflower rice
6 green onions, chopped
2 tablespoons olive oil
2 garlic cloves, minced
½ pound baby Portobello mushrooms, sliced
1 and ½ cups veggie stock

Directions:

In your slow cooker, combine the cauliflower rice with the green onions, oil, garlic, mushrooms and veggie stock, cover, cook on Low for 3 hours, divide between plates and serve as a side dish.
Enjoy!

Nutrition:

calories 172, fat 5, fiber 4, carbs 14, protein 6

Butternut Mix

Preparation time: 10 minutes
Cooking time: 4 hours
Servings: 8

Ingredients:

1 yellow onion, chopped
1 cup carrots, chopped
1 tablespoon olive oil
1 and ½ teaspoons curry powder
1 garlic clove, minced
¼ teaspoon ginger, grated
½ teaspoon cinnamon powder
1 butternut squash, cubed
2 cups veggie stock
¾ cup coconut milk

Directions:

Heat up a pan with the oil over medium-high heat, add onion, carrots and garlic, stir, cook for 4-5 minutes and transfer to your slow cooker.
Add curry powder, ginger, cinnamon, squash and stock, cover and cook on Low for 3 hours and 30 minutes.
Add milk, toss, cover, cook on Low for 30 minutes more, divide between plates and serve as a side dish.
Enjoy!

Nutrition:

calories 212, fat 6, fiber 5, carbs 14, protein 4

Sausage Side Dish

Preparation time: 10 minutes
Cooking time: 2 hours
Servings: 4

Ingredients:

1 pound pork sausage, minced
½ pound mushrooms, chopped
2 tablespoons olive oil
2 yellow onion, chopped
2 garlic cloves, minced
6 celery ribs, chopped
1 cup chicken stock
1 tablespoon sage, chopped
1 cup cranberries
½ cup sunflower seeds

Directions:

Grease your slow cooker with the oil, add sausage, mushrooms, onion, garlic, celery, stock, sage, cranberries and sunflower seeds, cover, cook on Low for 2 hours, divide between plates and serve as a side dish.
Enjoy!

Nutrition:

calories 200, fat 4, fiber 6, carbs 14, protein 7

Parsley Sweet Potatoes

Preparation time: 10 minutes
Cooking time: 6 hours
Servings: 6

Ingredients:

1 and ½ pounds sweet potatoes, peeled and cubed
1 carrot, sliced
1 celery rib, chopped
¼ cup yellow onion, chopped
2 cups chicken stock
1 tablespoon parsley, chopped
1 garlic clove, minced
A pinch of salt and black pepper

Directions:

In your slow cooker, combine the sweet potatoes with the carrot, celery, onion, stock, parsley, garlic, salt and pepper, toss, cover and cook on Low for 6 hours.
Divide between plates and serve.
Enjoy!

Nutrition:

calories 114, fat 4, fiber 3, carbs 15, protein 4

Sweet Cabbage

Preparation time: 10 minutes
Cooking time: 6 hours
Servings: 4

Ingredients:

1 onion, sliced
1 cabbage, shredded
2 apples, peeled, cored and roughly chopped
A pinch of sea salt
Black pepper to the taste
1 cup apple juice
½ cup chicken stock
3 tablespoons mustard
1 tablespoon coconut oil

Directions:

Grease your slow cooker with the coconut oil and place apples, cabbage and onions inside.
In a bowl, mix stock with mustard, a pinch of salt, black pepper and the apple juice and whisk well.
Pour this over into the slow cooker as well, cover and cook on Low for 6 hours.
Divide between plates and serve right away as a side dish.
Enjoy!

Nutrition:

calories 200, fat 4, fiber 2, carbs 8, protein 6

Delicious Sweet Potatoes and Bacon

Preparation time: 10 minutes
Cooking time: 3 hours
Servings: 4

Ingredients:

½ cup orange juice
4 pounds sweet potatoes, sliced
3 tablespoons agave nectar
½ teaspoon thyme, dried
½ teaspoon sage, crushed
A pinch of sea salt
2 tablespoons olive oil
4 bacon slices, cooked and crumbled

Directions:

In your slow cooker mix sweet potato slices with orange juice, agave nectar, thyme, sage, sea salt, olive oil and bacon, cover and cook on High for 3 hours.
Divide between plates and serve as a tasty side dish!
Enjoy!

Nutrition:

calories 189, fat 4, fiber 4, carbs 9, protein 5

Flavored Carrots

Preparation time: 10 minutes
Cooking time: 6 hours
Servings: 6

Ingredients:

2 pounds sweet carrots
½ cup peaches, chopped
2 tablespoons olive oil
¼ cup coconut sugar
½ teaspoon cinnamon powder
1 teaspoon vanilla extract
A pinch of nutmeg, ground
2 tablespoons water

Directions:

In your slow cooker, combine the carrots with peaches, oil, sugar, cinnamon, vanilla, nutmeg and water, toss, cover, cook on Low for 6 hours, divide between plates and serve.
Enjoy!

Nutrition:

calories 190, fat 7, fiber 4, carbs 16, protein 3

Easy Butternut Squash

Preparation time: 10 minutes
Cooking time: 4 hours
Servings: 12

Ingredients:

1 butternut squash, cubed
1 yellow onion, chopped
½ cup chicken stock
2 teaspoons thyme, chopped
3 garlic cloves, minced
A pinch of salt and black pepper
6 ounces baby spinach

Directions:

In your slow cooker, combine the squash with the onion, stock, thyme, garlic, salt and pepper, toss, cover and cook on Low for 4 hours.
Add the spinach, toss, divide between plates and serve as a side dish.
Enjoy!

Nutrition:

calories 100, fat 2, fiber 5, carbs 15, protein 5

Tasty Mushroom Mix

Preparation time: 10 minutes
Cooking time: 4 hours
Servings: 6

Ingredients:

1 pound mushrooms, halved
2 tablespoons olive oil
1 yellow onion, sliced
1 teaspoon Italian seasoning
¼ cup veggie stock

Directions:

In your slow cooker, combine the mushrooms with the oil, onion, Italian seasoning and stock, toss, cover and cook on Low for 4 hours.
Divide between plates and serve as a side dish.
Enjoy!

Nutrition:

calories 120, fat 7, fiber 2, carbs 8, protein 5

Green Beans And Bacon

Preparation time: 10 minutes
Cooking time: 6 hours
Servings: 10

Ingredients:

8 bacon strips, chopped
2 pounds green beans, trimmed and halved
3 sweet potatoes, peeled and cubed
1 yellow onion, chopped
¼ cup chicken stock
A pinch of salt and black pepper

Directions:

In your slow cooker, combine the bacon with the green beans, sweet potatoes, onion, stock, salt and pepper, cover, cook on Low for 6 hours, divide between plates and serve.
Enjoy!

Nutrition:

calories 116, fat 4, fiber 4, carbs 14, protein 5

Spinach And Cauliflower Rice

Preparation time: 10 minutes
Cooking time: 3 hours
Servings: 8

Ingredients:

1 yellow onion, chopped
2 garlic cloves, minced
2 tablespoons olive oil
4 cups chicken stock
¼ teaspoon thyme, dried
20 ounces spinach, halved
2 cups cauliflower rice

Directions:

In your slow cooker, combine the oil with the onion, garlic, stock, thyme and cauliflower rice, toss, cover and cook on Low for 2 hours and 30 minutes.
Add the spinach, toss, cover, cook on Low for 30 minutes more, divide between plates and serve.
Enjoy!

Nutrition:

calories 200, fat 4, fiber 7, carbs 15, protein 7

Walnut Sweet Potatoes

Preparation time: 10 minutes
Cooking time: 5 hours
Servings: 10

Ingredients:

8 sweet potatoes, peeled and cut into wedges
¾ cup walnuts, chopped
½ cup coconut sugar
½ cup maple syrup
¼ cup apple juice

Directions:

In your slow cooker, combine the sweet potatoes with the walnuts, coconut sugar, maple syrup and apple juice, cover, cook on Low for 5 hours, divide between plates and serve as a side dish.
Enjoy!

Nutrition:

calories 212, fat 4, fiber 6, carbs 15, protein 6

Delicious Glazed Carrots

Preparation time: 10 minutes
Cooking time: 3 hours
Servings: 8

Ingredients:

2 pounds carrots, sliced
½ cup water
½ cup raw honey
A pinch of sea salt
½ teaspoon cinnamon, ground
A pinch of nutmeg, ground

Directions:

Put carrots in your slow cooker.
Add water, raw honey, salt, cinnamon and nutmeg, toss well, cover and cook on High for 3 hours.
Stir again, divide between plates and serve as a side dish.
Enjoy!

Nutrition:

calories 170, fat 3, fiber 4, carbs 7, protein 3

Garlic Mushrooms

Preparation time: 10 minutes
Cooking time: 4 hours
Servings: 4

Ingredients:

2 bay leaves
4 garlic cloves, minced
24 ounces mushroom caps
¼ teaspoon thyme dried
½ teaspoon basil, dried
½ teaspoon oregano, dried
1 cup veggie stock
Black pepper to the taste
2 tablespoons olive oil
2 tablespoons parsley, chopped

Directions:

Grease your slow cooker with the olive oil.
Add mushrooms, garlic, bay leaves, thyme, basil, oregano, black pepper and stock.
Cover and cook on Low for 4 hours.
Divide between plates and serve with parsley sprinkled on top.
Enjoy!

Nutrition:

calories 122, fat 6, fiber 1, carbs 8, protein 5

Delicious Brussels Sprouts

Preparation time: 10 minutes
Cooking time: 3 hours
Servings: 4

Ingredients:

1 cup red onion, sliced
2 pounds Brussels sprouts, halved
A pinch of sea salt
Black pepper to the taste
2 tablespoons olive oil
¼ cup apple cider
¼ cup maple syrup
1 tablespoon thyme, chopped

Directions:

Put the oil in your slow cooker.
Add Brussels sprouts, a pinch of salt, black pepper to the taste, onion, cider, maple syrup and thyme.
Toss everything to coat, cover and cook on High for 3 hours.
Divide between plates and serve warm.
Enjoy!

Nutrition:

calories 100, fat 4, fiber 2, carbs 10, protein 3

Delicious Beets and Carrots

Preparation time: 10 minutes
Cooking time: 6 hours
Servings: 4

Ingredients:

¾ cup pomegranate juice
A pinch of sea salt
2 tablespoons agave nectar
2 teaspoons ginger, grated
3 pounds red beets, peeled and cut into wedges
4 carrots, peeled and sliced

Directions:

Put pomegranate juice in a pot and heat up over medium heat.
Add a pinch of salt and the agave nectar, stir and cook for 2 minutes.
Put beets and carrots in your slow cooker and ginger and stir gently.
Add pomegranate juice, toss a bit, cover and cook on Low for 6 hours.
Divide beets and carrots between plates and serve warm or cold.
Enjoy!

Nutrition:

calories 100, fat 1, fiber 2, carbs 5, protein 3

Shredded Sweet Potatoes

Preparation time: 10 minutes
Cooking time: 4 hours
Servings: 8

Ingredients:

1 yellow onion, chopped
2 tablespoons olive oil
2 shallots, chopped
¼ cup parsley, chopped
2 teaspoons chipotle pepper, ground
3 pounds sweet potatoes, peeled and shredded
A pinch of salt and black pepper
8 ounces coconut cream

Directions:

Grease your slow cooker with the oil, add onion, shallots, chipotle pepper, potatoes, salt, pepper, cream and parsley, cover, cook on Low for 4 hours, divide between plates and serve as a side dish.
Enjoy!

Nutrition:

calories 199, fat 8, fiber 6, carbs 17, protein 16

Orange And Sage Sweet Potatoes

Preparation time: 10 minutes
Cooking time: 6 hours
Servings: 8

Ingredients:

4 pounds sweet potatoes, peeled and sliced
½ cup orange juice
3 tablespoons coconut sugar
A pinch of salt and black pepper
½ teaspoon thyme, chopped
½ teaspoon sage, dried

Directions:

Arrange the sweet potatoes in your slow cooker, add sugar, salt, pepper, orange juice, thyme and sage, cover, cook on Low for 6 hours, divide between plates and serve as a side dish.
Enjoy!

Nutrition:

calories 182, fat 4, fiber 7, carbs 16, protein 4

Cauliflower And Broccoli Mix

Preparation time: 10 minutes
Cooking time: 6 hours
Servings: 8

Ingredients:

4 cups broccoli florets
4 cup cauliflower florets
12 ounces coconut cream
1 teaspoon thyme, chopped
1 yellow onion, chopped
A pinch of salt and black pepper
½ cup almonds, chopped

Directions:

In your slow cooker, combine the broccoli with the cauliflower, cream, thyme, onion, salt, pepper and almonds, cover, cook on Low for 6 hours.
Divide between plates and serve as a side dish.
Enjoy!

Nutrition:

calories 177, fat 12, fiber 3, carbs 10, protein 8

Cauliflower Rice With Cherries

Preparation time: 10 minutes
Cooking time: 5 hours
Servings: 12

Ingredients:

3 cups cauliflower rice
3 cups chicken stock
1 cup carrot, shredded
4 ounces mushrooms, sliced
2 teaspoon marjoram, crushed
2 tablespoons olive oil
2/3 cup dried cherries, pitted
2/3 cup green onions, chopped
A pinch of salt and black pepper

Directions:

In your slow cooker, combine the cauliflower rice with the stock, carrot, mushrooms, marjoram, oil, cherries, onions, salt and pepper, toss, cover, cook on Low for 5 hours, stir again, divide between plates and serve as a side dish.
Enjoy!

Nutrition:

calories 170, fat 5, fiber 6, carbs 14, protein 6

Simple Carrots And Parsnips

Preparation time: 10 minutes
Cooking time: 8 hours
Servings: 8

Ingredients:

2 pounds carrots, cut into chunks
2 tablespoons orange zest, grated
1 pounds parsnips, cut into chunks
1 cup orange juice
1 cup veggie stock
A pinch of salt and black pepper
¼ cup parsley, chopped
1 tablespoon olive oil

Directions:

Grease your slow cooker with the oil, add carrots, orange zest, parsnips, orange juice, stock, salt, pepper, parsley , salt and pepper, toss, cover, cook on Low for 8 hours, divide between plates and serve as a side dish.
Enjoy!

Nutrition:

calories 170, fat 4, fiber 6, carbs 16, protein 4

Eggplant And Kale Mix

Preparation time: 10 minutes
Cooking time: 4 hours
Servings: 6

Ingredients:

4 cups eggplants, cubed
14 ounces canned roasted tomatoes and garlic, chopped
¾ cup yellow bell pepper, cubed
1 red onion, chopped
4 cups kale, torn
3 tablespoons red vinegar
2 tablespoons olive oil
1 teaspoon mustard
1 garlic clove, minced
¼ cup basil, torn
A pinch of salt and black pepper

Directions:

In your slow cooker, combine the oil with the vinegar, mustard, basil, garlic, salt and pepper and whisk.
Add the eggplants, tomatoes and garlic, bell pepper, onion and kale, toss, cover, cook on Low for 4 hours, divide between plates and serve as a side dish.
Enjoy!

Nutrition:

calories 200, fat 6, fiber 7, carbs 15, protein 6

Special Acorn Squash and Cranberry Sauce

Preparation time: 10 minutes
Cooking time: 7 hours
Servings: 4

Ingredients:

¼-cup raisins
2 acorn squash, peeled and cut into medium wedges
16 ounces canned cranberry sauce, unsweetened
¼ teaspoon cinnamon, ground
A pinch of sea salt
Black pepper to the taste

Directions:

Place acorn pieces in your slow cooker, add cranberry sauce, raisins, cinnamon, salt and pepper, stir, cover and cook on Low for 7 hours.
Divide between plates and serve hot as a Paleo side.
Enjoy!

Nutrition:

calories 230, fat 3, fiber 3, carbs 10, protein 2

Crazy Eggplant Delight

Preparation time: 10 minutes
Cooking time: 6 hours
Servings: 4

Ingredients:

1 eggplant, roughly chopped
1 tablespoon olive oil
2 garlic cloves, minced
2 carrots, chopped
1 yellow onion, chopped
10 ounces canned tomatoes, roughly chopped
1 tablespoon ras all hanout
A pinch of cayenne pepper
1 teaspoon cumin, ground
A handful cilantro, chopped

Directions:

Put the oil in your slow cooker.
Add eggplant, garlic, carrots, onion, tomatoes, cumin, ras eh hanout and cayenne.
Toss everything, cover and cook on Low for 6 hours.
Sprinkle cilantro on top, divide between plates and serve with a tasty pork steak.
Enjoy!

Nutrition:

calories 120, fat 4, fiber 2, carbs 10, protein 3

Tasty Zucchini

Preparation time: 10 minutes
Cooking time: 6 hours
Servings: 6

Ingredients:

2 cups zucchinis, sliced
1 teaspoon Italian seasoning
Black pepper to the taste
2 cups yellow squash, peeled and cut into wedges
1 teaspoon garlic powder
2 tablespoons olive oil
A pinch of sea salt
¼ cup pork rinds, crushed

Directions:

Put the oil in your slow cooker.
Add zucchini and squash pieces, Italian seasoning, black pepper, salt and garlic powder, toss well, cover and cook on Low for 6 hours.
Divide between plates and serve with pork rind sprinkled on top.
Enjoy!

Nutrition:

calories 100, fat 2, fiber 4, carbs 8, protein 5

Zucchini, Squash And Mushrooms Mix

Preparation time: 10 minutes
Cooking time: 3 hours
Servings: 8

Ingredients:

12 ounces zucchini, sliced
8 ounces yellow summer squash, cubed
2 cups cremini mushrooms, sliced
1 red sweet pepper, chopped
2 leeks, chopped
2 garlic cloves, minced
2 tablespoons veggie stock
2 tablespoons red curry paste
1/3 cup coconut milk
1 tablespoon ginger, grated
¼ cup basil, chopped

Directions:

In your slow cooker, combine the zucchini with the squash, mushrooms, sweet pepper, leeks, garlic, stock, curry paste, coconut milk, ginger and basil, toss, cover, cook on Low for 3 hours, divide between plates and serve as a side dish. Enjoy!

Nutrition:

calories 100, fat 2, fiber 3, carbs 9, protein 5

Easy Brussels Sprouts

Preparation time: 10 minutes
Cooking time: 4 hours
Servings: 6

Ingredients:

2 tablespoons coconut sugar
½ cup balsamic vinegar
2 tablespoons olive oil
2 pounds Brussels sprouts, halved
A pinch of salt and black pepper
2 tablespoons parsley

Directions:

Grease your slow cooker with the oil, add sugar, vinegar, salt and pepper and whisk well.
Add the sprouts and the parsley, toss, cover, cook on Low for 4 hours, divide between plates and serve as a side dish. Enjoy!

Nutrition:

calories 198, fat 5, fiber 6, carbs 16, protein 8

Herbed Carrots

Preparation time: 10 minutes
Cooking time: 4 hours
Servings: 4

Ingredients:

1 pound carrots, sliced
2 tablespoons olive oil
1 tablespoon dill, chopped
1 tablespoon parsley, chopped
1 tablespoons oregano, chopped
A pinch of salt and black pepper

Directions:

In your slow cooker, combine the carrots with the oil, dill, parsley, oregano, salt and pepper, toss, cover, cook on Low for 4 hours, divide between plates and serve as a side dish. Enjoy!

Nutrition:

calories 171, fat 3, fiber 8, carbs 14, protein 6

Pear And Sausage Mix

Preparation time: 10 minutes
Cooking time: 3 hours
Servings: 6

Ingredients:

24 ounces pork sausages, chopped
1 yellow onion, chopped
4 celery ribs, chopped
3 tablespoons olive oil
1 teaspoon sage, dried
1 teaspoon Italian seasoning
5 pears, cored and cubed
1 cup cranberries
3 eggs
2 cups chicken stock

Directions:

Heat up a pan with the oil over medium-high heat, add the sausage and the onion, stir, cook for 5 minutes and transfer to your slow cooker.
Add celery, sage, seasoning, pears, cranberries and eggs and stir well.
Add the stock, cover, cook on Low for 3 hours, divide between plates and serve as a side dish. Enjoy!

Nutrition:

calories 212, fat 4, fiber 5, carbs 14, protein 8

Cranberry And Sausage Mix

Preparation time: 10 minutes
Cooking time: 4 hours
Servings: 6

Ingredients:

1 tablespoon olive oil
3 celery stalks, chopped
2 leeks, chopped
2 carrots, chopped
½ teaspoon thyme, dried
1 pounds Italian sausage, chopped
½ cup cranberries, dried
½ cup walnuts, chopped
2 cups chicken stock
¼ cup parsley, chopped

Directions:

Heat up a pan with the oil over medium-high heat, add sausage, stir, brown for 5 minutes and transfer to your slow cooker.
Add celery, leeks, carrots, thyme, cranberries, walnuts, stock and parsley, toss, cover, cook on Low for 4 hours, divide between plates and serve as a side dish.
Enjoy!

Nutrition:

calories 199, fat 4, fiber 6, carbs 15, protein 9

Brussels Sprouts And Pine Nuts

Preparation time: 10 minutes
Cooking time: 3 hours
Servings: 4

Ingredients:

2 pounds Brussels sprouts, halved
2 cups chicken stock
A pinch of salt and black pepper
2 tablespoons balsamic vinegar
2 tablespoons olive oil
¼ cup pine nuts, toasted
2 tablespoons cilantro, chopped

Directions:

In your slow cooker, combine the sprouts with the stock, salt, pepper, vinegar, oil, pine nuts and cilantro, toss, cover and cook on High for 3 hours.
Divide between plates and serve as a side dish.
Enjoy!

Nutrition:

calories 199, fat 4, fiber 4, carbs 12, protein 8

Scalloped Sweet Potatoes

Preparation time: 10 minutes
Cooking time: 4 hours
Servings: 12

Ingredients:

2 pounds sweet potatoes, peeled and cubed
10 ounces coconut cream
1 and ½ cups coconut milk
½ cup ghee, melted+ 1 teaspoon
¼ cup yellow onion, chopped
A pinch of salt and black pepper

Directions:

In a bowl, mix sweet potato cubes with coconut cream, coconut milk, ghee, onion, salt and pepper, stir well, and pour in your slow cooker after you've greased it with 1 teaspoon ghee, cover Crockpot and cook on Low for 4 hours.
Leave scalloped potatoes aside to cool down, slice, divide between plates and serve as a side dish.
Enjoy!

Nutrition:

calories 234, fat 12, fiber 1, carbs 20, protein 6

Broccoli Side Dish

Preparation time: 10 minutes
Cooking time: 3 hours
Servings: 10

Ingredients:

6 cups broccoli florets, chopped
10 ounces coconut cream
¼ cup yellow onion, chopped
1 and ½ cups cashew cheese, shredded
2 tablespoons ghee

Directions:

Add ghee to your slow cooker, add broccoli florets, onion and coconut cream and toss.
Sprinkle cashew cheese on top, cover and cook on High for 3 hours.
Divide between plates and serve as a side dish.
Enjoy!

Nutrition:

calories 158, fat 11, fiber 3, carbs 11, protein 5

Green Beans

Preparation time: 10 minutes
Cooking time: 2 hours
Servings: 12

Ingredients:

16 cups green beans, halved
½ cup ghee, melted
½ cup coconut sugar
¾ teaspoon coconut aminos
A pinch of salt and black pepper

Directions:

In your slow cooker, mix green beans with coconut sugar, aminos, salt, pepper and melted ghee, toss well, cover and cook on Low for 3 hours.
Divide between plates and serve as a side dish. Enjoy!

Nutrition:

calories 160, fat 4, fiber 5, carbs 12, protein 3

Spinach And Carrots Mix

Preparation time: 10 minutes
Cooking time: 4 hours
Servings: 6

Ingredients:

5 carrots, sliced
12 ounces baby spinach leaves
2 garlic cloves, minced
1 yellow onion, chopped
A pinch of salt and black pepper
½ teaspoon oregano, dried
1 cup veggie stock
2 teaspoons lemon peel, grated
3 tablespoons lemon juice
¼ cup walnuts, chopped

Directions:

In your slow cooker, combine the carrots with spinach, garlic, onion, salt, pepper, oregano, stock, lemon peel, lemon juice and walnuts, toss, cover, cook on Low for 4 hours, divide between plates and serve as a side dish. Enjoy!

Nutrition:

calories 209, fat 8, fiber 14, carbs 13, protein 11

Marjoram Cauliflower Rice

Preparation time: 10 minutes
Cooking time: 5 hours
Servings: 10

Ingredients:

3 cups cauliflower rice
1 and ½ cups chicken stock
1 cup carrot, shredded
4 ounces mushrooms, sliced
2 tablespoons olive oil
3 teaspoons marjoram, dried and crushed
A pinch of salt and black pepper
1 cup green onions, chopped

Directions:

In your slow cooker, combine the cauliflower rice with the stock, carrot, mushrooms, oil, marjoram, salt, pepper and onions, toss, cover, cook on Low for 5 hours, divide between plates and serve as a side dish. Enjoy!

Nutrition:

calories 179, fat 5, fiber 3, carbs 13, protein 5

Simple Garlic Squash Mix

Preparation time: 10 minutes
Cooking time: 3 hours and 30 minutes
Servings: 12

Ingredients:

2 pounds butternut squash, peeled and cubed
1 yellow onion, chopped
1 ounces veggie stock
A pinch of salt and black pepper
5 garlic cloves, minced

Directions:

In your slow cooker, combine the squash with the onion, stock, salt, pepper and garlic, toss, cover, cook on High for 3 hours and 30 minutes, divide between plates and serve as a side dish. Enjoy!

Nutrition:

calories 206, fat 3, fiber 7, carbs 16, protein 7

Broccoli Medley

Preparation time: 10 minutes
Cooking time: 5 hours
Servings: 6

Ingredients:

30 ounces broccoli florets
2 tablespoons olive oil
2 tablespoons rosemary, chopped
A pinch of salt and black pepper
2 cups cherry tomatoes, halved
2 garlic cloves, minced
12 small baby carrots, peeled
1 and ½ cups veggie stock
1 yellow onion, roughly chopped
4 cups baby spinach

Directions:

In your slow cooker, combine the broccoli with the oil, rosemary, salt and pepper and toss. Add tomatoes, garlic, carrots, onion and stock, toss, cover and cook on Low for 4 hours and 40 minutes.
Add the spinach, cover, cook on Low for 20 minutes more, divide between plates and serve as a side dish.
Enjoy!

Nutrition:

calories 223, fat 7, fiber 11, carbs 18, protein 9

Brussels Sprouts And Apple Sauce

Preparation time: 10 minutes
Cooking time: 3 hours
Servings: 10

Ingredients:

1 cup red onion, chopped
2 pounds Brussels sprouts, halved
A pinch of salt and black pepper
1 cup apple juice
3 tablespoons olive oil
1 tablespoon rosemary, chopped

Directions:

In your slow cooker, combine the onion with the sprouts, salt, pepper, oil, rosemary and apple juice, toss, cover, cook on High for 3 hours, divide everything between plates and serve as a side dish.
Enjoy!

Nutrition:

calories 180, fat 4, fiber 4, carbs 13, protein 8

Celery And Beets

Preparation time: 10 minutes
Cooking time: 7 hours
Servings: 8

Ingredients:

1 cup pomegranate juice
2 teaspoons ginger, grated
2 and ½ pounds beets, peeled and cut into wedges
12 ounces celery root, cut into medium wedges

Directions:

In your slow cooker, combine the beets with celery, pomegranate and ginger, toss, cover, cook on Low for 7 hours, divide between plates and serve as a side dish.
Enjoy!

Nutrition:

calories 175, fat 4, fiber 4, carbs 16, protein 8

Cauliflower Pilaf

Preparation time: 10 minutes
Cooking time: 3 hours
Servings: 6

Ingredients:

1 cup cauliflower rice
6 green onions, chopped
3 tablespoons ghee, melted
2 garlic cloves, minced
½ pound Portobello mushrooms, sliced
2 cups warm water
A pinch of salt and black pepper

Directions:

In your slow cooker, mix cauliflower rice with green onions, melted ghee, garlic, mushrooms, water, salt and pepper, stir well, cover and cook on Low for 3 hours.
Divide between plates and serve as a side dish.
Enjoy!

Nutrition:

calories 200, fat 5, fiber 3, carbs 14, protein 4

Butternut Squash Side Dish

Preparation time: 10 minutes
Cooking time: 4 hours
Servings: 8

Ingredients:

1 tablespoon olive oil
1 cup carrots, chopped
1 yellow onion, chopped
1 teaspoon stevia
1 and ½ teaspoons curry powder
1 garlic clove, minced
1 big butternut squash, peeled and cubed
A pinch of sea salt and black pepper
¼ teaspoon ginger, grated
½ teaspoon cinnamon powder
3 cups coconut milk

Directions:

Add the oil to your slow cooker and spread on the bottom.
Add carrots, onion, stevia, curry powder, garlic, squash, salt, pepper, ginger, cinnamon and coconut milk, stir well, cover and cook on Low for 4 hours.
Stir, divide between plates and serve as a side dish.
Enjoy!

Nutrition:

calories 200, fat 4, fiber 4, carbs 17, protein 4

Sausage Side Dish

Preparation time: 10 minutes
Cooking time: 2 hours and 30 minutes
Servings: 12

Ingredients:

½ cup ghee, melted
1 pound pork sausage, ground
½ pound mushrooms, sliced
6 celery ribs, chopped
2 yellow onions, chopped
2 garlic cloves, minced
1 tablespoon sage, chopped
1 cup cranberries, dried
½ cup cauliflower florets, chopped
½ cup veggie stock

Directions:

Heat up a pan with the ghee over medium high heat, add sausage, stir and cook for a couple of minutes.
Transfer this to your slow cooker, add mushrooms, celery, onion, garlic, sage, cranberries, cauliflower and stock, stir, cover and cook on High for 2 hours and 30 minutes.
Divide between plates and serve as a side dish.
Enjoy!

Nutrition:

calories 200, fat 3, fiber 6, carbs 9, protein 4

Creamy Apples And Sweet Potatoes

Preparation time: 10 minutes
Cooking time: 7 hours
Servings: 8

Ingredients:

2 green apples, cored and cut into wedges
3 pounds sweet potatoes, peeled and cut into wedges
1 cup coconut cream
½ cup dried cherries
2 tablespoons avocado oil
1 and ½ teaspoon pumpkin pie spice

Directions:

In your slow cooker, combine the apples with the sweet potatoes, cream, cherries, oil and pumpkin pie spice, toss, cover, cook on Low for 7 hours, divide between plates and serve as a side dish.
Enjoy!

Nutrition:

calories 211, fat 8, fiber 5, carbs 14, protein 7

Creamy Carrots

Preparation time: 10 minutes
Cooking time: 3 hours
Servings: 6

Ingredients:

50 ounces baby carrots, peeled
1 cup coconut milk
1 tablespoon coconut sugar
8 ounces coconut cream
A pinch of white pepper

Directions:

In your slow cooker, combine the carrots with the coconut milk, coconut sugar, coconut cream and white pepper, toss, cover, cook on High for 3 hours, divide between plates and serve as a side dish.
Enjoy!

Nutrition:

calories 180, fat 5, fiber 5, carbs 12, protein 4

Cauliflower Rice And Mango

Preparation time: 10 minutes
Cooking time: 5 hours
Servings: 6

Ingredients:

1 yellow onion, chopped
1 tablespoon olive oil
1 red bell pepper, chopped
1 jalapeno, chopped
2 garlic cloves, minced
1 teaspoon ginger, grated
½ teaspoon oregano, dried
4 cup cauliflower rice
1 cup veggie stock
A pinch of salt and black pepper
2 mangos, peeled and cubed

Directions:

Grease your slow cooker with the oil, add the onion, bell pepper, jalapeno, garlic, ginger, oregano, cauliflower rice, stock, salt, pepper and mangos, cover, cook on Low for 5 hours, divide between plates and serve as a side dish. Enjoy!

Nutrition:

calories 190, fat 6, fiber 7, carbs 15, protein 8

Zucchini And Squash Mix

Preparation time: 10 minutes
Cooking time: 7 hours
Servings: 10

Ingredients:

1 butternut squash, peeled and cubed
4 cups zucchini, cubed
10 ounces tomato sauce
1 yellow onion, chopped
½ cup veggie stock
2 garlic cloves, minced
½ teaspoon turmeric powder
½ teaspoon cumin, ground
½ teaspoon red pepper flakes, crushed
¼ teaspoon sweet paprika

Directions:

In your slow cooker, combine the squash with the zucchini, tomato sauce, onion, stock, garlic, turmeric, cumin, paprika and pepper flakes, cover, cook on Low for 7 hours, divide between plates and serve as a side dish. Enjoy!

Nutrition:

calories 170, fat 3, fiber 4, carbs 14, protein 7

Indian Broccoli Mix

Preparation time: 10 minutes
Cooking time: 6 hours
Servings: 8

Ingredients:

6 cups broccoli florets
1 cup veggie stock
1 yellow onion, chopped
1 tablespoon ginger, grated
2 garlic cloves, minced
1 Thai pepper, chopped
1 tablespoon cumin, ground
1 tablespoon coriander, ground
2 tablespoons garam masala
Juice of ½ lemon

Directions:

In your slow cooker, combine the broccoli with the stock, onion, ginger, garlic, Thai pepper, cumin, coriander, garam masala and lemon juice, toss, cover, cook on Low for 6 hours, divide between plates and serve as a side dish. Enjoy!

Nutrition:

calories 195, fat 5, fiber 7, carbs 14, protein 7

Hot Cauliflower Mix

Preparation time: 10 minutes
Cooking time: 6 hours
Servings: 4

Ingredients:

6 cups cauliflower florets
1 yellow onion, chopped
8 ounces canned tomatoes, chopped
2 ounces canned roasted green chilies, chopped
½ cup hot sauce
2 teaspoons cumin, ground
1 tablespoon chili powder
A pinch of salt and black pepper

Directions:

In your slow cooker, combine the cauliflower with the onion, tomatoes, chilies, hot sauce, cumin, salt, pepper and chili powder, toss, cover, cook on Low for 6 hours, divide between plates and serve as a side dish. Enjoy!

Nutrition:

calories 214, fat 6, fiber 6, carbs 15, protein 7

Sweet Potatoes and Parsley

Preparation time: 10 minutes
Cooking time: 6 hours
Servings: 8

Ingredients:

2 pounds sweet potatoes, cut into medium pieces
1 carrot, chopped
1 celery rib, chopped
¼ cup yellow onion, chopped
2 cups veggie stock
1 tablespoon parsley, chopped
2 tablespoons ghee, melted
1 garlic clove, minced
A pinch of salt and black pepper

Directions:

In your slow cooker, mix sweet potatoes with carrot, celery, onion, garlic, salt, pepper and stock, stir, cover and cook on Low for 6 hours. Transfer this to a bowl, add melted ghee and parsley, stir, divide between plates and serve as a side dish.
Enjoy!

Nutrition:

calories 114, fat 3, fiber 4, carbs 18, protein 3

Glazed Carrots

Preparation time: 10 minutes
Cooking time: 6 hours
Servings: 6

Ingredients:

½ cup peach preserves
½ cup ghee, melted
2 pounds baby carrots
2 tablespoon stevia
1 teaspoon vanilla extract
A pinch of salt and black pepper
A pinch of nutmeg, ground
½ teaspoon cinnamon powder
2 tablespoons water

Directions:

Put baby carrots in your slow cooker, add melted ghee, peach preserves, stevia, vanilla, salt, pepper, nutmeg, cinnamon and water, toss well, cover and cook on Low for 6 hours. Divide between plates and serve as a side dish.
Enjoy!

Nutrition:

calories 283, fat 14, fiber 4, carbs 28, protein 3

Sweet Potatoes Side Salad

Preparation time: 10 minutes
Cooking time: 7 hours
Servings: 10

Ingredients:

6 bacon strips, chopped
2 pounds sweet potatoes, cubed
7 ounces cashew cheese, shredded
10 ounces coconut cream
½ cup almond milk
3 tablespoons red onion, chopped
1 tablespoon garlic, minced
1 tablespoon thyme, chopped
A pinch of salt and black pepper

Directions:

In your slow cooker, mix bacon with sweet potato cubes, cashew cheese, coconut cream, almond milk, onion, garlic, thyme, salt and pepper, stir, cover and cook on Low for 7 hours. Divide on plates and serve as a side salad.
Enjoy!

Nutrition:

calories 230, fat 12, fiber 3, carbs 20, protein 6

Green Beans And Tomatoes Mix

Preparation time: 10 minutes
Cooking time: 6 hours
Servings: 6

Ingredients:

1 cup veggie stock
30 ounces green beans, halved
12 ounces canned tomatoes, chopped
1 green bell pepper, chopped
A pinch of salt and black pepper
1 yellow onion, chopped
1 tablespoon chili powder
2 teaspoons cumin, ground
¼ teaspoon smoked paprika

Directions:

In your slow cooker, combine the stock with the green beans, tomatoes, bell pepper, salt, pepper, onion, cumin, chili powder and paprika, toss, cover, cook on Low for 6 hours, divide between plates and serve as a side dish.
Enjoy!

Nutrition:

calories 172, fat 6, fiber 4, carbs 11, protein 4

Chard Mix

Preparation time: 10 minutes
Cooking time: 3 hours
Servings: 6

Ingredients:

1 yellow onion, chopped	2 bunches Swiss chard, leaves torn
1 tablespoon olive oil	2 garlic cloves, minced
1 carrot, chopped	½ cup veggie stock
1 celery stalk, chopped	1 tablespoon coconut aminos
A pinch of salt and black pepper	

Directions:

In your slow cooker, combine the oil with the onion, carrot, celery, Swiss chard, salt, pepper, stock, garlic and aminos, toss, cover, cook on Low for 3 hours, divide between plates and serve as a side dish.
Enjoy!

Nutrition:

calories 182, fat 5, fiber 5, carbs 7, protein 5

Celery, Bok Choy And Chestnuts

Preparation time: 10 minutes
Cooking time: 4 hours
Servings: 6

Ingredients:

4 celery stalks, chopped	½ teaspoon red pepper flakes
1 yellow onion, chopped	1 tablespoon coconut aminos
1 cup carrot, chopped	½ cup veggie stock
12 ounces water chestnuts	2 bunches bok choy, chopped
2 teaspoons garlic, minced	3 scallions, chopped
2 teaspoons ginger, grated	1 teaspoon olive oil

Directions:

Grease your slow cooker with the oil, add celery, onion, carrot, chestnuts, garlic, ginger, pepper flakes, coconut aminos, stock, bok choy and scallions, toss, cover, cook on Low for 4 hours, divide between plates and serve as a side dish.
Enjoy!

Nutrition:

calories 190, fat 4, fiber 6, carbs 9, protein 4

Spicy Carrots

Preparation time: 10 minutes
Cooking time: 3 hours
Servings: 6

Ingredients:

1 pound carrots, peeled and cut into wedges	½ teaspoon turmeric, ground
1 cup red onion, chopped	1 cup veggie stock
2 garlic cloves, minced	3 tablespoon tomato paste
2 celery ribs, chopped	¼ cup cilantro, chopped
1 teaspoon coriander, ground	1 tablespoon spicy red pepper sauce
1 teaspoon cumin, ground	1 tablespoon lemon juice
A pinch of salt and black pepper	

Directions:

In your slow cooker, combine the carrots with the onion, garlic, celery, coriander, cumin, salt, pepper, turmeric, stock, tomato paste, cilantro, spicy sauce and lemon juice, toss, cover, cook on High for 3 hours, divide between plates and serve as a side dish.
Enjoy!

Nutrition:

calories 198, fat 4, fiber 4, carbs 12, protein 7

Simple Tomato Mix

Preparation time: 10 minutes
Cooking time: 4 hours
Servings: 6

Ingredients:

2 and ¼ pounds tomatoes, cut into wedges	2 teaspoons basil, dried
½ cups veggie stock	A pinch of salt and black pepper
1 yellow onion, chopped	½ teaspoon cumin, ground
2 tablespoons tomato paste	

Directions:

In your slow cooker, combine the tomatoes with the stock, onion, tomato paste, basil, salt, pepper and cumin, toss, cover, cook on Low for 4 hours, divide between plates and serve as a side dish.
Enjoy!

Nutrition:

calories 212, fat 4, fiber 4, carbs 12, protein 6

Spicy Collard Greens

Preparation time: 10 minutes
Cooking time: 3 hours
Servings: 4

Ingredients:

12 cups collard greens, chopped
3 tablespoons olive oil
1 red onion, chopped
2 garlic cloves, minced
1 chipotle pepper, chopped
1 cup veggie stock

Directions:

In your slow cooker, combine the collard greens with the oil, onion, garlic, chipotle pepper and stock, toss, cover, cook on Low for 3 hours, divide between plates and serve as a side dish. Enjoy!

Nutrition:

calories 194, fat 12, fiber 4, carbs 10, protein 6

Fresh Butternut Squash Side Salad

Preparation time: 10 minutes
Cooking time: 4 hours
Servings: 12

Ingredients:

3 pounds butternut squash, peeled and cubed
1 yellow onion, chopped
2 teaspoons thyme, chopped
3 garlic cloves, minced
A pinch of salt and black pepper
10 ounces veggie stock
6 ounces baby spinach

Directions:

In your slow cooker, mix squash cubes with onion, thyme, salt, pepper and stock, stir, cover and cook on Low for 4 hours.
Transfer squash mix to a bowl, add spinach, more salt and pepper if you want, toss, divide between plates and serve as a side dish. Enjoy!

Nutrition:

calories 100, fat 1, fiber 4, carbs 18, protein 4

Rich Mushrooms Mix

Preparation time: 10 minutes
Cooking time: 4 hours
Servings: 6

Ingredients:

1 yellow onion, chopped
1 pounds mushrooms, halved
½ cup ghee, melted
1 teaspoon Italian seasoning
A pinch of salt and black pepper
1 teaspoon sweet paprika

Directions:

In your slow cooker, mix mushrooms with onion, ghee, Italian seasoning, salt, pepper and paprika, toss, cover and cook on Low for 4 hours.
Divide between plates and serve as a side dish. Enjoy!

Nutrition:

calories 100, fat 6, fiber 1, carbs 8, protein 4

Cauliflower Rice and Spinach

Preparation time: 10 minutes
Cooking time: 3 hours
Servings: 8

Ingredients:

2 garlic cloves, minced
2 tablespoons ghee, melted
1 yellow onion, chopped
¼ teaspoon thyme, dried
3 cups veggie stock
20 ounces spinach, chopped
6 ounces coconut cream
A pinch of salt and black pepper
2 cups cauliflower rice

Directions:

Heat up a pan with the ghee over medium heat, add onion, stir and cook for 4 minutes.
Add garlic and thyme, stir and cook for 1 minute more.
Add stock, stir, bring to a simmer and take off heat.
Add spinach, coconut cream, salt and pepper, stir and transfer everything to your slow cooker.
Add cauliflower rice as well, stir a bit, cover and cook on High for 3 hours.
Divide between plates and serve as a side dish. Enjoy!

Nutrition:

calories 200, fat 4, fiber 4, carbs 8, protein 2

Maple Sweet Potatoes Side Dish

Preparation time: 10 minutes
Cooking time: 5 hours
Servings: 10

Ingredients:

8 sweet potatoes, halved and sliced
1 cup walnuts, chopped
½ cup cherries, dried and chopped
½ cup maple syrup
¼ cup apple juice
A pinch of salt

Directions:

Arrange sweet potatoes in your slow cooker, add walnuts, dried cherries, maple syrup, apple juice and a pinch of salt, toss a bit, cover and cook on Low for 5 hours.
Divide between plates and serve as a side dish.
Enjoy!

Nutrition:

calories 271, fat 6, fiber 4, carbs 26, protein 6

Creamy Spinach

Preparation time: 10 minutes
Cooking time: 5 hours
Servings: 6

Ingredients:

20 ounces spinach
2 cups coconut cream
1 cup cashew cheese, shredded
¼ cup ghee, melted

Directions:

In your slow cooker, mix spinach with coconut cream and ghee and toss well.
Add cashew cheese, cover and cook on Low for 5 hours.
Divide between plates and serve as a side dish.
Enjoy!

Nutrition:

calories 230, fat 12, fiber 2, carbs 9, protein 12

Flavored Artichokes

Preparation time: 10 minutes
Cooking time: 6 hours and 30 minutes
Servings: 4

Ingredients:

2 celery stalks, chopped
1 carrot, chopped
1 yellow onion, chopped
3 garlic cloves, minced
½ teaspoon oregano, dried
½ teaspoon rosemary, dried
½ teaspoon thyme, dried
½ teaspoon garlic powder
A pinch of salt and black pepper
30 ounces canned artichoke hearts, roughly chopped
½ cup veggie stock

Directions:

In your slow cooker, combine the celery with the carrot, onion, garlic, oregano, rosemary, thyme, garlic powder, salt, pepper, artichokes and stock, toss, cover, cook on Low for 6 hours and 30 minutes, divide between plates and serve as a side dish.
Enjoy!

Nutrition:

calories 197, fat 3, fiber 5, carbs 12, protein 7

Beets And Cabbage Mix

Preparation time: 10 minutes
Cooking time: 8 hours
Servings: 4

Ingredients:

6 beets, cut into wedges
10 ounces canned tomatoes, chopped
3 garlic cloves, minced
1 yellow onion, chopped
Salt and black pepper to the taste
2 tablespoons parsley, chopped
6 tablespoons red vinegar
3 cups green cabbage, shredded
4 ounces tomato paste

Directions:

In your slow cooker, combine the beets with the tomatoes, garlic, onion, salt, pepper, parsley, vinegar, cabbage and tomato paste, toss, cover, cook on Low for 8 hours, divide between plates and serve as a side dish.
Enjoy!

Nutrition:

calories 200, fat 3, fiber 6, carbs 14, protein 8

Chinese Brussels Sprouts

Preparation time: 10 minutes
Cooking time: 3 hours
Servings: 4

Ingredients:

2 pounds Brussels sprouts, halved
1 tablespoon walnuts, chopped
1 teaspoon red pepper flakes
¼ cup coconut aminos
2 teaspoons onion powder

1 tablespoon sweet paprika
2 tablespoons olive oil
1 tablespoon balsamic vinegar
A pinch of salt and black pepper

Directions:

In your slow cooker, combine the sprouts with the walnuts, pepper flakes, aminos, onion powder, paprika, oil, vinegar, salt and pepper, toss, cover, cook on High for 3 hours, divide between plates and serve as a side dish. Enjoy!

Nutrition:

calories 199, fat 4, fiber 3, carbs 13, protein 7

Balsamic Beets And Capers

Preparation time: 10 minutes
Cooking time: 6 hours
Servings: 4

Ingredients:

4 beets, peeled and sliced
1 cup veggie stock
2 tablespoons capers
2 tablespoons balsamic vinegar

A bunch of parsley, chopped
A pinch of salt and black pepper
1 tablespoon olive oil
1 garlic clove, chopped

Directions:

In your slow cooker, combine the beets with the stock, capers, vinegar, salt, pepper, oil and garlic, toss, cover, cook on Low for 6 hours, add parsley, toss again, divide between plates and serve as a side dish. Enjoy!

Nutrition:

calories 181, fat 3, fiber 7, carbs 12, protein 6

Creamy Asparagus

Preparation time: 10 minutes
Cooking time: 2 hours
Servings: 4

Ingredients:

2 pounds green asparagus, halved
½ cup veggie stock
½ cup coconut milk
3 tablespoons olive oil

A pinch of salt and black pepper
1 yellow onion, chopped
¼ teaspoon lemon juice

Directions:

In your slow cooker, combine the asparagus with the stock, milk, oil, salt, pepper, lemon juice and onion, toss, cover, cook on High for 2 hours, divide between plates and serve as a side dish. Enjoy!

Nutrition:

calories 180, fat 3, fiber 2, carbs 12, protein 7

Leeks And Fennel Mix

Preparation time: 10 minutes
Cooking time: 4 hours
Servings: 4

Ingredients:

3 fennel bulbs, chopped
4 leeks, roughly chopped
½ cup veggie stock

1 teaspoon thyme, dried
1 tablespoon olive oil
A pinch of salt and black pepper

Directions:

In your slow cooker, combine the fennel with the leeks, stock, thyme, salt, pepper and oil, toss, cover, cook on Low for 4 hours, divide between plates and serve as a side dish. Enjoy!

Nutrition:

calories 192, fat 2, fiber 5, carbs 11, protein 7

Chipotle Shredded Sweet Potatoes

Preparation time: 10 minutes
Cooking time: 4 hours
Servings: 10

Ingredients:

1 sweet onion, chopped
2 tablespoons olive oil
¼ cup parsley, chopped
2 shallots, chopped
2 teaspoons chipotle pepper, crushed
A pinch of salt and black pepper
4 big sweet potatoes, shredded
8 ounces coconut cream
16 ounces bacon, cooked and chopped
½ teaspoon sweet paprika
Cooking spray

Directions:

Heat up a pan with the oil over medium high heat, add shallots and onion, stir, cook for 6 minutes and transfer to a bowl.
Add parsley, chipotle pepper, salt, pepper, sweet potatoes, coconut cream, paprika and bacon, stir and pour everything in your slow cooker after you've greased it with some cooking spray.
Cover, cook on Low for 4 hours, leave aside to cool down a bit, slice, divide between plates and serve as a side dish.
Enjoy!

Nutrition:

calories 260, fat 14, fiber 6, carbs 20, protein 15

Sweet Potato Mash

Preparation time: 10 minutes
Cooking time: 5 hours
Servings: 6

Ingredients:

2 pounds sweet potatoes, peeled and sliced
1 tablespoon cinnamon powder
1 cup apple juice
1 teaspoon nutmeg, ground
¼ teaspoon cloves, ground
½ teaspoon allspice
1 tablespoon ghee, melted

Directions:

In your slow cooker, mix sweet potatoes with cinnamon, apple juice, nutmeg, cloves and allspice, stir, cover and cook on Low for 5 hours.
Mash using a potato masher, add ghee, whisk well, divide between plates and serve as a side dish.
Enjoy!

Nutrition:

calories 111, fat 2, fiber 2, carbs 16, protein 3

Kale Side Dish

Preparation time: 10 minutes
Cooking time: 6 hours
Servings: 6

Ingredients:

8 ounces ham hock slices
1 and ½ cups water
1 cup chicken stock
12 cups kale leaves, torn
A pinch of salt and cayenne pepper
2 tablespoons olive oil
1 yellow onion, chopped
2 tablespoons apple cider vinegar
Cooking spray

Directions:

Put ham in a heat proof bowl, add the water and the stock, cover and microwave for 3 minutes.
Heat up a pan with the oil over medium high heat, add onion, stir and cook for 5 minutes.
Drain ham and add it to your slow cooker, add sautéed onions, kale, salt, cayenne and vinegar, toss, cover and cook on Low for 6 hours.
Divide between plates and serve as a side dish.
Enjoy!

Nutrition:

calories 200, fat 4, fiber 7, carbs 10, protein 3

Incredible Veggie Mix

Preparation time: 10 minutes
Cooking time: 3 hours
Servings: 4

Ingredients:

2 red bell peppers, roughly chopped
1 sweet potato, peeled and cubed
½ cup garlic cloves
3 zucchinis, sliced
2 tablespoons olive oil
1 teaspoon Italian seasoning
A pinch of salt and black pepper

Directions:

In your slow cooker, mix red bell peppers with sweet potato, garlic, zucchinis, oil, salt, pepper and Italian seasoning, toss, cover and cook on High for 3 hours.
Divide between plates and serve as a side dish.
Enjoy!

Nutrition:

calories 120, fat 3, fiber 4, carbs 6, protein 3

Cauliflower Mash

Preparation time: 10 minutes
Cooking time: 5 hours
Servings: 6

Ingredients:

1 cauliflower head, florets separated
1/3 cup dill, chopped
6 garlic cloves
2 tablespoons ghee, melted
A pinch of salt and black pepper

Directions:

Put cauliflower in your slow cooker, add dill, garlic and water to cover cauliflower, cover and cook on High for 5 hours.
Drain cauliflower and dill, add salt, pepper and ghee, mash using a potato masher, whisk well and serve as a side dish.
Enjoy!

Nutrition:

calories 187, fat 4, fiber 5, carbs 7, protein 3

Simple Scallions And Endives

Preparation time: 10 minutes
Cooking time: 3 hours
Servings: 4

Ingredients:

2 tablespoons olive oil
3 scallions, chopped
4 endives, roughly chopped
½ cup veggie stock
3 garlic cloves, minced
1 tablespoon ginger, grated
A pinch of salt and black pepper

Directions:

In your slow cooker, combine the oil with scallions, endives, stock, garlic, ginger, salt and pepper, toss, cover, cook on High for 3 hours, divide between plates and serve as a side dish.
Enjoy!

Nutrition:

calories 203, fat 4, fiber 7, carbs 13, protein 9

Cauliflower And Brown Mushrooms

Preparation time: 10 minutes
Cooking time: 5 hours
Servings: 6

Ingredients:

2 yellow onions, chopped
1 cauliflower head, florets separated
1 cup veggie stock
20 ounces brown mushrooms, halved
A pinch of salt and black pepper
3 garlic cloves, minced
2 teaspoons thyme, chopped
½ teaspoon sweet paprika
1 tablespoon lemon juice

Directions:

In your slow cooker, mix the onions with the cauliflower, mushrooms, stock, salt, pepper, thyme, garlic, paprika and lemon juice, toss, cover, cook on Low for 5 hours, divide between plates and serve as a side dish.
Enjoy!

Nutrition:

calories 210, fat 5, fiber 7, carbs 14, protein 8

Sweet Potatoes with Orange and Sage

Preparation time: 10 minutes
Cooking time: 6 hours
Servings: 10

Ingredients:

4 pounds sweet potatoes, peeled and cut into medium slices
½ cup orange juice
2 tablespoons coconut sugar
A pinch of salt and black pepper
1 teaspoon sage, dried
½ teaspoon thyme, dried
2 tablespoons ghee, melted
4 bacon slices, cooked and crumbled

Directions:

Place sweet potatoes in your slow cooker.
In a bowl, mix orange juice with coconut sugar, salt, pepper, sage, thyme and ghee and whisk really well.
Add this over sweet potatoes, also add bacon, cover and cook on Low for 6 hours.
Divide between plates and serve as a side dish.
Enjoy!

Nutrition:

calories 189, fat 4, fiber 4, carbs 29, protein 4

Paleo Slow Cooker Snack and Appetizer Recipes

Simple Meatballs

Preparation time: 10 minutes
Cooking time: 8 hours
Servings: 4

Ingredients:

1 and ½ pounds beef, ground
1 egg, whisked
16 ounces canned tomatoes, crushed
14 ounces canned tomato puree
¼ cup parsley, chopped
2 garlic cloves, minced
1 yellow onion, chopped
Black pepper to the taste

Directions:

In a bowl, mix beef with egg, parsley, garlic, black pepper and onion and stir well.
Shape 16 meatballs, place them in your slow cooker, add tomato puree and crushed tomatoes on top, cover and cook on Low for 8 hours.
Arrange them on a platter and serve.
Enjoy!

Nutrition:

calories 160, fat 5, fiber 3, carbs 10, protein 7

Chicken Spread

Preparation time: 10 minutes
Cooking time: 2 hours
Servings: 10

Ingredients:

12 ounces chicken breasts, skinless, boneless, cooked and shredded
10 ounces coconut cream
1 cup coconut milk
1 cup hot sauce
A pinch of salt and black pepper
½ teaspoon garlic powder
¼ cup scallions, chopped
½ teaspoon onion powder

Directions:

In your slow cooker, combine the chicken with the cream, coconut milk, hot sauce, salt, pepper, garlic powder, scallions and onion powder, toss, cover, cook on Low for 2 hours, stir again, divide into bowls and serve as a spread.
Enjoy!

Nutrition:

calories 214, fat 4, fiber 7, carbs 16, protein 17

Tasty Chicken Wings

Preparation time: 10 minutes
Cooking time: 3 hours
Servings: 6

Ingredients:

2 tablespoons garlic, minced
2 and ¼ cups pineapple juice
3 tablespoons coconut aminos
2 tablespoons tapioca flour
1 tablespoon ginger, minced
1 teaspoon sesame oil
A pinch of sea salt
3 pounds chicken wings
A pinch of red pepper flakes, crushed
2 tablespoons 5 spice powder
Sesame seeds, toasted for serving
Chopped cilantro, for serving

Directions:

Put 2 cups pineapple juice in your slow cooker, add sesame oil, a pinch of salt, coconut aminos, ginger and garlic and whisk well.
In a bowl, mix tapioca flour with the rest of the pineapple juice, whisk and also add to your slow cooker.
Whisk everything and then add chicken wings.
Season them with pepper flakes and 5 spice, toss everything, cover and cook on High for 3 hours.
Transfer chicken wings to a platter and sprinkle cilantro and sesame seeds on top.
Transfer sauce from the slow cooker to a pot and heat it up for 2 minutes over medium high heat.
Whisk well, pour into small bowls and serve your wings with it.

Nutrition:

calories 200, fat 4, fiber 4, carbs 9, protein 20

Pepperoni Dip

Preparation time: 10 minutes
Cooking time: 1 hour
Servings: 6

Ingredients:

13 ounces coconut cream
8 ounces pepperoni, sliced
A pinch of black pepper

Directions:

In your slow cooker, combine the cream with the pepperoni and black pepper, cover, cook on Low for 1 hours, stir, divide into bowls and serve.

Nutrition:

calories 231, fat 4, fiber 6, carbs 16, protein 11

Different Chicken Dip

Preparation time: 10 minutes
Cooking time: 3 hours and 30 minutes
Servings: 8

Ingredients:

1 yellow onion, chopped	12 ounces coconut cream
2 teaspoons olive oil	½ cup chili sauce
1 red bell pepper, chopped	2 tablespoons chives, chopped
3 cups rotisserie chicken, cooked and shredded	

Directions:

Heat up a pan with the oil over medium-high heat, add the onion, stir, cook for 5 minutes and transfer to your slow cooker.
Add bell pepper, cream, chicken, chili sauce and chives, toss, cover, cook on Low for 3 hours and 30 minutes, divide into bowls and serve as a party dip.
Enjoy!

Nutrition:

calories 251, fat 5, fiber 7, carbs 17, protein 18

Carrot Dip

Preparation time: 10 minutes
Cooking time: 5 hours
Servings: 8

Ingredients:

2 pound carrots, peeled and chopped	A pinch of salt and black pepper
¼ cup olive oil	4 garlic cloves, minced
2 teaspoons cumin, ground	½ cup veggie stock

Directions:

Grease your slow cooker with half of the oil, add carrots, cumin, salt, pepper, garlic and stock, toss, cover, cook on Low for 5 hours, transfer to your blender, add the rest of the oil, pulse well, divide into bowls and serve.
Enjoy!

Nutrition:

calories 211, fat 6, fiber 4, carbs 13, protein 7

Moroccan Carrot Spread

Preparation time: 10 minutes
Cooking time: 5 hours
Servings: 8

Ingredients:

16 ounces carrots, chopped	A pinch of salt and black pepper
2 garlic cloves, minced	2 tablespoons lemon juice
½ teaspoon sweet paprika	3 tablespoons olive oil
½ teaspoon ginger powder	2 tablespoons green olives, pitted and chopped
½ teaspoon cinnamon powder	¼ cup veggie stock

Directions:

In your slow cooker, combine the carrots with the stock, garlic, paprika, ginger, cinnamon, salt and pepper, toss, cover, cook on Low for 5 hours, transfer to your blender, add lemon juice and oil, pulse well, transfer to bowls, sprinkle olives on top and serve.
Enjoy!

Nutrition:

calories 166, fat 3, fiber 7, carbs 14, protein 4

Eggplant Spread

Preparation time: 10 minutes
Cooking time: 1 hour and 30 minutes
Servings: 6

Ingredients:

2 pounds eggplants, peeled and cubed	1 garlic clove, minced
1 tablespoon sesame paste	¼ teaspoon liquid smoke
3 tablespoons lemon juice	½ teaspoon olive oil
	A handful parsley, chopped

Directions:

In your slow cooker, combine the eggplants with the sesame paste, lemon juice, garlic, liquid smoke, oil and parsley, toss, cover, cook on High for 1 hour and 30 minutes, pulse using an immersion blender, divide into bowls and serve.
Enjoy!

Nutrition:

calories 211, fat 4, fiber 8, carbs 15, protein 7

Simple Jalapeno Poppers

Preparation time: 10 minutes
Cooking time: 3 hours
Servings: 4

Ingredients:

½ pound chorizo, chopped
10 jalapenos, tops cut off and deseeded
1 small white onion, chopped
½ pound beef, ground
¼ teaspoon garlic powder
1 tablespoon maple syrup
1 tablespoon mustard
1/3 cup water

Directions:

IN a bowl, mix beef with chorizo, garlic powder and onion and stir.
Stuff your jalapenos with the mix and place them in your slow cooker.
Add the water, cover and cook on High for 3 hours.
Transfer jalapeno poppers to a lined baking sheet.
IN a bowl, mix maple syrup with mustard and whisk well.
Brush poppers with this mix, introduce in preheated broiler and cook for 10 minutes.
Arrange on a platter and serve.
Enjoy!

Nutrition:

calories 200, fat 2, fiber 3, carbs 8, protein 3

Tasty Fish Sticks

Preparation time: 10 minutes
Cooking time: 2 hours
Servings: 4

Ingredients:

2 eggs, whisked
1 pound cod fillets, cut into medium strips
1 and ½ cups almond flour
A pinch of sea salt
Black pepper to the taste
½ cup tapioca flour
¼ teaspoon paprika
Cooking spray

Directions:

In a bowl, mix almond flour, salt, pepper, tapioca and paprika and stir.
Put the eggs in another bowl.
Dip fish sticks in the eggs and then dredge in flour mix.
Spray your slow cooker with cooking spray and arrange fish sticks in it.
Cover and cook on High for 2 hours.
Arrange on a platter and serve.
Enjoy!

Nutrition:

calories 200, fat 2, fiber 4, carbs 7, protein 12

Spicy Pecans

Preparation time: 10 minutes
Cooking time: 2 hours and 15 minutes
Servings: 5

Ingredients:

1 pound pecans, halved
2 tablespoons olive oil
1 teaspoon basil, dried
1 tablespoon chili powder
1 teaspoon oregano, dried
¼ teaspoon garlic powder
1 teaspoon thyme, dried
½ teaspoon onion powder
A pinch of cayenne pepper

Directions:

In your slow cooker, mix pecans with oil, basil, chili powder, oregano, garlic powder, onion powder, thyme and cayenne and toss to coat.
Cover and cook on High for 15 minutes.
Switch slow cooker to Low and cook for 2 hours.
Divide into bowls and serve as a snack.
Enjoy!

Nutrition:

calories 78, fat 3, fiber 2, carbs 9, protein 2

Tasty Sausage Appetizer

Preparation time: 10 minutes
Cooking time: 2 hours
Servings: 15

Ingredients:

2 pounds sausages, sliced
18 ounces unsweetened Paleo apple jelly
9 ounces Dijon mustard

Directions:

Place sausage slices in your slow cooker, add apple jelly and mustard and toss to coat really well.
Cover and cook on Low for 2 hours stirring every 20 minutes.
Arrange sausage slices on a platter and serve as a Paleo appetizer.
Enjoy!

Nutrition:

calories 140, fat 3, fiber 1, carbs 9, protein 10

Mini Sausages Delight

Preparation time: 10 minutes
Cooking time: 4 hours
Servings: 24

Ingredients:

1 pound mini sausages, smoked

12 ounces Paleo chili sauce
1 cup Paleo grape jelly

Directions:

Put mini sausages in your slow cooker.
In a bowl, mix chili sauce with grape jelly and whisk really well.
Add this to your slow cooker, toss sausages to coat and cook on Low for 4 hours.
Serve them on a platter.
Enjoy!

Nutrition:

calories 200, fat 2, fiber 3, carbs 6, protein 12

Asparagus Spread

Preparation time: 10 minutes
Cooking time: 2 hours and 30 minutes
Servings: 8

Ingredients:

1 bunch asparagus, roughly chopped
4 garlic cloves, minced
5 ounces coconut cream
½ teaspoon garlic powder

½ teaspoon red pepper flakes
¼ teaspoon onion powder
¼ teaspoon paprika
6 ounces baby spinach
2 teaspoons olive oil
½ cup veggie stock

Directions:

In your slow cooker, combine the asparagus with the garlic, cream, garlic powder, pepper flakes, onion powder, paprika, spinach, stock and oil, toss, cover, cook on Low for 2 hours and 30 minutes, pulse using an immersion blender and serve.
Enjoy!

Nutrition:

calories 221, fat 4, fiber 7, carbs 16, protein 8

Great Broccoli Dip

Preparation time: 10 minutes
Cooking time: 2 hours
Servings: 8

Ingredients:

1 yellow onion, chopped
6 bacon slices, cooked and chopped
2 garlic cloves, minced
¼ teaspoon red pepper flakes, crushed
4 cups broccoli florets, chopped

8 ounces coconut cream
1 tablespoon scallions, chopped
½ cup avocado mayonnaise
½ cup coconut milk
A pinch of salt and black pepper

Directions:

In your slow cooker, combine the onion with the bacon, garlic, pepper flakes, broccoli, cream, scallions, mayo, milk, salt and pepper, stir, cover, cook on Low for 2 hours, stir again really well, divide into bowls and serve.
Enjoy!

Nutrition:

calories 261, fat 11, fiber 8, carbs 8, protein 12

Crab And Onion Dip

Preparation time: 10 minutes
Cooking time: 4 hours
Servings: 12

Ingredients:

24 ounces coconut cream
12 ounces canned crabmeat, drained
¼ cup coconut milk

4 green onions, chopped
2 teaspoons horseradish, prepared
A pinch of salt and black pepper

Directions:

In your slow cooker, combine the cream with the crabmeat, milk, onions, salt, pepper and horseradish, stir, cover, cook on Low for 4 hours, divide into bowls and serve.
Enjoy!

Nutrition:

calories 167, fat 8, fiber 1, carbs 2, protein 7

Spinach And Bacon Dip

Preparation time: 10 minutes
Cooking time: 2 hours
Servings: 12

Ingredients:

16 ounces coconut cream	10 ounces spinach, chopped
1 cup coconut milk	2 tomatoes, chopped
15 ounces canned artichokes, drained and chopped	½ cup bacon, cooked and crumbled
	4 green onions, chopped

Directions:

In your slow cooker, combine the cream with coconut milk, spinach, artichokes, tomatoes and green onions, stir, cover, cook on Low for 2 hours, divide into bowls, sprinkle bacon on top and serve.
Enjoy!

Nutrition:

calories 200, fat 6, fiber 8, carbs 9, protein 6

Tomato And Artichoke Spread

Preparation time: 10 minutes
Cooking time: 2 hours
Servings: 12

Ingredients:

10 ounces spinach, chopped	½ cup sun-dried tomatoes, chopped
8 ounces coconut cream	¼ cup yellow onion, chopped
½ cup artichoke hearts, chopped	1 garlic clove, minced

Directions:

In your slow cooker, combine the spinach with the cream, artichokes, tomatoes, onion and garlic, stir, cover, cook on Low for 2 hours, stir again, divide into bowls and serve.
Enjoy!

Nutrition:

calories 200, fat 6, fiber 9, carbs 15, protein 9

Butternut Squash Spread

Preparation time: 10 minutes
Cooking time: 6 hours
Servings: 4

Ingredients:

½ cup butternut squash, peeled and cubed	2 tablespoons coconut milk
½ cup canned white beans, drained	A pinch of rosemary, dried
1 tablespoon water	A pinch of sage, dried
	A pinch of salt and black pepper

Directions:

In your slow cooker, mix beans with squash, water, coconut milk, sage, rosemary, salt and pepper, toss, cover and cook on Low for 6 hours.
Blend using an immersion blender, divide into bowls and serve cold as a party spread.
Enjoy!

Nutrition:

calories 182, fat 5, fiber 7, carbs 12, protein 5

Amazing Eggplant Dip

Preparation time: 10 minutes
Cooking time: 4 hours and 10 minutes
Servings: 4

Ingredients:

1 eggplant	1 celery stick, chopped
1 zucchini, chopped	1 tomato, chopped
2 tablespoons olive oil	2 tablespoons tomato paste
2 tablespoons balsamic vinegar	1 and ½ teaspoons garlic, minced
1 tablespoon parsley, chopped	A pinch of sea salt
1 yellow onion, chopped	Black pepper to the taste

Directions:

Brush eggplant with half of the oil, place on preheated grill and cook over medium high heat for 5 minutes on each side.
Leave aside to cool down and then chop it.
Grease your slow cooker with the rest of the oil and add eggplant pieces.
Also add, zucchini, vinegar, onion, celery, tomato, parsley, tomato paste, garlic, salt and pepper and stir everything.
Cover and cook on High for 4 hours.
Stir your spread again very well, divide into bowls and serve.
Enjoy!

Nutrition:

110, fat 1, fiber 2, carbs 7, protein 5

Incredible Spinach Dip

Preparation time: 10 minutes
Cooking time: 2 hours
Servings: 4

Ingredients:

1 cup almond milk	28 ounces canned
1 cup cashews,	artichokes, drained
soaked for 2 hours and	and chopped
drained	8 ounces spinach
2 tablespoons lemon	8 ounces canned
juice	water chestnuts,
2 garlic cloves,	drained
chopped	Black pepper to the
2 teaspoons mustard	taste
	Avocado mayonnaise

Directions:

In your food processor, mix cashews with garlic, almond milk, mustard and lemon juice and blend well.
Transfer this to your slow cooker, add chestnuts, spinach, black pepper and artichokes.
Stir, cover and cook on High for 2 hours.
Leave your dip to cool down, add avocado mayo, stir well, divide into bowls and serve.
Enjoy!

Nutrition:

calories 200, fat 4, fiber 2, carbs 8, protein 5

Coconut Meatballs

Preparation time: 10 minutes
Cooking time: 4 hours
Servings: 4

Ingredients:

1 and ½ pounds beef	14 ounces canned
2 small yellow onions,	coconut milk
chopped	2 tablespoons hot
1 egg	sauce
A pinch of sea salt	1 teaspoon basil, dried
Black pepper to the	1 tablespoon green
taste	curry paste
3 tablespoons cilantro,	1 tablespoon coconut
chopped	aminos

Directions:

Put the meat in a bowl, add 1 small onion, egg, salt, pepper and 1 tablespoon cilantro, stir well, shape medium-sized meatballs and place them in your slow cooker.
Add hot sauce, aminos, coconut milk, curry paste and basil, toss to cover all meatballs and cook on Low for 4 hours.
Arrange meatballs on a platter and serve with the sauce drizzled all over.
Enjoy!

Nutrition:

calories 200, fat 6, fiber 2, carbs 8, protein 4

Delicious Chicken Meatballs

Preparation time: 10 minutes
Cooking time: 7 hours
Servings: 8

Ingredients:

46 ounces canned	2 tablespoons olive oil
tomatoes, crushed	1 bay leaf
1 yellow onion, halved	1 basil spring, chopped
5 garlic cloves, minced	¼ teaspoon red
2 tablespoons tomato	pepper flakes, crushed
paste	
For the meatballs:	
1 pound chicken,	1 teaspoon oregano,
ground	dried
1/3 cup almond milk	2 tablespoons parsley,
1 egg	chopped
1/3 cup cashew	A pinch of salt and
cheese, shredded	black pepper

Directions:

In your slow cooker, mix canned tomatoes with onion, garlic, tomato paste, olive oil, bay leaf, basil and pepper flakes, stir, cover and cook on Low for 6 hours.
In a bowl, mix chicken meat with almond milk, egg, cashews cheese, oregano, parsley, salt and pepper, stir well and shape medium meatballs out of this mix.
Add meatballs to your slow cooker and cook everything on High for 1 more hour.
Arrange meatballs on a platter, drizzle sauce all over and serve as an appetizer.
Enjoy!

Nutrition:

calories 231, fat 4, fiber 5, carbs 8, protein 2

Apple Vinegar Cashew Dip

Preparation time: 10 minutes
Cooking time: 7 hours
Servings: 2

Ingredients:

1 cup cashews,	1 cup veggie stock
soaked and blended	1 tablespoon water
1 teaspoon apple cider	
vinegar	

Directions:

In your slow cooker, combine the cashews with the vinegar, stock and water, cover, cook on Low for 6 hours, blend using an immersion blender and serve as a dip.
Enjoy!

Nutrition:

calories 191, fat 6, fiber 5, carbs 11, protein 9

Smoked Cauliflower And Cashew Dip

Preparation time: 10 minutes
Cooking time: 7 hours
Servings: 4

Ingredients:

2 cups cauliflower florets
½ cup cashews
2 cups almond milk
1 teaspoon garlic powder
¼ teaspoon smoked paprika

Directions:

In your slow cooker, combine the cauliflower with the cashews, milk, garlic powder and paprika, cover, cook on Low for 7 hours, transfer to your blender, pulse well, divide into bowls and serve.
Enjoy!

Nutrition:

calories 201, fat 7, fiber 4, carbs 14, protein 7

Cauliflower, Tomatoes And Mushrooms Dip

Preparation time: 10 minutes
Cooking time: 5 hours
Servings: 4

Ingredients:

½ cauliflower head, blended
54 ounces canned tomatoes, crushed
15 ounces white mushrooms, chopped
6 garlic cloves, minced
2 tablespoons balsamic vinegar
2 tablespoons tomato paste
2 tablespoons basil, chopped
1 and ½ teaspoons rosemary, dried
A pinch of salt and black pepper

Directions:

In your slow cooker, combine the cauliflower with the tomatoes, mushrooms, garlic, vinegar, tomato paste, basil, rosemary, salt and pepper, cover, cook on Low for 5 hours, stir again, divide into bowls and serve as a dip
Enjoy!

Nutrition:

calories 221, fat 7, fiber 6, carbs 10, protein 6

Bell Peppers Appetizer Salad

Preparation time: 10 minutes
Cooking time: 3 hours
Servings: 4

Ingredients:

1 red bell pepper, cut into medium wedges
1 green bell pepper, cut into medium wedges
1 orange bell pepper, cut into wedges
3 zucchinis, sliced
½ cup garlic, minced
2 tablespoons olive oil
A pinch of salt and black pepper
1 teaspoon Italian seasoning

Directions:

In your slow cooker, combine the red bell pepper with the green and orange one, also add the zucchinis, garlic, oil, salt, pepper and Italian seasoning, toss a bit, cover, cook on High for 3 hours, divide into bowls and serve as an appetizer.
Enjoy!

Nutrition:

calories 202, fat 3, fiber 3, carbs 12, protein 7

Cauliflower Hummus

Preparation time: 10 minutes
Cooking time: 5 hours
Servings: 4

Ingredients:

4 tablespoons sesame seeds paste
5 tablespoons olive oil
1 cup veggie stock
2 cauliflower heads, florets separated
1 red bell pepper, chopped
4 tablespoons lemon juice
1 teaspoon garlic powder
Black pepper to the taste
½ teaspoon cumin, ground

Directions:

In your slow cooker, combine the cauliflower with half of the oil, stock, bell pepper, black pepper, garlic powder and cumin, toss, cover, cook on Low for 5 hours, transfer to your blender, add the rest of the oil, the sesame paste and the lemon juice, pulse well, divide into bowls and serve.
Enjoy!

Nutrition:

calories 190, fat 4, fiber 2, carbs 3, protein 8

Bell Peppers Pate

Preparation time: 10 minutes
Cooking time: 5 hours
Servings: 8

Ingredients:

2 cups veggie stock
6 big red bell peppers, deseeded
A pinch of salt and black pepper
2 garlic cloves, minced
3 tablespoons olive oil
½ cup lemon juice
1 cup sesame seeds paste

Directions:

In your slow cooker, combine the stock with the bell peppers, salt and pepper, cover, cook on Low for 5 hours, drain, transfer the bell peppers to your blender, add the garlic, oil, lemon juice and sesame seeds paste, pulse well, divide into bowls and serve.
Enjoy!

Nutrition:

calories 160, fat 1, fiber 2, carbs 5, protein 8

Candied Pecans

Preparation time: 10 minutes
Cooking time: 3 hours
Servings: 4

Ingredients:

1 cup coconut sugar
1 and ½ tablespoon cinnamon powder
1 egg white
2 teaspoons vanilla extract
4 cups pecans
¼ cup water
Cooking spray

Directions:

In a bowl, mix coconut sugar with cinnamon and stir.
In another bowl, mix egg white with vanilla and whisk well.
Grease your slow cooker with cooking spray and add pecans.
Add egg white mix and toss.
Add coconut sugar mix, toss again, cover and cook on Low for 3 hours.
Divide pecans into bowls and serve as a snack.
Enjoy!

Nutrition:

calories 172, fat 3, fiber 5, carbs 8, protein 2

Peanuts Snack

Preparation time: 10 minutes
Cooking time: 12 hours
Servings: 10

Ingredients:

2 pounds green peanuts
10 cups water
A pinch of sea salt
2 tablespoons Cajun seasoning

Directions:

In your slow cooker, mix peanuts with water, salt and Cajun seasoning, stir, cover and cook on Low for 12 hours.
Drain, transfer to bowls and serve as a snack.
Enjoy!

Nutrition:

calories 90, fat 2, fiber 3, carbs 5, protein 3

Chicken Wings

Preparation time: 10 minutes
Cooking time: 4 hours
Servings: 4

Ingredients:

¼ cup coconut aminos
¼ cup balsamic vinegar
2 garlic cloves, minced
2 tablespoon stevia
1 teaspoon sriracha sauce
3 tablespoons lime juice
Zest from 1 lime, grated
1 teaspoon ginger powder
2 teaspoons sesame seeds
2 pounds chicken wings
2 tablespoons chives, chopped

Directions:

In your slow cooker, mix aminos with vinegar, garlic, stevia, sriracha, lime juice, lime zest and ginger and stir well.
Add chicken wings, toss well, cover and cook on High for 4 hours.
Arrange chicken wings on a platter, sprinkle chives and sesame seeds on top and serve as a casual appetizer.
Enjoy!

Nutrition:

calories 212, fat 3, fiber 6, carbs 12, protein 3

Artichokes And Spinach Spread

Preparation time: 10 minutes
Cooking time: 5 hours
Servings: 4

Ingredients:

1 cup coconut milk
2 garlic cloves, minced
28 ounces artichokes, canned, drained and chopped
2 tablespoons lemon juice
2 teaspoons mustard
8 ounces spinach
Black pepper to the taste

Directions:

In your slow cooker, combine the coconut milk with the garlic, artichokes, lemon juice, spinach, mustard and black pepper, toss, cover, cook on Low for 6 hours, pulse using an immersion blender, divide into bowls and serve.
Enjoy!

Nutrition:

calories 200, fat 4, fiber 2, carbs 14, protein 8

Chicken Strips

Preparation time: 10 minutes
Cooking time: 6 hours
Servings: 2

Ingredients:

3 tablespoons curry powder
1 cup veggie stock
3 chicken breasts, boneless, skinless and cut into thin strips
2 teaspoons turmeric powder
1 tablespoon cumin, ground
1 tablespoon garlic powder

Directions:

In your slow cooker, combine the chicken with the veggie stock, curry powder, turmeric powder, cumin and garlic powder, toss, cover and cook on Low for 6 hours.
Divide into bowls and serve as a snack.
Enjoy!

Nutrition:

calories 180, fat 2, fiber 3, carbs 14, protein 8

Squid Appetizer

Preparation time: 10 minutes
Cooking time: 3 hours and 30 minutes
Servings: 4

Ingredients:

14 ounces veggie stock
3 tablespoons coconut aminos
4 squid, tentacles separated and chopped
1 cup cauliflower rice

Directions:

In a bowl, mix tentacles with cauliflower rice, stir and stuff squid with this mix.
Place stuffed squid in your slow cooker, add aminos and stock, cover, cook on High for 3 hours and 30 minutes, arrange on a platter and serve as an appetizer.
Enjoy!

Nutrition:

calories 200, fat 3, fiber 6, carbs 14, protein 6

Mussels Salad

Preparation time: 10 minutes
Cooking time: 2 hours and 30 minutes
Servings:

Ingredients:

1 pound mussels
½ cup veggie stock
2 teaspoons cayenne pepper
3 tablespoons lemon juice
½ cup olive oil
1 garlic clove, minced
2 handfuls mixed salad greens
1 avocado, pitted, peeled and cubed
1 red bell pepper, cut into thin strips

Directions:

In your slow cooker, combine the mussels with the stock, cayenne and lemon juice, cover, cook on Low for 2 hours and 30 minutes, drain the mussels, transfer them to a salad bowl, ad the oil, the garlic, salad greens, avocado and bell pepper, toss, divide into small cups and serve as an appetizer.
Enjoy!

Nutrition:

calories 245, fat 4, fiber 4, carbs 16, protein 8

Squash And Spinach Appetizer Salad

Preparation time: 10 minutes
Cooking time: 6 hours
Servings: 4

Ingredients:

2 red onions, cut into medium wedges
1 butternut squash, cut into medium wedges
½ cup veggie stock
6 cups spinach
A pinch of black pepper
2 tablespoons balsamic vinegar
1/3 cup walnuts, chopped
1 teaspoon Dijon mustard
½ tablespoons oregano, dried
1 garlic clove, minced
6 tablespoons olive oil

Directions:

In your slow cooker, combine the onions with the squash, stock, black pepper, walnuts, garlic and oregano, toss, cover, cook on Low for 6 hours, transfer to a salad bowl, add the spinach, vinegar, mustard and the oil, toss, divide between appetizer plates and serve.
Enjoy!

Nutrition:

calories 211, fat 1, fiber 2, carbs 14, protein 8

Olives Salad

Preparation time: 10 minutes
Cooking time: 2 hours
Servings: 6

Ingredients:

1 cup black olives, pitted
1 cup kalamata olives, pitted
1 cup green olives, pitted
3 cups salad greens
5 garlic cloves, minced
A pinch of black pepper
2 tablespoons olive oil
½ cup veggie stock
1 teaspoon Italian seasoning
1 teaspoon lemon zest, grated

Directions:

In your slow cooker, combine the black olives with the green ones and the kalamata ones.
Add the garlic, black pepper, seasoning, lemon zest and stock, cover and cook on Low for 2 hours.
Transfer to a salad bowl, add the oil and the salad greens, toss, divide into small cups and serve as an appetizer.
Enjoy!

Nutrition:

calories 200, fat 2, fiber 2, carbs 14, protein 6

Meatballs Appetizer

Preparation time: 10 minutes
Cooking time: 2 hours and 30 minutes
Servings: 6

Ingredients:

1 egg
1 pound chicken, ground
½ teaspoon garlic powder
½ teaspoon onion powder
2 green onions, chopped
A pinch of salt and black pepper
¾ cup Paleo buffalo sauce

Directions:

In a bowl, mix chicken with egg, onion powder, garlic powder, green onions, salt and pepper and stir well.
Shape meatballs, add them to your slow cooker, also add buffalo sauce, cover and cook on Low for 2 hours and 30 minutes.
Arrange meatballs on a platter and serve them with the sauce on the side.
Enjoy!

Nutrition:

calories 221, fat 4, fiber 6, carbs 8, protein 6

Cauliflower and Jalapeno Dip

Preparation time: 10 minutes
Cooking time: 2 hours and 15 minutes
Servings: 6

Ingredients:

4 bacon slices, chopped and cooked
2 jalapenos, chopped
½ cup coconut cream
2 cups cauliflower rice
¼ cup cashew cheese, grated
A pinch of salt and black pepper
2 tablespoons chives, chopped

Directions:

In your slow cooker, mix bacon with jalapenos, coconut cream, cauliflower, salt and pepper, stir, cover and cook on Low for 2 hours.
Add cashew cheese and chives, cover and cook on Low for 15 minutes more.
Divide into bowls and serve.
Enjoy!

Nutrition:

calories 182, fat 3, fiber 3, carbs 7, protein 6

BBQ Kielbasa

Preparation time: 10 minutes
Cooking time: 4 hours
Servings: 6

Ingredients:

2 cup tomato sauce
½ cup stevia
2 teaspoons mustard
1 teaspoon hot sauce

1 yellow onion, chopped
2 pounds kielbasa, sliced

Directions:

In your slow cooker, mix kielbasa slices with tomato sauce, stevia, mustard, hot sauce and onion, stirs, cover and cook on Low for 4 hours. Divide kielbasa slices into bowls and serve as a snack.
Enjoy!

Nutrition:

calories 200, fat 3, fiber 4, carbs 7, protein 3

Zucchini Bites

Preparation time: 10 minutes
Cooking time: 2 hours
Servings: 4

Ingredients:

½ cup tomato sauce
1 zucchini, sliced
Black pepper to the taste

A pinch of cumin, ground
1 tablespoon parsley, chopped

Directions:

In your slow cooker, combine the zucchini with the tomato sauce, black pepper, cumin and parsley, cover, cook on Low for 2 hours, divide into small bowls and serve.
Enjoy!

Nutrition:

calories 170, fat 5, fiber 2, carbs 8, protein 7

Apples, Spinach And Chard Salad

Preparation time: 10 minutes
Cooking time: 2 hours
Servings: 4

Ingredients:

1 apple, cored and sliced
1 yellow onion, sliced
3 tablespoons olive oil
6 garlic cloves, minced
A pinch of salt and black pepper

¼ cup pine nuts, toasted
¼ cup balsamic vinegar
3 cups spinach leaves
3 cups chard
½ cup veggie stock

Directions:

In your slow cooker, combine the apple with the onion, oil, garlic, salt, pepper, pine nuts, stock, vinegar, spinach and chard, toss, cover, cook on Low for 2 hours, divide into bowls and serve as an appetizer.
Enjoy!

Nutrition:

calories 200, fat 1, fiber 4, carbs 12, protein 6

Coconut And Spinach Dip

Preparation time: 10 minutes
Cooking time: 2 hours
Servings: 4

Ingredients:

1 bunch spinach, chopped
½ cup veggie stock
2 tablespoons mint, chopped

1 scallion, chopped
¾ cup coconut cream
Black pepper to the taste

Directions:

In your slow cooker, combine the spinach with the stock, mint, scallions, cream and black pepper, cover, cook on Low for 2 hours, blend using an immersion blender, divide into bowls and serve as a dip.
Enjoy!

Nutrition:

calories 200, fat 5, fiber 5, carbs 12, protein 7

Walnuts Snack

Preparation time: 10 minutes
Cooking time: 1 hour and 30 minutes
Servings: 10

Ingredients:

3 tablespoons cinnamon powder
3 tablespoons coconut sugar
4 and ½ cups walnuts
1 cup water
2 teaspoons vanilla extract

Directions:

In your slow cooker, combine the walnuts with cinnamon, sugar, water and vanilla, toss, cover, cook on High for 1 hour and 30 minutes, divide into bowls and serve cold as a snack.
Enjoy!

Nutrition:

calories 180, fat 3, fiber 4, carbs 7, protein 7

Cauliflower Bites

Preparation time: 10 minutes
Cooking time: 4 hours
Servings: 2

Ingredients:

1 cauliflower head, florets separated
A pinch of salt and black pepper
2 tablespoons veggie stock
½ teaspoon chives, dried
½ teaspoon onion powder
2 tablespoons avocado oil

Directions:

In your slow cooker, combine the cauliflower florets with salt, pepper, stock, chives, onion powder and avocado oil, cover, cook on Low for 4 hours, divide into bowls and serve as a snack
Enjoy!

Nutrition:

calories 160, fat 6, fiber 7, carbs 12, protein 8

Nuts Snack

Preparation time: 5 minutes
Cooking time: 1 hour and 30 minutes
Servings: 6

Ingredients:

1 cup raw cashews, halved
2 and ¼ cup walnuts
1/3 cup coconut sugar
5 tablespoons coconut oil, melted
1 cup coconut flakes, unsweetened
1 teaspoon vanilla extract

Directions:

In your slow cooker, combine the cashews with the walnuts, sugar, oil, coconut flakes and vanilla extract, toss, cover, cook on High for 1 hour and 30 minutes.
Divide into bowls and serve as a snack.
Enjoy!

Nutrition:

calories 192, fat 7, fiber 3, carbs 10, protein 6

Special Mushrooms Appetizer

Preparation time: 10 minutes
Cooking time: 8 hours
Servings: 8

Ingredients:

1 shallot, chopped
2 garlic cloves, minced
2 tablespoons parsley, chopped
1 and ½ pounds button mushrooms
½ cup chicken stock
½ cup coconut cream
A pinch of salt and black pepper

Directions:

In your slow cooker, mix shallot with garlic, parsley, stock, cream, salt and pepper and whisk well.
Add mushrooms, cover and cook on Low for 8 hours.
Arrange mushrooms on a platter and serve them as an appetizer.
Enjoy!

Nutrition:

calories 130, fat 3, fiber 3, carbs 7, protein 3

Nuts Mix

Preparation time: 10 minutes
Cooking time: 4 hours
Servings: 20

Ingredients:

4 tablespoons ghee, melted
1 ounce Italian seasoning
1 teaspoon cinnamon powder
A pinch of cayenne pepper
2 cups cashews
2 cups pecans
2 cups almonds
2 cups walnuts

Directions:

In your slow cooker, mix melted ghee with Italian seasoning, cinnamon powder, cayenne, cashews, pecans, almonds and walnuts, toss well, cover and cook on Low for 4 hours. Divide into bowls and serve as a party snack. Enjoy!

Nutrition:

calories 200, fat 4, fiber 3, carbs 14, protein 4

Veggie Salsa

Preparation time: 10 minutes
Cooking time: 5 hours
Servings: 8

Ingredients:

2 eggplants, cubed
3 celery stalks, chopped
1 pound plum tomatoes, chopped
1 zucchini, halved and sliced
1 red bell pepper, chopped
1 cup sweet onion, chopped
3 tablespoons tomato paste
½ cup raisins
1 tablespoon stevia
1 teaspoon red pepper flakes, crushed
¼ cup basil, chopped
¼ cup parsley, chopped
A pinch of salt and black pepper
¼ cup green olives, pitted and chopped
¼ cup capers
2 tablespoons red wine vinegar

Directions:

In your slow cooker, mix eggplants with celery, tomatoes, zucchini, bell pepper, sweet onion, tomato paste, raisins, stevia, pepper flakes, basil, parsley, salt, pepper, olives, capers and vinegar, stir, cover and cook on Low for 5 hours. Divide into small bowls and serve as an appetizer. Enjoy!

Nutrition:

calories 80, fat 1, fiber 2, carbs 6, protein 1

Squash Cubes

Preparation time: 10 minutes
Cooking time: 4 hours
Servings: 4

Ingredients:

2 pounds butternut squash, cut into medium cubes
¼ cup veggie stock
1 teaspoon chili powder
1 teaspoon garlic powder
1 teaspoon sweet paprika
Black pepper to the taste

Directions:

In your slow cooker, combine the squash with the stock, chili powder, garlic powder, paprika and black pepper, cover, cook on Low for 4 hours, divide into cubes and serve as a snack. Enjoy!

Nutrition:

calories 202, fat 2, fiber 2, carbs 4, protein 6

Thyme Zucchini Snack

Preparation time: 10 minutes
Cooking time: 2 hours
Servings: 4

Ingredients:

1 zucchini, sliced
A pinch of salt and black pepper
1 tablespoon thyme, chopped
1 teaspoon garlic powder
3 tablespoons veggie stock
1 tablespoon olive oil

Directions:

In your slow cooker, combine the zucchini slices with salt, pepper, thyme, garlic, stock and oil, cover, cook on High for 2 hours, toss gently, divide into bowls and serve as a snack. Enjoy!

Nutrition:

calories 190, fat 4, fiber 3, carbs 9, protein 6

Carrot Bites

Preparation time: 10 minutes
Cooking time: 3 hours
Servings: 12

Ingredients:

½ teaspoon cinnamon powder
1 cup baby carrots halved
1 tablespoon coconut sugar
¼ cup water
2 tablespoons coconut flakes

Directions:

In your slow cooker, combine the carrots with cinnamon, sugar, water and coconut flakes, cover, cook on High for 3 hours, divide into bowls and serve cold
Enjoy!

Nutrition:

calories 160, fat 2, fiber 2, carbs 4, protein 8

Bacon Olives

Preparation time: 10 minutes
Cooking time: 2 hours
Servings: 36

Ingredients:

36 almond stuffed green olives
A pinch of black pepper
36 bacon pieces
¼ cup veggie stock

Directions:

Wrap each olive in a bacon piece and secure them with a toothpick
Arrange the wrapped olives in your slow cooker, add black pepper and the stock, cover, cook on High for 2 hours, divide the olives into bowls and serve as a snack
Enjoy!

Nutrition:

calories 180, fat 2, fiber 4, carbs 6, protein 5

Stuffed Mushrooms

Preparation time: 10 minutes
Cooking time: 4 hours
Servings: 4

Ingredients:

1 pound Mexican chorizo, chopped
1 pound mushroom caps
3 tablespoons coconut oil, melted
½ cup tomato sauce
1 yellow onion, chopped
A pinch of black pepper

Directions:

Stuff the mushrooms caps with mixed chorizo, black pepper and onion.
Arrange the mushrooms in your slow cooker greased with the oil, also add tomato sauce, cover, cook on Low for 4 hours, divide between plates and serve as an appetizer.
Enjoy!

Nutrition:

calories 205, fat 23, fiber 2, carbs 4, protein 13

Mushroom Appetizer Salad

Preparation time: 10 minutes
Cooking time: 5 hours
Servings: 4

Ingredients:

1 pound mushroom caps
½ teaspoon chili powder
1 teaspoon garam masala
1 teaspoon garlic paste
½ teaspoon turmeric powder
1 tablespoon olive oil
A pinch of salt and black pepper
½ cup veggie stock

Directions:

In your slow cooker, combine the mushrooms with the chili powder, garam masala, garlic paste, turmeric, oil, salt, pepper and stock, cover, cook on Low for 5 hours, divide into small cups and serve as an appetizer.
Enjoy!

Nutrition:

calories 170, fat 2, fiber 6, carbs 12, protein 7

Spinach Dip

Preparation time: 10 minutes
Cooking time: 4 hours
Servings: 24

Ingredients:

1 cup sweet onion, chopped
4 bacon slices, chopped and cooked
28 ounces canned artichoke hearts, chopped
10 ounces spinach
1 cup red bell pepper, chopped
1 cup Paleo mayonnaise
8 ounces coconut cream
3 garlic cloves, minced
½ teaspoon dried mustard

Directions:

In your slow cooker, mix onion with bacon, artichokes, spinach, bell pepper, mayo, coconut cream, garlic and dried mustard, stir, cover and cook on Low for 4 hours.
Divide into bowls and serve as a dip.
Enjoy!

Nutrition:

calories 200, fat 3, fiber 6, carbs 8, protein 3

Caramelized Onion Appetizer

Preparation time: 10 minutes
Cooking time: 6 hours
Servings: 32

Ingredients:

1 apple, peeled, cored and chopped
2 cups sweet onions, sliced
2 tablespoons ghee
½ cup cranberries
¼ cup balsamic vinegar
1 tablespoon stevia
½ teaspoon orange zest, grated
7 ounces cashew cheese, shredded

Directions:

In your slow cooker, mix apples with cranberries, onions, ghee, vinegar, stevia and orange zest, stir, cover and cook on Low for 6 hours.
Divide into bowls, sprinkle cashew cheese on to and serve as an appetizer.
Enjoy!

Nutrition:

calories 32, fat 2, fiber 1, carbs 3, protein 4

Lemony Snack

Preparation time: 10 minutes
Cooking time: 2 hours and 30 minutes
Servings: 24

Ingredients:

Cooking spray
1 cup walnuts, chopped
1 cup pumpkin seeds
2 tablespoons dill, dried
2 tablespoons olive oil
1 teaspoon rosemary, dried
1 tablespoon lemon peel, shredded

Directions:

Grease your slow cooker with cooking spray.
Add walnuts, pumpkin seeds, oil, dill, rosemary and lemon pee, toss, cover and cook on Low for 2 hours and 30 minutes.
Divide nuts and seeds into bowls and serve them as a snack.
Enjoy!

Nutrition:

calories 100, fat 2, fiber 2, carbs 3, protein 2

Sweet Potato Patties

Preparation time: 10 minutes
Cooking time: 5 hours
Servings: 12

Ingredients:

2 cups sweet potatoes, peeled, cubed and boiled
2 garlic cloves, minced
1 cup tomato sauce
4 tablespoons cilantro, chopped
A pinch of salt and black pepper
Juice of 1 lime

Directions:

In a bowl mix sweet potatoes with salt and pepper, mash well, add garlic, cilantro, salt and pepper, stir well and shape medium patties out of this mix.
Place all the patties in your slow cooker, add tomato sauce and the lime juice, cover, cook on Low for 5 hours, divide into bowls and serve as an appetizer.
Enjoy!

Nutrition:

calories 170, fat 2, fiber 2, carbs 12, protein 6

Chili Chicken Appetizer

Preparation time: 10 minutes
Cooking time: 5 hours
Servings: 12

Ingredients:

2 pounds chicken breasts, cubed	1 adobo chili pepper, chopped
	1/5 cup tomato sauce

Directions:

In your slow cooker, combine the chicken with the chili pepper and tomato sauce, toss, cover, cook on Low for 5 hours, divide into bowls and serve.
Enjoy!

Nutrition:

calories 200, fat 3, fiber 2, carbs 8, protein 10

Tomato Salsa

Preparation time: 10 minutes
Cooking time: 6 hours
Servings: 4

Ingredients:

4 cups tomatoes, cubed	1 tablespoon oregano, chopped
2 teaspoons capers	1 tablespoon cilantro, chopped
6 ounces green olives, pitted and sliced	A pinch of salt and black pepper
4 garlic cloves, minced	
2 teaspoons balsamic vinegar	

Directions:

In your slow cooker, combine the tomatoes with the capers, olives, garlic, vinegar, oregano, cilantro, salt and pepper, cover, cook on Low for 6 hours, divide into bowls and serve cold.
Enjoy!

Nutrition:

calories 190, fat 6, fiber 5, carbs 12, protein 6

Fish Bites

Preparation time: 10 minutes
Cooking time: 2 hours
Servings: 4

Ingredients:

1 pound cod fillets, cubed	2 tablespoons olive oil
1 and ½ cups almond flour	1 cup tomato sauce
	A pinch of salt and black pepper

Directions:

In a bowl, combine the fish cubes with the flour, salt and pepper and toss.
Heat up a pan with the oil over medium-high heat, add the fish, sear for 1 minute on each side, transfer to your slow cooker, also add the sauce, cover, cook on Low for 2 hours, divide into bowls and serve as an appetizer.
Enjoy!

Nutrition:

calories 201, fat 2, fiber 4, carbs 5, protein 8

Shrimp And Tomato Appetizer Bowls

Preparation time: 10 minutes
Cooking time: 2 hours
Servings: 4

Ingredients:

2 pound shrimp, peeled and deveined	10 ounces canned tomato paste
1 yellow onion, chopped	

Directions:

In your slow cooker, combine the shrimp with the onion and tomato paste, cover, cook on Low for 2 hours, divide into bowls and serve warm.
Enjoy!

Nutrition:

calories 190, fat 3, fiber 2, carbs 11, protein 9

Stuffed Chicken

Preparation time: 10 minutes
Cooking time: 6 hours
Servings: 4

Ingredients:

4 chicken breasts, skinless and boneless
1 tablespoon olive oil
1 small yellow onion, chopped
1 small red bell pepper, chopped
2 teaspoons garlic, minced
6 ounces spinach
1 tablespoon lemon juice
1 cup veggie stock
A pinch of salt and black pepper
A handful parsley, chopped

Directions:

In a bowl, combine the onion with the bell pepper, garlic, spinach, salt and pepper, stir, cut a pocket in each chicken breast and stuff them with the spinach mix.
Add the oil to your slow cooker, add stuffed chicken, lemon juice and stock, cover, cook on Low for 6 hours, divide between plates, sprinkle parsley on top and serve as an appetizer.
Enjoy!

Nutrition:

calories 205, fat 4, fiber 3, carbs 12, protein 17

Spicy Sausage Appetizer

Preparation time: 10 minutes
Cooking time: 2 hours
Servings: 12

Ingredients:

2 pounds spicy pork sausage, sliced
18 ounces Paleo apple jelly
9 ounces mustard

Directions:

In your slow cooker, mix apple jelly with mustard and whisk really well.
Add spicy sausage slices, toss really well, cover and cook on Low for 2 hours.
Divide sausage slices between bowls and serve them as an appetizer.
Enjoy!

Nutrition:

calories 231, fat 4, fiber 6, carbs 7, protein 5

Beef and Pork Party Meatballs

Preparation time: 10 minutes
Cooking time: 5 hours
Servings: 20

Ingredients:

1 pound pork sausage, ground
1 pound lean beef, ground
2 eggs
½ cup yellow onion, chopped
2 tablespoons parsley, chopped
A pinch of salt and black pepper
½ teaspoon garlic powder
12 ounces canned apricot preserves
¾ cup BBQ sauce

Directions:

In a bowl, mix pork sausage meat with beef meat, eggs, onion, parsley, salt, pepper and garlic powder, stir well and shape 40 meatballs out of this mix.
In your slow cooker mix, apricot preserves with BBQ sauce and whisk well.
Add meatballs, toss them in the pot, cover and cook on Low for 5 hours.
Arrange meatballs, sauce on a platter, and serve them as an appetizer.
Enjoy!

Nutrition:

calories 216, fat 4, fiber 6, carbs 8, protein 4

Zucchini Spread

Preparation time: 10 minutes
Cooking time: 2 hours
Servings: 4

Ingredients:

4 cups zucchinis, chopped
1 cup chicken stock
¼ cup olive oil
A pinch of salt and black pepper
4 garlic cloves, minced
½ cup lemon juice
1 tablespoon cumin, ground

Directions:

1. In your slow cooker, combine the zucchinis with the stock, oil, salt, pepper, garlic, lemon juice and cumin, cover, cook on High for 2 hours, blend using an immersion blender, divide into bowls and serve cold.

Nutrition:

calories 140, fat 5, fiber 4, carbs 11, protein 7

Cocktail Meatballs

Preparation time: 10 minutes
Cooking time: 5 hours
Servings: 30

Ingredients:

2 pounds ground beef, ground
1 tablespoon coconut flour
2 eggs
½ cup parsley, chopped
1/3 cup tomato paste
3 tablespoons onion, chopped
2 tablespoon coconut aminos
A pinch of salt and black pepper
¼ teaspoon garlic powder
12 ounces chili sauce
14 ounces canned cranberry sauce
1 tablespoon stevia
1 tablespoon lemon juice

Directions:

In a bowl, mix beef with coconut flour, eggs, parsley, tomato paste, onion, coconut aminos, salt, pepper and garlic powder, stir well and shape 60 small meatballs out of this mix.
In your slow cooker, mix chili sauce with cranberry sauce, stevia and lemon juice and whisk really well.
Add meatballs, cover and cook on Low for 5 hours.
Arrange meatballs on a platter, drizzle sauce all over and serve as an appetizer.
Enjoy!

Nutrition:

calories 251, fat 4, fiber 6, carbs 10, protein 3

Hot Dip

Preparation time: 10 minutes
Cooking time: 2 hours
Servings: 6

Ingredients:

5 ancho chilies, chopped
2 garlic cloves, minced
A pinch of salt and black pepper
¼ cup veggie stock
2 tablespoons balsamic vinegar
1 tablespoon oregano, chopped
½ teaspoon cumin, ground

Directions:

In your slow cooker, combine the chilies with the garlic, salt, pepper, stock, vinegar, oregano and cumin, stir, cover, cook on High for 2 hours, blend using an immersion blender, divide into bowls and serve.
Enjoy!

Nutrition:

calories 115, fat 3, fiber 4, carbs 8, protein 5

Chicken Bites

Preparation time: 2 hours
Cooking time: 3 hours
Servings: 12

Ingredients:

2 cups chicken, ground
A pinch of salt and black pepper
2 green onions, chopped
2 celery stalks, chopped
1 egg, whisked
2 garlic cloves, minced
1 tablespoon parsley, chopped
1 cup tomato sauce
2 tablespoons olive oil

Directions:

In a bowl, combine the chicken with salt, pepper, green onions, celery, garlic, parsley, salt, pepper and egg, stir well and shape medium meatballs out if this mix.
Heat up a pan with the oil over medium-high heat, add the meatballs, cook them for 2-3 minutes, transfer them to your slow cooker, add the tomato sauce, cover, cook on High for 3 hours, divide into bowls and serve as an appetizer.
Enjoy!

Nutrition:

calories 210, fat 7, fiber 2, carbs 6, protein 10

Seafood Salad

Preparation time: 10 minutes
Cooking time: 5 hours
Servings: 3

Ingredients:

11 ounces octopus tentacles
2 cups veggie stock
1 pound shrimp, peeled and deveined
Juice of 1 lemon
4 celery stalks, chopped
3 tablespoons olive oil
Salt and black pepper to the taste
4 tablespoons parsley, chopped

Directions:

In your slow cooker, combine the octopus with the stock, lemon juice, celery, oil, salt and pepper, cover and cook on Low for 4 hours.
Add the shrimp and the parsley, toss, cover, cook on Low for 1 more hour, divide into bowls and serve cold.
Enjoy!

Nutrition:

calories 200, fat 10, fiber 3, carbs 14, protein 8

Apple Dip

Preparation time: 10 minutes
Cooking time: 1 hour and 30 minutes
Servings: 4

Ingredients:

1 shallot, chopped
1 tablespoon coconut oil, melted
¼ teaspoon cardamom powder
2 tablespoons ginger, minced
½ teaspoon cinnamon powder
2 red hot chilies, chopped
3 apples, cored and chopped
3 tablespoons coconut sugar
1 and ¼ tablespoon balsamic vinegar

Directions:

Grease your slow cooker with the oil, add shallot, cardamom, ginger, cinnamon, chilies, apples, sugar and vinegar, stir, cover, cook on High for 1 hour and 30 minutes, blend using an immersion blender, divide into bowls and serve. Enjoy!

Nutrition:

calories 140, fat 2, fiber 1, carbs 9, protein 6

Artichokes Salad

Preparation time: 10 minutes
Cooking time: 2 hours
Servings: 4

Ingredients:

4 big artichokes, halved
A pinch of salt and black pepper
1 cup baby arugula
2 tablespoons lemon juice
¼ cup olive oil
2 teaspoons balsamic vinegar
1 teaspoon oregano, dried
2 garlic cloves, minced
1 cup chicken stock

Directions:

In your slow cooker, combine the artichokes with salt, pepper, garlic and stock, cover, cook on High for 2 hours, transfer the artichokes to a bowl, add arugula, lemon juice, oil, vinegar and oregano, toss and serve as an appetizer. Enjoy!

Nutrition:

calories 202, fat 4, fiber 2, carbs 9, protein 9

Mini Hot Dogs

Preparation time: 10 minutes
Cooking time: 4 hours
Servings: 24

Ingredients:

1 pound mini smoked pork sausages
12 ounces chili sauce
1 cup grape jelly

Directions:

In your slow cooker, mix pork sausages with chili sauce and grape jelly, toss, cover and cook on Low for 4 hours.
Arrange mini hot dogs on a platter and serve them as an appetizer.
Enjoy!

Nutrition:

calories 251, fat 4, fiber 6, carbs 7, protein 3

Chicken Dip

Preparation time: 10 minutes
Cooking time: 3 hours and 30 minutes
Servings: 10

Ingredients:

1 pound chicken breast, skinless, boneless and sliced
3 tablespoons sriracha sauce
¼ cup chicken stock
2 tablespoons stevia
1 teaspoon hot sauce
8 ounces coconut cream

Directions:

In your slow cooker, mix chicken with sriracha sauce, stock, stevia and hot sauce, stir, cover and cook on High for 3 hours.
Shred meat, return to pot, also add coconut cream, cover and cook on High for 30 minutes more.
Divide into bowls and serve as a party dip.
Enjoy!

Nutrition:

calories 231, fat 3, fiber 6, carbs 10, protein 3

Crab Dip

Preparation time: 10 minutes
Cooking time: 2 hours
Servings: 6

Ingredients:

4 ounces coconut cream
1 pound crab meat
1 jalapeno, chopped
1 red bell pepper, chopped
4 tablespoons lemon juice
2 garlic cloves, minced
½ teaspoon mustard powder

Directions:

In your slow cooker, mix coconut cream with crab meat, jalapeno, bell pepper, lemon juice, garlic and mustard, stir, cover and cook on High for 2 hours.
Stir again, divide into bowls and serve as a party dip.
Enjoy!

Nutrition:

calories 182, fat 3, fiber 6, carbs 7, protein 3

Radish Dip

Preparation time: 10 minutes
Cooking time: 3 hours
Servings: 2

Ingredients:

14 ounces radishes, halved
4 tablespoons coconut cream
4 bacon slices, chopped
2 tablespoons veggie stock
1 tablespoon green onion, chopped
A pinch of salt and black pepper

Directions:

In your slow cooker, combine the radishes with the cream, bacon, stock, green onions, salt and pepper, cover, cook on High for 3 hours, blend using an immersion blender, divide into bowls and serve.
Enjoy!

Nutrition:

calories 240, fat 3, fiber 3, carbs 8, protein 11

Collard Greens Appetizer

Preparation time: 10 minutes
Cooking time: 4 hours
Servings: 4

Ingredients:

4 cups collard greens, torn
1 cup veggie stock
1 yellow onion, chopped
A pinch of salt and black pepper
2 tablespoons coconut aminos
2 teaspoons ginger, grated

Directions:

In your slow cooker, combine the greens with the stock, onion, salt, pepper, aminos and ginger, cover, cook on High for 1 hour and 30 minutes, divide into small bowls and serve as an appetizer.
Enjoy!

Nutrition:

calories 190, fat 2, fiber 4, carbs 7, protein 11

Tomato Dip

Preparation time: 10 minutes
Cooking time: 5 hours
Servings: 12

Ingredients:

8 pounds tomatoes, peeled and chopped
2 sweet onions, chopped
6 garlic cloves, minced
6 ounces tomato paste
¼ cup white vinegar
2 tablespoons coconut sugar
1 and ½ tablespoons Italian seasoning
A pinch of salt and black pepper
½ cup basil, chopped
1 tablespoon thyme, chopped

Directions:

In your slow cooker, mix tomatoes with onions, garlic, tomato paste, vinegar, coconut sugar, Italian seasoning, salt, pepper, basil and thyme, stir, cover and cook on High for 5 hours.
Blend using an immersion blender, divide into bowls and serve as a party dip.
Enjoy!

Nutrition:

calories 182, fat 3, fiber 6, carbs 8, protein 3

Paleo Slow Cooker Main Dish Recipes

Flavored Tilapia

Preparation time: 10 minutes
Cooking time: 2 hours
Servings: 4

Ingredients:

1 asparagus bunch, spears trimmed	4 tilapia fillets
12 tablespoons lemon juice	A pinch of lemon pepper
	2 tablespoons olive oil

Directions:

Divide tilapia fillets on 4 parchment paper pieces.
Divide asparagus on top, drizzle the lemon juice and sprinkle a pinch of pepper.
Drizzle the oil all over, wrap fish and asparagus and place in your slow cooker.
Cover and cook on High for 2 hours.
Unwrap fish, divide between plates and serve.
Enjoy!

Nutrition:

calories 200, fat 3, fiber 1, carbs 8, protein 6

Special Seafood Chowder

Preparation time: 10 minutes
Cooking time: 8 hours and 30 minutes
Servings: 4

Ingredients:

2 cups water	A pinch of cayenne pepper
½ fennel bulb, chopped	1 bottle clam juice
2 sweet potatoes, cubed	2 tablespoons tapioca powder
1 yellow onion, chopped	1 cup coconut milk
2 bay leaves	1 pounds salmon fillets, cubed
1 tablespoon thyme, dried	5 sea scallops, halved
1 celery rib, chopped	24 shrimp, peeled and deveined
Black pepper to the taste	¼ cup parsley, chopped

Directions:

In your slow cooker, mix water with fennel, potatoes, onion, bay leaves, thyme, celery, clam juice, cayenne, black pepper and tapioca powdered, stir, cover and cook on Low for 8 hours.
Add salmon, coconut milk, scallops, shrimp and parsley, cover and cook on Low for 30 minutes more.
Ladle chowder into bowls and serve.
Enjoy!

Nutrition:

calories 354, fat 10, fiber 2, carbs 10, protein 12

Easy Chicken Soup

Preparation time: 10 minutes
Cooking time: 4 hours
Servings: 4

Ingredients:

64 ounces chicken stock	½ teaspoon thyme, dried
1 yellow onion, chopped	3 carrots, chopped
2 celery stalks, chopped	2 tablespoons olive oil
2 tablespoons parsley, chopped	2 chicken breasts, skinless and boneless
2 zucchinis, chopped	A pinch of salt and black pepper

Directions:

Drizzle the oil in your slow cooker, add chicken breasts, carrots, onion, celery, zucchini, thyme, salt, pepper and stock, toss, cover and cook on High for 4 hours.
Shred the meat, divide it and the soup into bowls and serve with parsley sprinkled on top
Enjoy!

Nutrition:

calories 211, fat 4, fiber 7, carbs 14, protein 12

Italian Beef Roast

Preparation time: 10 minutes
Cooking time: 8 hours
Servings: 6

Ingredients:

5 pounds beef chuck roast	1 tablespoon coconut aminos
2 tablespoons Italian seasoning	10 peperoncinis
1 cup beef stock	3 tablespoons olive oil

Directions:

Put the roast in your slow cooker, add Italian seasoning and toss.
Also add stock, aminos, peperoncinis and the oil, toss, cover and cook on Low for 8 hours.
Shred the meat, divide it and cooking juices between plates and serve.
Enjoy!

Nutrition:

calories 314, fat 5, fiber 7, carbs 17, protein 20

Pork Shoulder Mix

Preparation time: 10 minutes
Cooking time: 7 hours
Servings: 6

Ingredients:

3 pounds pork shoulder
¼ cup balsamic vinegar
4 cups chicken stock
2 tablespoons chili sauce
1 tablespoon ginger, grated
Juice of 1 lime
2 cups baby mushrooms, sliced

A pinch of salt and black pepper
1 teaspoon cinnamon powder
1 teaspoon lemon pepper
1 tablespoon star anise seeds
½ teaspoons fennel seeds
¼ teaspoon clove, ground

Directions:

Rub the pork shoulder with salt, pepper, cinnamon, lemon pepper, star anise seeds, fennel seeds and clove and put in your slow cooker.
Add vinegar, stock, chili sauce, ginger, lime juice and baby mushrooms, cover and cook on Low for 7 hours.
Slice the pork shoulder, divide it and the mushrooms between plates, drizzle the cooking juices all over and serve.
Enjoy!

Nutrition:

calories 312, fat 4, fiber 5, carbs 16, protein 16

Pumpkin Soup

Preparation time: 10 minutes
Cooking time: 8 hours
Servings: 4

Ingredients:

2 pounds pumpkin, peeled and cubed
6 ounces coconut milk
2 tablespoons curry powder

A pinch of salt and black pepper
1 tablespoon coconut oil, melted

Directions:

Put the coconut oil in your slow cooker, add the pumpkin, coconut milk, curry powder, salt and pepper, toss, cover, cook on Low for 8 hours, pulse using an immersion blender, divide into bowls and serve.
Enjoy!

Nutrition:

calories 217, fat 6, fiber 9, carbs 15, protein 11

Easy Slow Cooked Beef

Preparation time: 10 minutes
Cooking time: 6 hours
Servings: 4

Ingredients:

2 pounds beef roast
1 poblano pepper, chopped
7 ounces tomato paste
1 yellow onion, chopped
1 cup beef stock
2 tablespoons cumin, ground

2 tablespoons olive oil
1 tablespoon oregano, chopped
1 tablespoon sweet paprika
1 tablespoon garlic, minced
½ cup cilantro, chopped

Directions:

Heat up a pan with the oil over medium-high heat, add the roast, brown it for 2 minutes on each side and transfer to your slow cooker.
Add poblano, tomato paste, onion, stock, cumin, oregano, paprika, garlic and cilantro, toss a bit, cover and cook on Low for 6 hours.
Divide the roast and the cooking juices between plates and serve.
Enjoy!

Nutrition:

calories 312, fat 4, fiber 6, carbs 16, protein 15

Cabbage Soup

Preparation time: 10 minutes
Cooking time: 4 hours
Servings: 4

Ingredients:

3 chicken breasts, skinless, boneless and cubed
2 celery stalks, chopped
2 carrots, chopped
½ cup zucchini, chopped
2 tablespoons olive oil

1 yellow onion, chopped
3 garlic cloves, minced
1 teaspoon basil, dried
1 green cabbage head, shredded
4 cups chicken stock
½ teaspoon oregano, dried

Directions:

In your slow cooker, mix the oil with the carrots, celery, chicken, zucchini, onion, garlic, basil, oregano and stock, toss, cover and cook on High for 2 hours.
Add the cabbage, cover, cook on High for 2 hours more, ladle into bowls and serve.
Enjoy!

Nutrition:

calories 281, fat 4, fiber 7, carbs 17, protein 9

Great Veggie Mix

Preparation time: 10 minutes
Cooking time: 8 hours
Servings: 4

Ingredients:

1 cauliflower head, florets separated	2 tablespoons curry powder
1 cup green beans, chopped	A pinch of salt and black pepper
2 carrots, sliced	1 tablespoon red pepper flakes
1 yellow onion, chopped	1 teaspoon garam masala
6 ounces coconut milk	2 tablespoons almond meal
2 garlic cloves, minced	

Directions:

In your slow cooker, combine the cauliflower with the green beans, carrots, onion, garlic, salt, pepper, coconut milk, pepper flakes, garam masala and almond meal, toss well, cover, cook on Low for 8 hours, divide into bowls and serve. Enjoy!

Nutrition:

calories 261, fat 6, fiber 8, carbs 15, protein 11

Easy Beef Stew

Preparation time: 10 minutes
Cooking time: 8 hours
Servings: 5

Ingredients:

2 pounds beef stew meat, cubed	2 carrots, chopped
2 cups chicken stock	3 garlic cloves, minced
1 yellow onion, chopped	3 bay leaves
1 tablespoon balsamic vinegar	1 tablespoons sweet paprika
2 celery stalks, chopped	1 teaspoon rosemary, dried
	A pinch of salt and black pepper

Directions:

In your slow cooker, combine the beef with the stock, onion, vinegar, celery, carrots, garlic, bay leaves, paprika, rosemary, salt and pepper, toss, cover and cook on Low for 8 hours. Divide the stew into bowls and serve. Enjoy!

Nutrition:

calories 243, fat 4, fiber 7, carbs 16, protein 14

Simple Chili

Preparation time: 10 minutes
Cooking time: 7 hours
Servings: 4

Ingredients:

1 yellow onion, chopped	1 tablespoon oregano, chopped
2 pounds beef, ground	2 tablespoons chili powder
4 garlic cloves, minced	½ teaspoon cumin, ground
2 green bell peppers, chopped	½ tablespoon basil, chopped
1 tomato, chopped	½ teaspoon adobo sauce
3 celery stalks, chopped	A pinch of salt and black pepper
28 ounces canned tomatoes, crushed	A drizzle of olive oil
¼ cup green chilies, chopped	
15 ounces tomato sauce	

Directions:

Heat up a pan with the oil over medium-high heat, add onion and garlic, toss and cook for 2 minutes,
Add the beef, brown it for a few minutes more and transfer everything to your slow cooker.
Add bell peppers, celery, tomato, crushed tomatoes, green chilies, tomato sauce, oregano, chili powder, cumin, basil, adobo sauce, salt and pepper, toss, cover and cook on Low for 7 hours.
Divide into bowls and serve. Enjoy!

Nutrition:

calories 291, fat 5, fiber 8, carbs 16, protein 18

Dill Sea Bass

Preparation time: 10 minutes
Cooking time: 2 hours
Servings: 4

Ingredients:

Juice of 1 lemon	2 tablespoons dill, chopped
1 pound sea bass fillet	A pinch of salt and black pepper
¼ cup tomato sauce	

Directions:

In your slow cooker, combine the sea bass with the tomato sauce, lemon juice, dill, salt and pepper, cover and cook on Low for 2 hours. Divide between plates and serve. Enjoy!

Nutrition:

calories 210, fat 3, fiber 6, carbs 8, protein 5

Italian Chicken

Preparation time: 10 minutes
Cooking time: 6 hours
Servings: 4

Ingredients:

3 pounds chicken pieces
2 tablespoons olive oil
1 yellow onion, chopped
1 and ½ teaspoons oregano, dried
¼ cup tomato paste
3 garlic cloves, minced
¼ teaspoon red pepper flakes
6 ounces canned tomatoes, chopped
½ cup chicken stock
2 pounds white mushrooms, sliced

Directions:

Heat up a pan with the oil over medium-high heat, add the chicken, brown on all sides for 2 minutes and transfer to your slow cooker.
Add the onion and the garlic to the pan, cook them over medium heat for 2 minutes more and also add to your slow cooker.
Add oregano, tomato paste, pepper flakes, tomatoes, stock and mushrooms to the slow cooker as well, cover the pot and cook on Low for 6 hours.
Divide between plates and serve.
Enjoy!

Nutrition:

calories 251, fat 4, fiber 6, carbs 15, protein 8

Elegant Salmon Dish

Preparation time: 10 minutes
Cooking time: 3 hours
Servings: 2

Ingredients:

2 medium salmon fillets
A pinch of sea salt
Black pepper to the taste
2 tablespoons coconut aminos
2 tablespoons maple syrup
16 ounces mixed broccoli and cauliflower florets
2 tablespoons lemon juice
1 teaspoon sesame seeds

Directions:

Put the cauliflower and broccoli florets in your slow cooker and top with salmon fillets.
In a bowl, mix maple syrup with aminos and lemon juice and whisk really well.
Pour this over salmon fillets, season with black pepper to the taste, sprinkle sesame seeds on top and cook on Low for 3 hours.
Divide everything between plates and serve.
Enjoy!

Nutrition:

calories 230, fat 4, fiber 2, carbs 7, protein 6

Seafood Stew

Preparation time: 10 minutes
Cooking time: 3 hours and 30 minutes
Servings: 6

Ingredients:

3 garlic cloves, minced
28 ounces canned tomatoes, crushed
1 pound sweet potatoes, peeled and cubed
4 cups veggie stock
1 small yellow onion, chopped
1 teaspoon cilantro, dried
1 teaspoon thyme, dried
1 teaspoon basil, dried
A pinch of sea salt
Black pepper to the taste
¼ teaspoon red pepper flakes
A pinch of cayenne pepper
2 pounds mixed scallops and peeled and deveined shrimp

Directions:

Put tomatoes in your slow cooker.
Add garlic, sweet potatoes, stock, onion, cilantro, thyme, basil, salt, pepper, cayenne and pepper flakes, stir, cover and cook on High for 3 hours.
Add scallops and shrimp, stir gently, cover and cook on High for 30 minutes more.
Divide into bowls and serve.
Enjoy!

Nutrition:

calories 230, fat 3, fiber 2, carbs 8, protein 6

Divine Shrimp Scampi

Preparation time: 10 minutes
Cooking time: 1 hour and 30 minutes
Servings: 4

Ingredients:

2 tablespoons olive oil
¼ cup chicken stock
1 tablespoon garlic, minced
2 tablespoons parsley, chopped
Juice of ½ lemon
A pinch of sea salt
Black pepper to the taste
1 pound shrimp, peeled and deveined

Directions:

Put the oil in your slow cooker.
Add stock, garlic, parsley, lemon juice, salt and pepper and whisk really well.
Add shrimp, stir, cover and cook on High for 1 hour and 30 minutes.
Divide into bowls and serve.
Enjoy!

Nutrition:

calories 140, fat 4, fiber 3, carbs 9, protein 3

Steamed Pompano

Preparation time: 10 minutes
Cooking time: 1 hour
Servings: 4

Ingredients:

2 tablespoons agave nectar
1 pompano
2 tablespoons coconut aminos
¼ cup sesame oil
¼ cup veggie stock
1 small ginger piece, grated
6 garlic cloves, minced
2 tablespoons Paleo Worcestershire sauce
1 bunch leeks, chopped
1 bunch cilantro, chopped

Directions:

Put the oil in your slow cooker.
Add leeks and top with the fish.
In a bowl, mix stock with ginger, garlic, cilantro and coconut aminos and whisk well.
Add this to the pot as well, cover and cook on High for 1 hour.
Divide fish among plates and serve with the sauce drizzled on top.
Enjoy!

Nutrition:

calories 300, fat 8, fiber 2, carbs 8, protein 6

Special Poached Milkfish

Preparation time: 10 minutes
Cooking time: 4 hours
Servings: 2

Ingredients:

1 pound milkfish
6 garlic cloves, minced
1 small ginger pieces, chopped
½ tablespoon black peppercorns
1 cup pineapple juice
1 cup pineapple, chopped
¼ cup white vinegar
4 jalapeno peppers, chopped
A pinch of sea salt
Black pepper to the taste

Directions:

Put the fish in your slow cooker and season with a pinch of salt and some black pepper.
Add garlic, ginger, peppercorns, pineapple juice, pineapple chunks, vinegar and jalapenos.
Stir gently, cover and cook on Low for 4 hours.
Divide fish between 2 plates and top with the pineapple mix.
Enjoy!

Nutrition:

calories 240, fat 4, fiber 4, carbs 8, protein 3

Great Catfish Dish

Preparation time: 10 minutes
Cooking time: 6 hours
Servings: 3

Ingredients:

1 catfish, cut into 3 pieces
3 red chili peppers, chopped
½ cup coconut sugar
¼ cup coconut water
1 tablespoon coconut aminos
1 shallot, minced
A small ginger piece, grated
A handful coriander, chopped

Directions:

Put the catfish in your slow cooker.
Heat up a pan with the coconut sugar over medium high heat and stir until it caramelizes.
Add aminos, shallot, ginger, coconut water and chili pepper, stir and pour over the fish.
Add coriander, stir again, cover and cook on Low for 6 hours.
Divide between plates and serve with the sauce from the slow cooker drizzled on top.
Enjoy!

Nutrition:

calories 200, fat 4, fiber 4, carbs 8, protein 10

Asian Style Salmon

Preparation time: 10 minutes
Cooking time: 3 hours
Servings: 4

Ingredients:

4 salmon fillets, boneless
1 red bell pepper, cut into medium strips
1 tomato, cut into medium wedges
1 carrot, cut into matchsticks
2 tablespoons coconut aminos
2 tablespoons stevia
2 tablespoons lemon juice
1 teaspoon sesame seeds

Directions:

In your slow cooker, mix salmon with red bell pepper, tomato carrot, aminos, stevia and lemon juice, toss, cover and cook on Low for 3 hours.
Add sesame seeds, divide Asian fish mix between plates and serve.
Enjoy!

Nutrition:

calories 162, fat 4, fiber 7, carbs 8, protein 3

Lamb Stew

Preparation time: 10 minutes
Cooking time: 8 hours
Servings: 4

Ingredients:

1 yellow onion, chopped
1 tablespoon coconut oil, melted
1 and ½ pounds lamb meat, cubed
A pinch of salt and black pepper
1 carrot, sliced
1 teaspoon lemon zest, grated
1 teaspoon cinnamon powder
1 and ½ teaspoons coriander, ground
1 and ½ teaspoons cumin powder
½ teaspoon allspice
1 teaspoon onion powder
2 tablespoons lemon juice
2 garlic cloves, minced
6 apricots, sliced
1 tablespoons tomato paste
2 bay leaves
1 and ½ cups water
¼ cup almonds, chopped
2 tablespoons parsley, chopped

Directions:

Grease your slow cooker with the oil, add lamb meat, onion, carrot, salt, pepper, lemon zest, cinnamon, coriander, cumin, allspice, onion powder, lemon juice, garlic, apricots, tomato paste, bay leaves and water, toss, cover and cook on Low for 8 hours.
Add almonds and parsley, toss, divide into bowls and serve.
Enjoy!

Nutrition:

calories 312, fat 4, fiber 8, carbs 15, protein 8

Tasty Beef And Broccoli

Preparation time: 10 minutes
Cooking time: 4 hours
Servings: 4

Ingredients:

1 and ½ pounds beef flank steak, sliced and cubed
1 cup beef stock
2/3 cup coconut aminos
1/3 cup coconut sugar
1 tablespoon olive oil
1 tablespoons garlic, minced
¼ teaspoon chili powder
4 cups broccoli florets

Directions:

Grease your slow cooker with the oil, add beef, aminos, sugar, chili powder and garlic and whisk well.
Add beef and broccoli, toss, cover, cook on Low for 4 hours.
Divide into bowls and serve.
Enjoy!

Nutrition:

calories 271, fat 7, fiber 10, carbs 17, protein 16

Pork Loin Mix

Preparation time: 10 minutes
Cooking time: 8 hours
Servings: 6

Ingredients:

2 pounds pork tenderloin
1 yellow onion, chopped
3 garlic cloves, minced
1 jalapeno, chopped
A pinch of salt and black pepper
Juice of 1 lime
Juice of 1 orange
1 tablespoon oregano, dried
1 tablespoon olive oil
2 teaspoons cumin, ground

Directions:

Rub the pork tenderloin with the oregano, cumin, oil, salt and pepper and put it in your slow cooker.
Add onion, garlic, jalapeno, lime juice and orange juice, toss, cover and cook on Low for 8 hours.
Divide everything between plates and serve.
Enjoy!

Nutrition:

calories 241, fat 4, fiber 6, carbs 16, protein 18

Mexican Chicken Soup

Preparation time: 10 minutes
Cooking time: 6 hours
Servings: 6

Ingredients:

1 pound chicken breasts, boneless and skinless
4 cups chicken stock
15 ounces coconut milk
1 cup yellow onion, chopped
2 cups tomatoes, chopped
3 tablespoons chipotle peppers, chopped
1 teaspoon sweet paprika
2 tablespoons cumin, ground
1 tablespoon cilantro, chopped

Directions:

In your slow cooker, combine the chicken with chicken stock, coconut milk, onion, tomatoes, chipotle peppers, paprika, cumin and cilantro, toss, cover and cook on Low for 6 hours.
Shred the meat using 2 forks, divide the soup into bowls and serve.
Enjoy!

Nutrition:

calories 261, fat 6, fiber 8, carbs 15, protein 16

Easy Salsa Chicken

Preparation time: 10 minutes
Cooking time: 7 hours
Servings: 4

Ingredients:

4 chicken breasts, boneless and skinless
15 ounces mild salsa
1/3 cup water
1 and ½ tablespoons parsley, dried
1 teaspoon onion powder
1 teaspoon garlic powder
½ tablespoon cilantro, dried
½ tablespoon oregano, dried
½ teaspoon smoked paprika
½ teaspoon cumin, ground
1 teaspoon chili powder
A pinch of salt and black pepper

Directions:

In your slow cooker, combine the chicken with salsa, water, parsley, onion powder, garlic powder, cilantro, oregano, smoked paprika, cumin, chili powder, salt and pepper, toss, cover and cook on Low for 7 hours.
Divide into bowls and serve.
Enjoy!

Nutrition:

calories 271, fat 4, fiber 7,carbs 16, protein 20

Shredded Chicken Soup

Preparation time: 10 minutes
Cooking time: 4 hours
Servings: 4

Ingredients:

1 red bell pepper, chopped
2 tablespoons olive oil
1 yellow onion, chopped
1 jalapeno, chopped
3 garlic cloves, minced
4 chicken breasts, skinless and boneless
28 ounces canned tomatoes, chopped
4 cups chicken stock
1 teaspoon cumin, ground
1 tablespoons cilantro, chopped
¼ cup coconut milk

Directions:

In your slow cooker, combine the bell pepper with the oil, onion, jalapeno, garlic, chicken, tomatoes, stock and cumin, cover and cook on High for 3 hours and 30 minutes.
Add cilantro and coconut milk, shred the meat, toss, cover, cook on High for 30 minutes more, divide into bowls and serve.
Enjoy!

Nutrition:

calories 288, fat 4, fiber 7, carbs 16, protein 15

Easy Turkey Meatballs

Preparation time: 10 minutes
Cooking time: 2 hours and 30 minutes
Servings: 12

Ingredients:

1 and ½ pounds turkey meat, ground
½ cup coconut flour
1 egg
1 teaspoon chili powder
1 teaspoons onion powder
A pinch of salt and black pepper
Cooking spray
2 tablespoons white vinegar
2 tablespoons Worcestershire sauce
1 cup tomato sauce
2 tablespoons coconut sugar

Directions:

In a bowl, combine the meat with coconut flour, eggs, half of the chili powder, half of the onion powder, salt and pepper, stir well, shape medium meatballs, arrange them all on a lined baking sheet, spray them with cooking spray, introduce in the oven and bake them at 350 degrees F for 30 minutes.
In your slow cooker, combine the rest of the chili powder with the rest of the onion powder, vinegar, Worcestershire sauce, coconut sugar and tomato sauce and whisk.
Add meatballs, toss them a bit, cover and cook on Low for 2 hours.
Divide the meatballs and sauce into bowls and serve.
Enjoy!

Nutrition:

calories 266, fat 5, fiber 7, carbs 16, protein 18

Garlicky Wings

Preparation time: 10 minutes
Cooking time: 6 hours
Servings: 4

Ingredients:

3 pounds chicken wings
¾ cup honey
1 and ½ tablespoons garlic, minced
2 tablespoons olive oil
A pinch of salt and black pepper

Directions:

In your slow cooker, combine the chicken with the honey, garlic, oil, salt and pepper, toss, cover, cook on Low for 6 hours, divide between plates and serve.
Enjoy!

Nutrition:

calories 299, fat 6, fiber 7, carbs 13, protein 18

Chicken Curry

Preparation time: 10 minutes
Cooking time: 4 hours
Servings: 4

Ingredients:

14 ounces coconut milk
3 tablespoons red curry paste
1 tablespoon coconut aminos
1 tablespoon coconut sugar
1 tablespoon ginger, grated
3 garlic cloves, minced
1 pound chicken thighs, skinless, boneless and cut into pieces
1 butternut squash, cubed
1 yellow onion, chopped
2 cups kale, torn

Directions:

In your slow cooker, combine the coconut milk with curry paste, aminos, sugar, garlic and ginger and whisk well.
Add chicken, squash, onion and kale, toss, cover, cook on High for 4 hours, divide into bowls and serve.
Enjoy!

Nutrition:

calories 300, fat 11, fiber 8, carbs 18, protein 27

Sweet Chicken Mix

Preparation time: 10 minutes
Cooking time: 4 hours
Servings: 6

Ingredients:

1 and ½ pounds chicken breasts, skinless, boneless and cubed
1 tablespoon coconut oil, melted
2 tablespoons arrowroot powder
A pinch of salt and black pepper
3 tablespoons coconut aminos
2 tablespoons white vinegar
1 tablespoon tomato paste
2 tablespoons coconut sugar
1 teaspoon ginger, grated
2 garlic cloves, minced
¼ cup cashews, chopped
1 green onion, chopped

Directions:

In your slow cooker, combine the chicken with coconut oil, arrowroot powder, salt, pepper, aminos, vinegar, tomato paste, coconut sugar, ginger, garlic, cashews and green onion, toss, cover, cook on Low for 4 hours, divide between plates and serve.
Enjoy!

Nutrition:

calories 298, fat 7, fiber 7, carbs 16, protein 20

Chicken Stew

Preparation time: 10 minutes
Cooking time: 4 hours
Servings: 8

Ingredients:

1 pound chicken breasts, skinless, boneless and cubed
1 pound chicken thighs, skinless, boneless and cubed
2 cups mushrooms, sliced
2 cups water
1 cup small onions, peeled
1 and ½ cups carrots, sliced
1 cup celery, chopped
1 teaspoon sweet paprika
1 teaspoon sage, dried
A pinch of salt and black pepper
½ teaspoon thyme, dried
14 ounces chicken stock
6 ounces tomato paste

Directions:

In your slow cooker, combine the chicken breasts with chicken thighs, mushrooms, water, small onions, carrots, celery, paprika, sage, salt, pepper, thyme, chicken stock and tomato paste, toss, cover and cook on High for 4 hours.
Divide into bowls and serve.
Enjoy!

Nutrition:

calories 249, fat 6, fiber 6, carbs 22, protein 26

Stylish Tuna Dish

Preparation time: 10 minutes
Cooking time: 4 hours and 10 minutes
Servings: 2

Ingredients:

½ pound tuna loin, cubed
1 garlic clove, minced
4 jalapeno peppers, chopped
1 cup olive oil
3 red chili peppers, chopped
2 teaspoons black peppercorns, ground
A pinch of sea salt
Black pepper to the taste

Directions:

Put the oil in your slow cooker, add chili peppers, jalapenos, peppercorns, salt, pepper and garlic and whisk.
Cover and cook on Low for 4 hours.
Add tuna cubes, stir again and cook on High for 10 minutes more.
Divide between plates and serve.
Enjoy!

Nutrition:

calories 200, fat 4, fiber 3, carbs 10, protein 4

1 cup olive oil

3 red chili peppers, chopped
2 teaspoons black peppercorns, ground
A pinch of sea salt
Black pepper to the taste

Directions:

Put the oil in your slow cooker, add chili peppers, jalapenos, peppercorns, salt, pepper and garlic and whisk.
Cover and cook on Low for 4 hours.
Add tuna cubes, stir again and cook on High for 10 minutes more.
Divide between plates and serve.
Enjoy!

Nutrition:

calories 200, fat 4, fiber 3, carbs 10, protein 4

Wonderful Shrimp And Crawfish

Preparation time: 10 minutes
Cooking time: 5 hours and 6 minutes
Servings: 8

Ingredients:

1 pound shrimp, peeled and deveined
½ cup yellow onions, chopped
2 celery stalks, chopped
½ cup red bell pepper, chopped
4 green onions, chopped
¼ cup olive oil
1 tablespoon tapioca flour
1 and ½ tablespoons garlic, minced
10 ounces canned tomatoes and chilies, chopped
1 pound crawfish tails, cooked and peeled
2/3 cup water
6 ounces canned sugar free tomato paste
½ teaspoon oregano, dried
½ teaspoon basil, dried
½ teaspoon thyme, dried
Black pepper to the taste
A pinch of red pepper, crushed
½ cup parsley, chopped

Directions:

Heat up a pan with the oil over medium high heat, add onions, bell pepper, celery and green onions, stir and cook for a couple of minutes.
Add garlic and tomatoes, stir and transfer everything to your slow cooker.
Add tomato paste, water, flour, black pepper, oregano, basil, red pepper and thyme, stir, cover and cook on Low for 4 hours.
Add shrimp, crawfish and parsley, stir, cover and cook on Low for 1 more hour.
Divide into bowls and serve.
Enjoy!

Nutrition:

calories 240, fat 2, fiber 2, carbs 7, protein 2

Tasty Braised Squid

Preparation time: 10 minutes
Cooking time: 7 hours
Servings: 4

Ingredients:

1 pound squid, cleaned and cut into rings
1/2 cup coconut sugar
1 small ginger piece, grated
1 garlic head, crushed
3 tablespoons coconut aminos
1/4 cup veggie stock
2 leeks stalks, chopped
2 bay leaves
Black pepper to the taste

Directions:

Put the squid in your slow cooker.
Add sugar, ginger, garlic, aminos, leeks, stock, black pepper and bay leaves, stir, cover and cook on Low for 8 hours.
Divide into bowls and serve right away.
Enjoy!

Nutrition:

calories 190, fat 2, fiber 4, carbs 7, protein 5

Seabass and Coconut Cream

Preparation time: 10 minutes
Cooking time: 1 hour and 30 minutes
Servings: 2

Ingredients:

1 pound sea bass
2 scallion stalks, chopped
1 small ginger piece, grated
1 tablespoon coconut aminos
2 cups coconut cream
4 bok choy stalks, chopped
3 jalapeno peppers, chopped
A pinch of sea salt
Black pepper to the taste

Directions:

Put coconut cream in your slow cooker.
Add ginger, aminos, scallions, a pinch of salt, black pepper and jalapenos.
Stir, top with the fish and bok choy, cover and cook on High for 1 hour and 30 minutes.
Divide fish and cream between 2 plates and serve.
Enjoy!

Nutrition:

calories 200, fat 3, fiber 3, carbs 8, protein 5

Salmon With Cilantro And Lime

Preparation time: 10 minutes
Cooking time: 2 hours and 30 minutes
Servings: 4

Ingredients:

2 garlic cloves, minced
4 salmon fillets
¾ cup cilantro, chopped
3 tablespoons lime juice
1 tablespoon olive oil
A pinch of sea salt
Black pepper to the taste

Directions:

Grease your slow cooker with the oil and place salmon fillets inside, skin side down.
Add garlic, cilantro, lime juice, salt and pepper, cover and cook on Low for 2 hours and 30 minutes.
Divide salmon fillets on plates, drizzle the juices from the slow cooker all over and serve.
Enjoy!

Nutrition:

calories 180, fat 3, fiber 2, carbs 4, protein 8

Jamaican Salmon

Preparation time: 10 minutes
Cooking time: 2 hours
Servings: 2

Ingredients:

1 medium salmon fillets
A pinch of nutmeg, ground
A pinch of cloves, ground
A pinch of ginger powder
A pinch of sea salt
2 teaspoons coconut sugar
1 teaspoon onion powder
¼ teaspoon chipotle chili powder
½ teaspoon cayenne pepper
Black pepper to the taste
½ teaspoon cinnamon, ground
1/8 teaspoon thyme, dried

Directions:

In a bowl, mix salmon fillets with nutmeg, cloves, ginger, salt, coconut sugar, onion powder, chili powder, cayenne black pepper, cinnamon and thyme.
Rub fish with this mix, arrange fish on 2 tin foil pieces, wrap, place in your slow cooker, cover and cook on Low for 2 hours.
Unwrap fish, divide between plates and serve with a side salad.
Enjoy!

Nutrition:

calories 220, fat 4, fiber 2, carbs 7, protein 4

Simple Clams

Preparation time: 10 minutes
Cooking time: 6 hours
Servings: 4

Ingredients:

21 ounces canned clams, chopped
1/3 cup coconut milk
4 eggs, whisked
2 tablespoons olive oil
1/3 cup green bell pepper, chopped
½ cup yellow onion, chopped
Black pepper to the taste
A pinch of sea salt

Directions:

Put clams in your slow cooker.
Add milk, eggs, oil, onion, bell pepper, a pinch of salt and black pepper.
Stir, cover and cook on Low for 6 hours.
Divide into bowls and serve.
Enjoy!

Nutrition:

calories 190, fat 4, fiber 2, carbs 6, protein 7

Delicious Clam Chowder

Preparation time: 10 minutes
Cooking time: 3 hours and 30 minutes
Servings: 6

Ingredients:

6 bacon slices, cooked and chopped
1 yellow onion, chopped
3 carrots, chopped
13 ounces canned clams, chopped
2 sweet potatoes, chopped
1 and ¾ cups water
1 teaspoon Paleo Worcestershire sauce
¼ cup tapioca flour
24 ounces canned coconut milk

Directions:

In your slow cooker, mix water with clams, carrots, onion, bacon, potatoes and Worcestershire sauce, stir, cover and cook on High for 3 hours.
Add coconut milk mixed with tapioca flour, stir and cook on High for 30 minutes more.
Divide chowder into bowls and serve.
Enjoy!

Nutrition:

calories 140, fat 10, fiber 1, carbs 8, protein 10

Easy Seafood Soup

Preparation time: 10 minutes
Cooking time: 3 hours
Servings: 12

Ingredients:

10 ounces canned coconut cream
2 cups veggie stock
2 cups tomato sauce
1 cup Paleo shrimp cocktail sauce
12 ounces canned crab meat
1 and ½ cups water
1 pound small shrimp, peeled and deveined
1 pound jumbo shrimp, peeled and deveined
1 yellow onion, chopped
1 cup carrots, chopped
4 tilapia fillets, cubed
2 celery stalks, chopped
3 kale stalks, chopped
1 bay leaf
2 garlic cloves, minced
A pinch of sea salt
½ teaspoon cloves, ground
1 teaspoon rosemary, dried
1 teaspoon thyme, dried

Directions:

In your slow cooker, mix coconut cream with stock, tomato sauce, shrimp cocktail sauce and water and stir.
Add small and jumbo shrimp, fish cubes, onion, carrots, celery, kale, garlic, bay leaf, salt, cloves, thyme and rosemary, stir, cover and cook on Low for 3 hours.
Stir soup again, ladle into bowls and serve.
Enjoy!

Nutrition:

calories 220, fat 3, fiber 3, carbs 8, protein 13

Easy Seafood Gumbo

Preparation time: 10 minutes
Cooking time: 6 hours
Servings: 4

Ingredients:

1 pound shrimp, peeled and deveined
2 pounds mussels, cleaned and debearded
28 ounces canned clams
1 yellow onion, chopped
10 ounces canned tomato paste

Directions:

In your slow cooker, mix shrimp with mussels, clams, onion and tomato paste, stir, cover and cook on Low for 6 hours.
Ladle into bowls and serve.
Enjoy!

Nutrition:

calories 150, fat 3, fiber 2, carbs 7, protein 5

Coconut Curry Shrimp

Preparation time: 10 minutes
Cooking time: 4 hours and 30 minutes
Servings: 2

Ingredients:

1 small yellow onion, chopped
15 baby carrots
2 garlic cloves, minced
1 small green bell pepper, chopped
8 ounces canned coconut milk
3 tablespoons tomato paste
½ teaspoon red pepper, crushed
¾ tablespoons curry powder
¾ tablespoon tapioca flour
1 pound shrimp, cooked, peeled and deveined

Directions:

In your food processor, mix onion with garlic, bell pepper, tomato paste, coconut milk, red pepper and curry powder, blend well and add to your slow cooker.
Add baby carrots, stir, cover and cook on Low for 4 hours.
Add tapioca, stir, cover and cook on Low for 15 minutes more.
Add shrimp, stir and cook on Low for 15 minutes more.
Divide into bowls and serve.
Enjoy!

Nutrition:

calories 200, fat 4, fiber 3, carbs 4, protein 5

Lemon And Dill Trout

Preparation time: 10 minutes
Cooking time: 2 hours
Servings: 4

Ingredients:

2 lemons, sliced
¼ cup low sodium chicken stock
A pinch of sea salt
Black pepper to the taste
2 tablespoons dill, chopped
12 ounces spinach
4 medium trout

Directions:

Put the stock in your slow cooker and add the fish inside as well.
Season with a pinch of salt and black pepper to the taste, top with lemon slices, dill and spinach, cover and cook on High for 2 hours.
Divide fish, lemon and spinach between plates and drizzle some of the juice from the pot all over.
Enjoy!

Nutrition:

calories 240, fat 5, fiber 4, carbs 9, protein 14

Elegant Tilapia and Asparagus

Preparation time: 10 minutes
Cooking time: 2 hours
Servings: 4

Ingredients:

4 tilapia fillets, boneless	A pinch of lemon pepper seasoning
1 bundle asparagus	2 tablespoons olive oil
12 tablespoons lemon juice	

Directions:

Divide tilapia fillets on tin foil pieces.
Top each tilapia with asparagus spears, lemon juice, lemon pepper and oil and wrap them.
Arrange tilapia fillets in your slow cooker, cover and cook on High for 2 hours.
Unwrap tilapia and divide fish and asparagus between plates.
Enjoy!

Nutrition:

calories 172, fat 3, fiber 6, carbs 7, protein 3

Seafood Chowder

Preparation time: 10 minutes
Cooking time: 8 hours
Servings: 4

Ingredients:

½ fennel bulb, cored and chopped	1 cup coconut cream
2 bay leaves	1 pound salmon fillet, skinless, boneless and cut into medium chunks
1 yellow onion, chopped	5 sea scallops, halved
1 celery rib, chopped	24 shrimp, peeled and deveined
1 tablespoon thyme, chopped	¼ cup parsley, chopped
A pinch of salt and black pepper	
3 ounces clam juice	

Directions:

In your slow cooker, mix fennel with bay leaves, onion, celery, thyme, salt, pepper, clam juice, salmon, shrimp and coconut cream, stir, cover and cook on Low for 8 hours.
Add parsley, stir, divide into bowls and serve.
Enjoy!

Nutrition:

calories 172, fat 3, fiber 7, carbs 13, protein 3

Tasty Seafood Stew

Preparation time: 10 minutes
Cooking time: 7 hours
Servings: 4

Ingredients:

28 ounces canned tomatoes, crushed	1 teaspoon cilantro, dried
4 cups veggie stock	1 teaspoon basil, dried
3 garlic cloves, minced	A pinch of salt and black pepper
1 pound sweet potatoes, cubed	A pinch of red pepper flakes, crushed
½ cup yellow onion, chopped	2 pounds favorite seafood
1 teaspoon thyme, dried	

Directions:

In your slow cooker, mix tomatoes with stock, garlic, sweet potatoes, onion, thyme, cilantro, basil, salt, pepper and pepper flakes, stir, cover and cook on Low for 6 hours.
Add seafood, stir, cover and cook on High for 1 more hour.
Divide stew into bowls and serve.
Enjoy!

Nutrition:

calories 200, fat 4, fiber 4, carbs 6, protein 3

Shrimp Mix

Preparation time: 10 minutes
Cooking time: 2 hours and 30 minutes
Servings: 4

Ingredients:

1 cup chicken stock	2 teaspoons garlic, minced
2 tablespoons olive oil	20 shrimp, peeled and deveined
2 teaspoons parsley, chopped	

Directions:

In your slow cooker, mix stock with oil, parsley, garlic and shrimp, toss, cover and cook on Low for 2 hours and 30 minutes.
Divide into bowls and serve.
Enjoy!

Nutrition:

calories 162, fat 2, fiber 6, carbs 9, protein 2

Fish and Tomatoes

Preparation time: 10 minutes
Cooking time: 1 hour and 30 minutes
Servings: 4

Ingredients:

1 pound cod fillets, skinless and boneless	1 tablespoons rosemary, chopped
1 yellow onion, chopped	¼ cup veggie stock
1 red bell pepper, chopped	A pinch of red pepper flakes, crushed
3 garlic cloves, minced	A pinch of salt and black pepper
15 ounces canned tomatoes, chopped	

Directions:

In your slow cooker, mix tomatoes with onion, bell pepper, garlic, rosemary, stock, pepper flakes, salt and pepper and stir.
Add fish fillets on top, cover and cook on Low for 1 hour and 30 minutes.
Divide everything between plates and serve.
Enjoy!

Nutrition:

calories 200, fat 4, fiber 3, carbs 7, protein 4

Indian Chicken

Preparation time: 10 minutes
Cooking time: 6 hours
Servings: 6

Ingredients:

2 and ½ pounds chicken thighs, skinless, boneless and cubed	1 teaspoon ginger, grated
	½ teaspoon sweet paprika
½ cup cashews, chopped	2 garlic cloves, minced
2 cups tomato puree	1 yellow onion, chopped
2 and ½ tablespoons garam masala	½ cup cilantro, chopped

Directions:

In your slow cooker, combine the chicken with the cashews, tomato puree, garam masala, ginger, paprika, garlic and onion, toss, cover and cook on Low for 6 hours.
Add cilantro, stir, divide into bowls and serve.
Enjoy!

Nutrition:

calories 288, fat 4, fiber 8, carbs 17, protein 20

Turkey Breast And Figs Mix

Preparation time: 10 minutes
Cooking time: 9 hours
Servings: 5

Ingredients:

3 pounds turkey breast, boneless and skinless	½ cup cherries, pitted and halved
3 sweet potatoes, peeled and cut into chunks	½ cup cranberries
	1 tablespoon garlic powder
2 yellow onions, chopped	1 tablespoon parsley flakes
1 cup figs, halved	1 tablespoon sage
	½ cup water

Directions:

In your slow cooker, combine the turkey breast with sweet potatoes, onions, figs, cherries, cranberries, garlic powder, parsley flakes, sage and water, toss, cover and cook on Low for 9 hours.
Divide between plates and serve.
Enjoy!

Nutrition:

calories 225, fat 7, fiber 7, carbs 17, protein 17

Simple Summer Soup

Preparation time: 10 minutes
Cooking time: 4 hours
Servings: 4

Ingredients:

1 tablespoon olive oil	2 cups water
1 yellow onion, chopped	15 ounces canned tomatoes, chopped
4 garlic cloves, minced	6 ounces tomato paste
2 carrots, sliced	12 ounces
3 celery ribs, chopped	mushrooms, sliced
A handful basil, chopped	1 cup red cabbage, shredded
A handful oregano, chopped	2/3 cup red bell peppers
A handful parsley, chopped	A pinch of salt and black pepper
4 cups chicken stock	

Directions:

Grease your slow cooker with the oil, add onion, garlic, carrots, celery, basil, oregano, parsley, stock, water, tomatoes, tomato paste, mushrooms, cabbage, bell peppers, salt and pepper, toss, cover, cook on Low for 4 hours, divide into bowls and serve.
Enjoy!

Nutrition:

calories 288, fat 6, fiber 8, carbs 16, protein 20

Beef And Veggie Chili

Preparation time: 10 minutes
Cooking time: 8 hours
Servings: 6

Ingredients:

2 pounds beef meat, ground
1 garlic clove, minced
1 yellow onion, chopped
28 ounces canned tomato sauce
15 ounces canned tomatoes, chopped
3 cups beef stock
2 sweet potatoes, chopped
4 tablespoons chili powder
¼ teaspoon oregano, dried

Directions:

In your slow cooker, combine the beef with the garlic, onion, tomato sauce, tomatoes, stock, sweet potatoes, chili powder and oregano, toss, cover and cook on Low for 8 hours.
Divide into bowls and serve.
Enjoy!

Nutrition:

calories 261, fat 7, fiber 9, carbs 17, protein 18

Apple Pork Loin

Preparation time: 10 minutes
Cooking time: 8 hours
Servings: 4

Ingredients:

1 pound pork tenderloin
2 tablespoons olive oil
2 apples, cored and cubed
1 sweet potato, peeled and cubed
1 red onion, chopped
½ tablespoon cinnamon powder
A pinch of salt and black pepper

Directions:

Grease your slow cooker with the oil, add pork, apples, sweet potato, onion, cinnamon, salt and pepper, toss, cover and cook on Low for 8 hours.
Divide everything between plates and serve.
Enjoy!

Nutrition:

calories 300, fat 6, fiber 8, carbs 17, protein 20

Pork Chops And Sauce

Preparation time: 10 minutes
Cooking time: 7 hours and 10 minutes
Servings: 4

Ingredients:

1 teaspoon ginger, grated
2 garlic cloves, minced
1 yellow onion, chopped
1 and ½ cups tomato sauce
1 tablespoon olive oil
3 peaches, cut into chunks
2 tablespoons apple cider vinegar
A pinch of salt and black pepper
4 pork chops, bone-in

Directions:

Heat up a pan with the oil over medium-high heat, add ginger, garlic, onion, tomato sauce, vinegar, salt, pepper and peaches, stir well, bring to a simmer and cook for 10 minutes.
Transfer the sauce to your slow cooker, add the pork chops, cover and cook on Low for 7 hours.
Divide between plates and serve.
Enjoy!

Nutrition:

calories 281, fat 7, fiber 8, carbs 17, protein 8

Clam Chowder

Preparation time: 10 minutes
Cooking time: 4 hours
Servings: 6

Ingredients:

1 yellow onion, chopped
21 ounces canned clams, chopped
8 ounces veggie stock
½ teaspoon thyme, dried
A pinch of salt and black pepper
2 tablespoons olive oil
1 cup coconut cream
1 cup coconut milk
2 bacon slices, cooked and chopped

Directions:

Grease your slow cooker with the oil, add the onion, clams, stock, thyme, salt and pepper, stir, cover and cook on High for 3 hours and 30 minutes.
Add bacon, coconut milk and coconut cream, stir, cover, cook on High for 30 minutes, divide into bowls and serve.
Enjoy!

Nutrition:

calories 276, fat 7, fiber 9, carbs 16, protein 16

Slow Cooked Shrimp

Preparation time: 10 minutes
Cooking time: 1 hour
Servings: 4

Ingredients:

3 tablespoons olive oil
2 pounds shrimp, peeled and deveined
2 teaspoons garlic, minced
1 cup tomato sauce
A pinch of salt and black pepper

Directions:

In your slow cooker, combine the oil with the shrimp, garlic, tomato sauce, salt and pepper, toss, cover, cook on Low for 1 hour, divide into bowls and serve.
Enjoy!

Nutrition:

calories 200, fat 6, fiber 6, carbs 16, protein 9

Fish Curry

Preparation time: 10 minutes
Cooking time: 2 hours and 30 minutes
Servings: 4

Ingredients:

1/3 cup coconut oil, melted
2 hot green chilies, chopped
1 yellow onion, chopped
2 garlic cloves, minced
1 teaspoon ginger, grated
2 teaspoons coriander, ground
1 tablespoon cumin, ground
2 teaspoons mustard seeds
2 tomatoes, chopped
2 teaspoons turmeric powder
2 pounds cod fillets, cut into medium chunks
3 tablespoons cilantro, chopped

Directions:

Grease your slow cooker with the oil, add chilies, onion, garlic, ginger, coriander, cumin, mustard seeds, tomatoes, turmeric and cod, cover and cook on Low for 2 hours and 30 minutes.
Add cilantro, toss, divide into bowls and serve. Enjoy!

Nutrition:

calories 227, fat 6, fiber 8, carbs 15, protein 14

Tender Salmon

Preparation time: 10 minutes
Cooking time: 2 hours
Servings: 4

Ingredients:

4 salmon fillets, boneless
A pinch of salt and black pepper
½ teaspoon coriander, ground
1 tablespoon lemon juice
2 fennel bulbs, chopped
2 spring onions, chopped
1 and ½ cups veggie stock

Directions:

In your slow cooker, combine the salmon with salt, pepper, coriander, lemon juice, fennel, spring onions and stock, cover, cook on Low for 2 hours, divide between plates and serve.
Enjoy!

Nutrition:

calories 261, fat 6, fiber 8, carbs 15, protein 17

Italian Shrimp

Preparation time: 10 minutes
Cooking time: 1 hour and 30 minutes
Servings: 4

Ingredients:

2 tablespoons olive oil
¼ cup chicken stock
1 tablespoon garlic, minced
2 tablespoons parsley, chopped
Juice of ½ lemon
1 pound shrimp, peeled and deveined
A pinch of salt and black pepper

Directions:

In your slow cooker, combine the oil with the stock, garlic, parsley, lemon juice, salt, pepper and shrimp, toss, cover, cook on Low for 1 hour and 30 minutes, divide into bowls and serve.
Enjoy!

Nutrition:

calories 213, fat 4, fiber 7, carbs 14, protein 11

Shrimp And Crab Mix

Preparation time: 10 minutes
Cooking time: 1 hour and 30 minutes
Servings: 4

Ingredients:

1 tablespoon olive oil	15 ounces canned tomatoes, chopped
3 leeks, sliced	1 tablespoon coconut sugar
4 garlic cloves, minced	
A pinch of red pepper flakes	1 cup coconut cream
2 tablespoons tomato paste	1 pound shrimp, peeled and deveined
4 cups fish stock	1 cup crab meat
2 cups water	2 tablespoons parsley, chopped

Directions:

Grease your slow cooker with the oil, add the leeks, garlic, pepper flakes, tomato paste, stock, water, tomatoes, sugar, cream, shrimp and crab, toss, cover, cook on Low for 1 hour and 30 minutes, sprinkle parsley, divide into bowls and serve.
Enjoy!

Nutrition:

calories 221, fat 4, fiber 7, carbs 14, protein 11

Asian Style Salmon

Preparation time: 10 minutes
Cooking time: 2 hours
Servings: 2

Ingredients:

2 salmon fillets, boneless	2 tablespoons maple syrup
A pinch of salt and black pepper	16 ounces broccoli and cauliflower florets
3 tablespoons coconut aminos	2 tablespoons lemon juice

Directions:

In your slow cooker, combine the salmon with salt, pepper, aminos, maple syrup, broccoli, cauliflower and lemon juice, toss, cover and cook on Low for 2 hours.
Divide everything between plates and serve.
Enjoy!

Nutrition:

calories 210, fat 4, fiber 2, carbs 6, protein 5

Bell Peppers Soup

Preparation time: 5 minutes
Cooking time: 3 hours
Servings: 4

Ingredients:

6 red bell peppers, sliced	1 sweet potato, chopped
2 red onions, chopped	6 cups chicken stock
2 garlic cloves, minced	2 tablespoons olive oil
4 tomatoes, sliced	A pinch of salt and black pepper

Directions:

In your instant pot, combine the bell peppers with the onions, garlic, tomatoes, sweet potato, oil, salt, pepper and stock, stir, cover, cook on High for 3 hours, ladle into bowls and serve. Enjoy!

Nutrition:

calories 213, fat 4, fiber 3, carbs 9, protein 7

Saffron Halibut Mix

Preparation time: 10 minutes
Cooking time: 2 hours
Servings: 8

Ingredients:

14 ounces chicken stock	¼ cup parsley, chopped
4 sweet potatoes, cubed	¼ teaspoon saffron powder
3 carrots, chopped	1 pound halibut, boneless and cubed
1 yellow onion, chopped	
2 garlic cloves, minced	1 red bell pepper, chopped

Directions:

In your slow cooker, combine the stock with the sweet potatoes, carrots, onion, garlic, saffron, bell pepper and halibut, cover and cook on Low for 2 hours.
Add parsley, toss, divide everything into bowls and serve.
Enjoy!

Nutrition:

calories 230, fat 4, fiber 7, carbs 12, protein 9

Shiitake Mushroom And Tomatoes Mix

Preparation time: 10 minutes
Cooking time: 3 hours
Servings: 4

Ingredients:

12 ounces shiitake mushrooms, roughly chopped
1 tablespoon ginger, grated
2 cups veggie stock
½ cup red onion, chopped
1 cup carrot, chopped
5 garlic cloves, minced
A pinch of salt and black pepper
¼ teaspoon oregano, dry
28 ounces canned tomatoes, chopped
1 and ½ teaspoons turmeric powder
¼ cup cilantro, chopped

Directions:

In your slow cooker, combine the mushrooms with the ginger, stock, onion, carrot, garlic, salt, pepper, oregano, tomatoes, turmeric and cilantro, toss, cover and cook on High for 3 hours.
Divide into bowls and serve.
Enjoy!

Nutrition:

calories 170, fat 3, fiber 5, carbs 12, protein 6

Cauliflower Cream

Preparation time: 10 minutes
Cooking time: 5 hours
Servings: 8

Ingredients:

1 tablespoon ginger, grated
3 garlic cloves, minced
1 yellow onion, chopped
1 chili pepper, minced
A pinch of cinnamon powder
7 cups veggie stock
1 pound sweet potatoes, peeled and cubed
1 tablespoon curry powder
1 cauliflower head, florets separated
15 ounces canned tomatoes, chopped
A pinch of salt and black pepper

Directions:

In your slow cooker, combine the ginger with the garlic, onion, chili powder, cinnamon, stock, sweet potatoes, curry powder, cauliflower, salt, pepper and tomatoes, toss, cover and cook on Low for 5 hours.
Pulse using an immersion blender, divide into bowls and serve.
Enjoy!

Nutrition:

calories 213, fat 4, fiber 5, carbs 13, protein 7

Spring Cod And Sauce

Preparation time: 10 minutes
Cooking time: 2 hours and 30 minutes
Servings: 4

Ingredients:

4 spring onions, chopped
1 teaspoon ginger, grated
1 tablespoon olive oil
4 cod fillets, boneless and skinless
Juice of 1 orange
Zest of 1 orange, grated
A pinch of salt and black pepper
1 cup veggie stock

Directions:

In your slow cooker, combine the ginger with the spring onions and oil.
Add cod, orange juice, orange zest, salt, pepper and stock, cover, cook on Low for 2 hours and 30 minutes, divide everything between plates and serve.
Enjoy!

Nutrition:

calories 217, fat 3, fiber 2, carbs 11, protein 7

Cod With Tomatoes And Olives

Preparation time: 10 minutes
Cooking time: 2 hours and 30 minutes
Servings: 4

Ingredients:

1 garlic clove, minced
1 tablespoon olive oil
¼ cup veggie stock
17 ounces cherry tomatoes, halved
4 cod fillets, boneless and skinless
2 tablespoons capers, chopped
1 cup black olives, pitted and chopped
A pinch of salt and black pepper
1 tablespoon cilantro, chopped

Directions:

Grease your slow cooker with the oil, add garlic, stock, tomatoes, capers, olives, salt, pepper, cilantro and cod, cover and cook on Low for 2 hours and 30 minutes.
Divide everything between plates and serve.
Enjoy!

Nutrition:

calories 217, fat 3, fiber 4, carbs 12, protein 7

Shrimp And Asparagus

Preparation time: 10 minutes
Cooking time: 2 hours
Servings: 4

Ingredients:

1 teaspoon olive oil
5 ounces tomato paste
1 pound shrimp,
peeled and deveined
1 bunch asparagus
spears, trimmed
½ tablespoon Italian
seasoning

Directions:

Grease your slow cooker with the oil, add tomato paste, shrimp, Italian seasoning and asparagus, toss a bit, cover, cook on Low for 2 hours, divide into bowls and serve.
Enjoy!

Nutrition:

calories 182, fat 2, fiber 3, carbs 12, protein 11

Tomato Shrimp

Preparation time: 10 minutes
Cooking time: 1 hour and 30 minutes
Servings: 4

Ingredients:

1 pound shrimp,
peeled and deveined
2 tablespoons olive oil
1 garlic clove, minced
¼ teaspoon oregano,
dried
1 tablespoon cilantro,
chopped
10 ounces canned
tomatoes, chopped
½ cup tomato paste

Directions:

Grease your slow cooker with the oil, add shrimp, garlic, oregano, cilantro, tomatoes and tomato paste, toss, cover, cook on Low for 1 hour and 30 minutes, divide into bowls and serve.
Enjoy!

Nutrition:

calories 202, fat 5, fiber 6, carbs 11, protein 7

Shrimp And Horseradish Mix

Preparation time: 10 minutes
Cooking time: 1 hour and 30 minutes
Servings: 6

Ingredients:

2 pounds big shrimp,
peeled and deveined
Juice of ½ lemon
1 cup tomato paste
3 tablespoons
horseradish, prepared
¼ teaspoon hot
pepper sauce

Directions:

In your slow cooker, combine the shrimp with lemon juice, tomato paste, horseradish and pepper sauce, toss, cover, cook on Low for 1 hour and 30 minutes.
Divide into bowls and serve.
Enjoy!

Nutrition:

calories 210, fat 3, fiber 4, carbs 12, protein 7

Shrimp And Pineapple Sauce

Preparation time: 10 minutes
Cooking time: 1 hour and 30 minutes
Servings: 4

Ingredients:

2 tablespoons coconut
aminos
1 pound shrimp,
peeled and deveined
1 cup chicken stock
3 tablespoon coconut
sugar
3 tablespoons
balsamic vinegar
¾ cup pineapple juice

Directions:

In your slow cooker, combine the aminos with the stock, sugar, vinegar and pineapple juice and whisk really well.
Add the shrimp, toss, cover, cook on Low for 1 hour and 30 minutes, divide everything between plates and serve.
Enjoy!

Nutrition:

calories 202, fat 3, fiber 4, carbs 12, protein 6

Salmon And Caper Sauce

Preparation time: 10 minutes
Cooking time: 2 hours
Servings: 3

Ingredients:

3 salmon fillets, boneless
A pinch of salt and black pepper
1 tablespoon olive oil
1 tablespoon Italian seasoning
2 tablespoons capers
3 tablespoons lemon juice
4 garlic cloves, minced

Directions:

Grease your slow cooker with the oil, add salmon, salt, pepper, Italian seasoning, capers, lemon juice and garlic, toss a bit, cover and cook on Low for 2 hours.
Divide everything between plates and serve.
Enjoy!

Nutrition:

calories 245, fat 12, fiber 1, carbs 13, protein 8

Shrimp And Red Pepper Stew

Preparation time: 10 minutes
Cooking time: 2 hours
Servings: 6

Ingredients:

¼ cup yellow onion, chopped
2 tablespoons olive oil
1 garlic clove, minced
1 and ½ pounds shrimp, peeled and deveined
1 cup red peppers, roasted and chopped
6 ounces canned tomatoes, chopped
¼ cup cilantro, chopped
1 cup coconut milk
A pinch of salt and black pepper
2 tablespoons lime juice

Directions:

Grease your slow cooker with the oil, add the onion, garlic, red peppers, shrimp, tomatoes, lime juice, salt and pepper, cover and cook on Low for 1 hour and 30 minutes.
Add cilantro and coconut milk, toss, cover, cook on Low for 30 minutes more, divide everything into bowls and serve.
Enjoy!

Nutrition:

calories 21, fat 7 fiber 3, carbs 11, protein 13

Salmon And Shallot Sauce

Preparation time: 10 minutes
Cooking time: 2 hours
Servings: 2

Ingredients:

2 medium salmon fillets, boneless
A pinch of salt and black pepper
3 tablespoons olive oil
2 shallots, chopped
1 tablespoon lemon juice
2 tablespoons parsley, chopped

Directions:

In your blender, combine the shallots with the oil, salt, pepper, lemon juice and parsley and pulse well.
Put the salmon in your slow cooker, add the shallots sauce, toss gently, cover and cook on Low for 2 hours.
Divide everything between plates and serve.
Enjoy!

Nutrition:

calories 210, fat 8, fiber 2, carbs 14, protein 14

Tomatoes And Mussels Soup

Preparation time: 10 minutes
Cooking time: 2 hours
Servings: 6

Ingredients:

2 pounds mussels
50 ounces canned tomatoes, crushed
2 cup chicken stock
1 teaspoon red pepper flakes, crushed
3 garlic cloves, minced
1 handful parsley, chopped
1 yellow onion, chopped
A pinch of salt and black pepper
1 tablespoon olive oil

Directions:

Grease your slow cooker with the oil, add the mussels, tomatoes, stock, pepper flakes, garlic, onion, salt and pepper, cover and cook on Low for 2 hours.
Add parsley, stir, ladle the soup bowls and serve.
Enjoy!

Nutrition:

calories 180, fat 3, fiber 2, carbs 6, protein 8

Tuna And Sauce

Preparation time: 10 minutes
Cooking time: 1 hour and 30 minutes
Servings: 4

Ingredients:

½ cup cilantro, chopped
2 tablespoons olive oil
1 small red onion, chopped
¼ cup tomato juice
3 tablespoon balsamic vinegar
2 tablespoons parsley, chopped
2 tablespoons basil, chopped
1 jalapeno pepper, chopped
1 pound tuna steak
A pinch of salt and black pepper
1 teaspoon red pepper flakes
3 garlic cloves, minced

Directions:

Grease your slow cooker with the oil, add tomato juice, onion, balsamic vinegar, jalapeno, cilantro, parsley, basil, salt, pepper, tuna steak, pepper flakes and garlic, toss, cover, cook on Low for 1 hour and 30 minutes, divide between plates and serve.
Enjoy!

Nutrition:

calories 216, fat 4, fiber 4, carbs 14, protein 12

Italian Seafood Stew

Preparation time: 10 minutes
Cooking time: 4 hours and 30 minutes
Servings: 8

Ingredients:

29 ounces canned tomatoes, chopped
2 yellow onions, chopped
2 celery ribs, chopped
6 ounces tomato paste
½ cup veggie stock
4 garlic cloves, minced
1 tablespoon red vinegar
2 teaspoons Italian seasoning
2 tablespoons olive oil
1 pound haddock fillets, skinless, boneless and cubed
1 pound shrimp, peeled and deveined
6 ounces canned clams
6 ounces crab meat
2 tablespoons parsley, chopped

Directions:

In your slow cooker, mix tomatoes with onions, celery, tomato paste, stock, garlic, Italian seasoning and oil, whisk well, cover and cook on Low for 4 hours.
Add haddock, clams, shrimp, crab and parsley, stir gently, cover and cook on Low for 30 minutes more.
Divide into bowls and serve.
Enjoy!

Nutrition:

calories 205, fat 4, fiber 3, carbs 14, protein 26

Salmon with Onions and Carrots

Preparation time: 10 minutes
Cooking time: 9 hours
Servings: 4

Ingredients:

16 ounces baby carrots
4 onions, chopped
3 tablespoons olive oil
4 garlic cloves, minced
4 salmon fillets, boneless
½ teaspoon dill, chopped
A pinch of salt and black pepper

Directions:

In your slow cooker, mix oil with carrots, onions and garlic, stir, cover and cook on Low for 7 hours.
Add salmon, salt, pepper and dill, cover and cook on Low for 2 hours more.
Divide everything between plates and serve.
Enjoy!

Nutrition:

calories 200, fat 3, fiber 6, carbs 8, protein 2

Slow Cooker Shrimp Dish

Preparation time: 10 minutes
Cooking time: 8 hours
Servings: 8

Ingredients:

4 cups veggie stock
2 tablespoons Italian seasoning
1 pound sausage, sliced
A pinch of salt and black pepper
2 pound shrimp, deveined
2 tablespoons parsley, chopped
4 tablespoons olive oil

Directions:

In your slow cooker, mix stock with Italian seasoning, sausage, salt, pepper, oil and shrimp, toss, cover and cook on Low for 8 hours.
Add parsley, stir, divide into bowls and serve.
Enjoy!

Nutrition:

calories 172, fat 3, fiber 5, carbs 7, protein 3

Shrimp Soup

Preparation time: 10 minutes
Cooking time: 3 hours
Servings: 6

Ingredients:

1 and ½ cups celery, chopped
1 cup green bell pepper, chopped
1 and ½ cups onions, chopped
8 ounces tomato sauce
28 ounces canned tomatoes, chopped
28 ounces chicken stock
2 garlic cloves, minced
A pinch of salt and black pepper
¼ cup red vinegar
1 pound shrimp, deveined

Directions:

In your slow cooker, mix celery with bell pepper, onion, tomato sauce, tomatoes, stock, garlic, salt, pepper, vinegar and shrimp, stir, cover and cook on High for 3 hours.
Ladle soup into bowls and serve.
Enjoy!

Nutrition:

calories 162, fat 3, fiber 3, carbs 9, protein 3

Indian Chicken Dish

Preparation time: 10 minutes
Cooking time: 6 hours
Servings: 6

Ingredients:

2 cups tomato puree
½ cup cashews, chopped, soaked for a couple of hours and drained
¼ cup water
2 and ½ pounds chicken thighs, skinless, boneless and cubed
2 and ½ tablespoons garam masala
2 garlic cloves, minced
½ yellow onion, chopped
1 teaspoon ginger powder
A pinch of sea salt
A pinch of cayenne pepper
½ teaspoon sweet paprika
½ cup cilantro, chopped

Directions:

Put the tomato puree in your slow cooker.
Add chicken pieces, garlic, garam masala, onion, ginger powder, a pinch of salt, cayenne pepper and paprika.
Stir, cover and cook on Low for 6 hours.
Meanwhile, in your blender, mix cashews with the water and pulse really well.
Add this to your chicken, stir well, divide into bowls and sprinkle cilantro on top.
Enjoy!

Nutrition:

calories 189, fat 3, fiber 3, carbs 7, protein 14

Delicious Turkey Breast

Preparation time: 10 minutes
Cooking time: 8 hours
Servings: 4

Ingredients:

3 pounds turkey breast, bone in
1 cup black figs
3 sweet potatoes, cut into wedges
½ cup dried cherries, pitted
2 white onions, cut into wedges
½ cup dried cranberries
1/3 cup water
1 teaspoon onion powder
1 teaspoon garlic powder
1 teaspoon parsley flakes
1 teaspoon thyme, dried
1 teaspoon sage, dried
1 teaspoon paprika, dried
A pinch of sea salt
Black pepper to the taste

Directions:

Put the turkey breast in your slow cooker.
Add sweet potatoes, figs, cherries, onions, cranberries and water.
Also add parsley, garlic and onion powder, thyme, sage, paprika, salt and pepper.
Stir everything around the pot, cover and cook on Low for 8 hours.
Discard bone from turkey breast, slice meat and divide between plates.
Serve with the veggies, figs, cherries and berries on the side.
Enjoy!

Nutrition:

calories 220, fat 5, fiber 4, carbs 8, protein 15

American Roast

Preparation time: 10 minutes
Cooking time: 8 hours
Servings: 4

Ingredients:

5 pounds beef chuck roast
1 tablespoon coconut aminos
10 pepperoncini
1 cup beef stock
2 tablespoons ghee

Directions:

In your slow cooker, mix beef roast with aminos, pepperoncini, stock and ghee, toss well, cover and cook on Low for 8 hours.
Transfer roast to a cutting board, shred using 2 forks, return to pot, toss, divide between plates and serve with a side salad.
Enjoy!

Nutrition:

calories 362, fat 4, fiber 8, carbs 17, protein 17

Thai Chicken Soup

Preparation time: 10 minutes
Cooking time: 4 hours
Servings: 6

Ingredients:

14 ounces canned coconut milk
1 butternut squash, peeled and cubed
1 yellow onion, chopped
2 cups veggie stock
1 tablespoon Thai chili sauce
1 and ½ tablespoons red curry paste
1 tablespoon ginger, grated
A pinch of sea salt
1 pound chicken breast, skinless and boneless
2 garlic cloves, minced
2 red bell peppers, chopped
Juice from 1 lime
½ cup cilantro, chopped

Directions:

But the coconut milk in your slow cooker.
Add squash pieces, onion, stock, Thai chili sauce, curry paste, ginger, a pinch of salt and garlic and stir really well.
Add chicken breasts, toss to coat and cook on High for 4 hours.
Add lime juice, stir soup, divide it into bowls, top with chopped parsley and bell peppers and serve right away.
Enjoy!

Nutrition:

calories 276, fat 5, fiber 2, carbs 8, protein 16

Cod with Tomatoes and Olives

Preparation time: 10 minutes
Cooking time: 2 hours
Servings: 4

Ingredients:

4 cod fillets, boneless
1 cup black olives, pitted and chopped
1 tablespoon olive oil
1 garlic clove, minced
½ cup veggie stock
A pinch of salt and black pepper
1 pound cherry tomatoes, halved
A pinch of thyme, dried

Directions:

In your slow cooker, mix cod with black olives, oil, garlic, stock, salt, pepper, cherry tomatoes and thyme, cover and cook on High for 2 hours.
Divide everything between plates and serve.
Enjoy!

Nutrition:

calories 200, fat 3, fiber 4, carbs 8, protein 17

Unbelievable Turkey Chili

Preparation time: 10 minutes
Cooking time: 4 hours
Servings: 8

Ingredients:

1 red bell pepper, chopped
2 pound turkey meat ground
28 ounces canned tomatoes, chopped
1 red onion, chopped
1 green bell pepper, chopped
4 tablespoons tomato paste
1 tablespoon oregano, dried
3 tablespoon chili powder
3 tablespoons cumin, ground
A pinch of sea salt
Black pepper to the taste

Directions:

Heat up a pan over medium high heat, add turkey meat, brown it for a few minutes and transfer to your slow cooker.
Add red and green bell pepper, onion, tomatoes, tomato paste, chili powder, oregano, cumin, a pinch of salt and black pepper to the taste, stir, cover and cook on High for 4 hours.
Divide into bowls and serve.
Enjoy!

Nutrition:

calories 200, fat 6, fiber 4, carbs 8, protein 18

Salmon Fillets and Lemon Sauce

Preparation time: 10 minutes
Cooking time: 2 hours
Servings: 4

Ingredients:

4 salmon fillets
2 tablespoons chili pepper
Juice of 1 lemon
1 lemon, sliced
1 cup veggie stock
1 teaspoon sweet paprika
1 teaspoon basil, dried
Salt and black pepper to the taste

Directions:

In your slow cooker, mix chili pepper with lemon juice, stock, paprika, basil, salt and pepper and whisk.
Add salmon fillets, top them with lemon slices, cover and cook on High for 2 hours.
Divide salmon on plates, drizzle sauce from the Crockpot all over and serve.
Enjoy!

Nutrition:

calories 200, fat 4, fiber 7, carbs 16, protein 3

Turkey Breast And Sweet Potatoes

Preparation time: 10 minutes
Cooking time: 8 hours
Servings: 4

Ingredients:

3 pounds turkey breast, skinless and boneless
1 cup cranberries, chopped
2 sweet potatoes, chopped
½ cup raisins
½ cup walnuts, chopped
1 sweet onion, chopped
2 tablespoons limon juice
1 cup coconut sugar
1 teaspoon ginger, grated
½ teaspoon nutmeg, ground
1 teaspoon cinnamon powder
½ cup veggie stock
1 teaspoon poultry seasoning
Black pepper to the taste
3 tablespoons olive oil

Directions:

Heat up a pan with the oil over medium high heat, add cranberries, walnuts, raisins, onion, lemon juice, sugar, ginger, nutmeg, cinnamon, stock and black pepper, stir well and bring to a simmer.
Place turkey breast in your slow cooker and add sweet potatoes next to it.
Add cranberries mix and poultry seasoning, toss a bit, cover and cook on Low for 8 hours.
Slice turkey breast and divide on plates next to sweet potatoes.
Drizzle the sauce from the cooker all over and serve.

Nutrition:

calories 264, fat 4, fiber 6, carbs 8, protein 15

Mussels Stew

Preparation time: 10 minutes
Cooking time: 2 hours
Servings: 4

Ingredients:

2 pounds mussels, scrubbed
2 tablespoons olive oil
1 yellow onion, chopped
1 teaspoon parsley, dried
½ teaspoon red pepper flakes, crushed
2 teaspoons garlic, minced
14 ounces tomatoes, chopped
½ cup chicken stock

Directions:

In your slow cooker, mix mussels with oil, onion parsley, pepper flakes, garlic, tomatoes and stock, stir, cover and cook on High for 2 hours.
Divide into bowls and serve.

Nutrition:

calories 100, fat 2, fiber 3, carbs 7, protein 2

Palestinian Chicken

Preparation time: 10 minutes
Cooking time: 6 hours and 5 minutes
Servings: 6

Ingredients:

2 and ½ pounds chicken thighs, skinless and boneless
1 and ½ tablespoon olive oil
2 yellow onions, chopped
1 teaspoon cinnamon powder
¼ teaspoon cloves, ground
¼ teaspoon allspice, ground
A pinch of sea salt
Black pepper to the taste
A pinch of saffron
A handful pine nuts for serving
A handful mint, chopped for serving

Directions:

In a bowl, mix oil with onions, cinnamon, allspice, salt, pepper and saffron, whisk and introduce in the microwave for 5 minutes.
Stir again and transfer to your slow cooker.
Add the chicken, toss well, cover and cook on Low for 6 hours.
Sprinkle pine nuts and mint on top before serving,
Enjoy!

Nutrition:

calories 223, fat 3, fiber 2, carbs 6, protein 13
Cooking time: 2 hours and 30 minutes
Servings: 4

Ingredients:

18 ounces mackerel, cut into pieces
3 garlic cloves, minced
8 shallots, chopped
1 teaspoon shrimp powder
1 teaspoon turmeric powder
1 tablespoon chili paste
2 lemongrass sticks, halved
1 small piece of ginger, chopped
3 and ½ ounces water
5 tablespoons olive oil
1 and 1/3 tablespoons tamarind paste
Salt to the taste

Directions:

In your blender, mix garlic with shallots, chili paste, turmeric powder and shrimp powder, blend well and add to slow cooker.
Also add fish, oil, ginger, lemongrass, tamarind, water and salt, stir, cover and cook on Low for 2 hours and 30 minutes.
Divide between plates and serve.
Enjoy!

Nutrition:

calories 172, fat 8, fiber 4, carbs 12, protein 16

Cod Curry

Preparation time: 10 minutes
Cooking time: 2 hours
Servings: 6

Ingredients:

6 cod fillets, skinless, boneless and cut into medium cubes
1 tomato, chopped
14 ounces coconut milk
2 yellow onions, sliced
2 green bell peppers, chopped
2 garlic cloves, minced
½ teaspoon turmeric powder
6 curry leaves
A pinch of salt and black pepper
2 teaspoons cumin, ground
2 tablespoons lemon juice
1 tablespoons coriander, ground
1 tablespoon ginger, grated
1 teaspoon hot pepper flakes

Directions:

In your slow cooker, mix fish cubes with tomato, coconut milk, onions, green bell peppers, garlic, curry leaves, turmeric, salt, pepper, cumin, lemon juice, coriander, ginger and pepper flakes, toss a bit, cover and cook on High for 2 hours.
Divide into bowls and serve.
Enjoy!

Nutrition:

calories 201, fat 7, fiber 3, carbs 12, protein 13

Salmon Dinner Mix

Preparation time: 10 minutes
Cooking time: 2 hours
Servings: 4

Ingredients:

3 salmon fillets, skin on and boneless
Zest from 1 lemon, grated
4 scallions, chopped
3 black peppercorns
½ teaspoon fennel seeds
Salt and black pepper to the taste
1 bay leaf
1 teaspoon white wine vinegar
2 cups chicken stock
¼ cup dill, chopped

Directions:

In your slow cooker, mix lemon zest with scallions, peppercorns, fennel, salt, pepper, bay leaf, vinegar, stock and dill and stir.
Add salmon fillets, cover and cook on High for 2 hours.
Divide salmon and scallions mix from the pot on plates and serve.
Enjoy!

Nutrition:

calories 152, fat 3, fiber 2, carbs 4, protein 12

Salmon, Carrots and Broccoli

Preparation time: 10 minutes
Cooking time: 2 hours
Servings: 2

Ingredients:

2 salmon fillets, skin on
1 bay leaf
1 cup veggie stock
1 cinnamon stick
3 cloves
1 tablespoon olive oil
1 cup baby carrots
2 cups broccoli florets
Salt and black pepper to the taste

Directions:

In your slow cooker, mix stock with bay leaf, cinnamon, cloves, oil, carrots, broccoli, salt and pepper and toss.
Add salmon, toss a bit, cover and cook on High for 2 hours.
Divide salmon and veggies on plates, drizzle some of the cooking juices on top and serve.
Enjoy!

Nutrition:

calories 200, fat 4, fiber 6, carbs 14, protein 16

Salmon and Special Sauce

Preparation time: 10 minutes
Cooking time: 2 hours
Servings: 6

Ingredients:

6 salmon steaks
2 tablespoons olive oil
4 leeks, sliced
2 garlic cloves, minced
2 tablespoons parsley, chopped
1 cup clam juice
2 tablespoons lemon juice
Salt and white pepper to the taste
2 cups raspberries
1/3 cup dill, chopped

Directions:

In your slow cooker, mix oil with leeks, garlic, parsley, clam juice, lemon juice, salt, pepper, raspberries and dill and stir.
Add salmon steaks on top, cover and cook on High for 2 hours.
Divide salmon and raspberry sauce between plates and serve.
Enjoy!

Nutrition:

calories 321, fat 5, fiber 8, carbs 14, protein 16

Spicy Mackerel

Preparation time: 10 minutes
Cooking time: 2 hours and 30 minutes
Servings: 4

Ingredients:

18 ounces mackerel, cut into pieces
3 garlic cloves, minced
8 shallots, chopped
1 teaspoon shrimp powder
1 teaspoon turmeric powder
1 tablespoon chili paste
2 lemongrass sticks, halved
1 small piece of ginger, chopped
3 and ½ ounces water
5 tablespoons olive oil
1 and 1/3 tablespoons tamarind paste
Salt to the taste

Directions:

In your blender, mix garlic with shallots, chili paste, turmeric powder and shrimp powder, blend well and add to slow cooker.
Also add fish, oil, ginger, lemongrass, tamarind, water and salt, stir, cover and cook on Low for 2 hours and 30 minutes.
Divide between plates and serve.
Enjoy!

Nutrition:

calories 172, fat 8, fiber 4, carbs 12, protein 16

Squid Stew

Preparation time: 10 minutes
Cooking time: 2 hours
Servings: 4

Ingredients:

17 ounces squid
1 and ½ tablespoons red chili powder
Salt and black pepper to the taste
¼ teaspoon turmeric powder
2 cups veggie stock
4 garlic cloves, minced
1 teaspoon ginger powder
½ teaspoons cumin, ground
3 tablespoons olive oil
¼ teaspoon mustard seeds, toasted

Directions:

Put squids in your slow cooker, add chili powder, salt, pepper, turmeric, stock, garlic, ginger, cumin, oil and mustard seeds, stir, cover and cook on High for 2 hours.
Enjoy!

Nutrition:

calories 241, fat 1, fiber 7, carbs 12, protein 3

Lemony Mackerel

Preparation time: 10 minutes
Cooking time: 2 hours
Servings: 4

Ingredients:

4 mackerels
Juice from 1 lemon
Zest from 1 lemon, grated
1 tablespoon chives, finely chopped
Salt and black pepper to the taste
2 tablespoons ghee
1 tablespoon olive oil
1 cup veggie stock
Lemon wedges for serving

Directions:

In your instant pot, mix ghee with oil.
Add mackerels, salt and pepper and rub well.
Also, add stock, chives, lemon juice and lemon zest, cover and cook on Low for 2 hours.
Divide mackerel between plates and serve with lemon wedges on the side.
Enjoy!

Nutrition:

calories 162, fat 4, fiber 7, carbs 8, protein 4

Delicious Pulled Chicken

Preparation time: 10 minutes
Cooking time: 6 hours
Servings: 2

Ingredients:

2 tomatoes, chopped
2 red onions, chopped
2 chicken breasts
2 garlic cloves, minced
1 tablespoon maple syrup
1 teaspoon chili powder
1 teaspoon basil, dried
3 tablespoons water
1 teaspoon cloves
Lettuce leaves for serving

Directions:

In your slow cooker mix onion with tomatoes, chicken, garlic, maple syrup, chili powder, basil, water and cloves, toss well, cover and cook on Low for 6 hours.
Shred chicken and divide it along with the veggies on lettuce leaves.
Serve right away!
Enjoy!

Nutrition:

calories 200, fat 3, fiber 3, carbs 7, protein 6

Chicken Chili

Preparation time: 10 minutes
Cooking time: 7 hours
Servings: 4

Ingredients:

16 ounces jarred Paleo salsa
8 chicken thighs
1 yellow onion, chopped
16 ounces canned tomatoes, chopped
1 red bell pepper, chopped
2 tablespoons chili powder

Directions:

Put the salsa in your slow cooker.
Add chicken, onion, tomatoes, bell pepper and chili powder, stir, cover and cook on Low for 7 hours.
Divide chili among plates and serve.
Enjoy!

Nutrition:

calories 200, fat 3, fiber 3, carbs 7, protein 8

Roasted Chicken

Preparation time: 10 minutes
Cooking time: 8 hours
Servings: 8

Ingredients:

1 big chicken
1 garlic head, peeled
1 yellow onion, chopped
1 lemon, sliced
1 tablespoons sweet paprika
A pinch of sea salt
Black pepper to the taste
1 teaspoon thyme, dried
2 carrots, chopped

Directions:

Stuff your chicken with half of the garlic and stuff with half of the lemon slices.
Rub the bird with salt, pepper, thyme and paprika both outside and inside.
Place carrots on the bottom of your slow cooker, add the rest of the garlic, onion and lemon slices.
Place the bird on top, cover and cook on Low for 8 hours.
Transfer chicken to a platter, carve and serve with a side salad.
Enjoy!

Nutrition:

calories 200, fat 4, fiber 3, carbs 8, protein 16

Simple Italian Chicken

Preparation time: 10 minutes
Cooking time: 6 hours
Servings: 4

Ingredients:

¼ cup tomato paste
1 onion, chopped
2 tablespoons coconut oil
1 and ½ teaspoon oregano, dried
3 garlic cloves, minced
¼ teaspoon red pepper flakes
2 pounds mushrooms, sliced
½ cup chicken stock
10 ounces canned tomatoes, chopped
8 chicken thighs
A pinch of sea salt
Black pepper to the taste

Directions:

Heat up a pan with the oil over medium high heat, add onion and garlic, stir and cook for 2 minutes.
Transfer this to your slow cooker, add tomato paste, oregano, pepper flakes, mushrooms, tomatoes, stock, chicken pieces, some black pepper and a pinch of salt, stir well, cover and cook on Low for 6 hours.
Stir again, divide between plates and serve.

Nutrition:

calories 240, fat 4, fiber 3, carbs 8, protein 10

Wonderful Salsa Chicken

Preparation time: 10 minutes
Cooking time: 7 hours
Servings: 4

Ingredients:

4 chicken breasts, skinless and boneless
½ cup water
16 ounces Paleo salsa
1 and ½ tablespoons parsley, dried
1 teaspoon garlic powder
½ tablespoon cilantro, chopped
1 teaspoon onion powder
½ tablespoons oregano, dried
½ teaspoon paprika, smoked
1 teaspoon chili powder
½ teaspoon cumin, ground
Black pepper to the taste

Directions:

Put the water in your slow cooker and add chicken breasts.
Add salsa, parsley, garlic powder, cilantro, onion powder, oregano, paprika, chili powder, cumin and black pepper to the taste.
Stir, cover and cook on Low for 7 hours.
Divide chicken on plates, drizzle the sauces on top and serve.
Enjoy!

Nutrition:

calories 200, fat 4, fiber 2, carbs 7, protein 9

Superb Chicken Soup

Preparation time: 10 minutes
Cooking time: 4 hours and 10 minutes
Servings: 4

Ingredients:

1 jalapeno pepper, chopped	28 ounces canned tomatoes, chopped
2 tablespoons olive oil	2 teaspoons chili powder
1 yellow onion, chopped	4 cups low sodium chicken stock
1 red bell pepper, chopped	1 teaspoon cumin, ground
3 garlic cloves, minced	A handful cilantro, chopped
4 chicken breasts, skinless and boneless	Black pepper to the taste
4 ounces canned green chilies, chopped	

Directions:

Heat up a pan with the oil over medium high heat, add jalapeno, onion, bell pepper and garlic, stir and sauté them for 7 minutes.
Transfer these to your slow cooker, add, chicken breasts, chilies, tomatoes, chili powder, stock, cumin and black pepper, stir, cover and cook on High for 4 hours.
Add cilantro, stir your soup, take meat out and shred using 2 forks, ladle into soup bowls, divide shredded meat in each bowl and serve.
Enjoy!

Nutrition:

calories 140, fat 1, fiber 2, carbs 6, protein 7

Divine Turkey Breast

Preparation time: 10 minutes
Cooking time: 6 hours
Servings: 6

Ingredients:

6-pound turkey breast, skin and bone in	½ cup balsamic vinegar
4 cups cranberries, rinsed	½ cup maple syrup
3 apples, peeled, cored and sliced	A pinch of sea salt
	Black pepper to the taste

Directions:

Put the turkey breast in your slow cooker.
Add cranberries, apple slices, a pinch of salt, black pepper, vinegar and maple syrup.
Toss a bit, cover and cook on Low for 6 hours.
Slice turkey breast and divide on plates, mash cranberries and apples a bit and add them on top of the meat.
Serve right away.
Enjoy!

Nutrition:

calories 360, fat 4, fiber 3, carbs 9, protein 20

Cashew Chicken

Preparation time: 10 minutes
Cooking time: 4 hours
Servings: 6

Ingredients:

1 and ½ pound chicken breast, boneless, skinless and cubed	1 tablespoon unsweetened ketchup
	2 tablespoons white vinegar
1 tablespoon coconut oil	1 teaspoon ginger, grated
3 tablespoons coconut aminos	2 tablespoons palm sugar
2 tablespoons tapioca flour	½ cup cashews, chopped
Black pepper to the taste	2 garlic cloves, minced
	1 green onion, chopped

Directions:

Put chicken pieces in a bowl, season with black pepper, add tapioca flour and toss well.
Heat up a pan with the oil over medium high heat, add chicken, cook for 5 minutes and transfer to your slow cooker.
Add aminos, ketchup, vinegar, ginger, palm sugar and garlic, stir well, cover and cook on Low for 4 hours.
Add cashews and green onion, stir, divide into bowls and serve.
Enjoy!

Nutrition:

calories 200, fat 3, fiber 2, carbs 8, protein 12

Sweet Chicken

Preparation time: 10 minutes
Cooking time: 4 hours
Servings: 4

Ingredients:

2 pounds chicken thighs	1 cup apple juice
Salt and black pepper to the taste	1 teaspoon red pepper, crushed
¾ cup sweet Bbq sauce	2 teaspoons paprika
A pinch of cayenne pepper	½ teaspoon basil, dried

Directions:

In your slow cooker, mix chicken with salt, pepper, bbq sauce, cayenne, apple juice, red pepper, paprika and basil, stir, cover and cook on High for 4 hours.
Divide everything into bowls and serve.
Enjoy!

Nutrition:

calories 200, fat 3, fiber 6, carbs 10, protein 17

Chicken Stew

Preparation time: 10 minutes
Cooking time: 8 hours
Servings: 4

Ingredients:

1 yellow onion, chopped
2 pounds chicken breasts, skinless and boneless
4 ounces canned jalapenos, chopped
1 green bell pepper, chopped
4 ounces canned green chilies, chopped
7 ounces tomato sauce
14 ounces canned tomatoes, chopped
2 tablespoons coconut oil
3 garlic cloves, minced
1 tablespoon chili powder
1 tablespoon cumin, ground
2 teaspoons oregano, dried
A bunch of cilantro, chopped
A pinch of sea salt
Black pepper to the taste
1 avocado, pitted, peeled and sliced

Directions:

Put the oil in your slow cooker.
Add onion, chicken breasts, jalapenos, bell pepper, green chilies, tomato sauce, tomatoes, garlic, chili powder, cumin, oregano, a pinch of salt and black pepper, stir, cover and cook on Low for 8 hours.
Add cilantro, shred chicken breasts using 2 forks, return them to the pot, stir your stew one more time, divide into bowls and top with avocado slices.
Enjoy!

Nutrition:

calories 245, fat 4, fiber 5, carbs 9, protein 16

Ginger Duck

Preparation time: 10 minutes
Cooking time: 8 hours
Servings: 6

Ingredients:

1 duck, chopped into medium pieces
1 celery stalk, chopped
2 carrots, chopped
2 cups chicken stock
Salt and black pepper to the taste
1 tablespoon ginger, grated

Directions:

In your slow cooker, mix duck with celery, carrots, stock, salt, pepper and ginger, stir, cover and cook on Low for 8 hours.
Divide duck, ginger sauce between plates, and serve.
Enjoy!

Nutrition:

calories 200, fat 3, fiber 6, carbs 19, protein 17

Chicken And Sausage Delight

Preparation time: 10 minutes
Cooking time: 5 hours
Servings: 4

Ingredients:

4 chicken breasts, skinless and boneless
6 Italian sausages, sliced
5 garlic cloves, minced
1 white onion, chopped
1 teaspoon Italian seasoning
A drizzle of olive oil
1 teaspoon garlic powder
29 ounces canned tomatoes, chopped
15 ounces tomato sauce
1 cup water
½ cup balsamic vinegar

Directions:

Put chicken and sausage slices in your slow cooker.
Add garlic, onion, Italian seasoning and the oil and toss everything.
Also add tomatoes, tomato sauce, garlic powder, water and the vinegar, cover and cook on High for 5 hours.
Stir chicken and sausage mix again, divide between plates and serve.
Enjoy!

Nutrition:

calories 267, fat 4, fiber 3, carbs 7, protein 13

Savory Chicken

Preparation time: 10 minutes
Cooking time: 6 hours
Servings: 4

Ingredients:

2 red bell peppers, chopped
2 pounds chicken breasts, skinless and boneless
4 garlic cloves, minced
1 yellow onion, chopped
2 teaspoons paprika
1 cup low sodium chicken stock
2 teaspoons cinnamon powder
¼ teaspoon nutmeg, ground

Directions:

In a bowl, mix bell peppers with chicken breasts, garlic, onion, paprika, cinnamon and nutmeg and toss to coat.
Transfer everything to your slow cooker, add stock, cover and cook on Low for 6 hours.
Divide chicken and veggies between plates and serve.
Enjoy!

Nutrition:

calories 150, fat 3, fiber 5, carbs 7, protein 10

Delicious Stuffed Chicken Breasts

Preparation time: 10 minutes
Cooking time: 6 hours
Servings: 4

Ingredients:

4 chicken breasts, skinless and boneless	6 ounces spinach
1 tablespoon olive oil	1 and ½ teaspoon oregano, chopped
1 small yellow onion, chopped	1 tablespoon lemon juice
2 chili peppers, chopped	1 cup veggie stock
1 small red bell pepper, chopped	A pinch of sea salt
2 teaspoons garlic, minced	Black pepper to the taste
	A handful parsley, chopped

Directions:

Heat up a pan with the oil over medium high heat, add bell pepper, chili peppers and onions, stir and cook for 3 minutes.
Add spinach and garlic, stir and cook for a couple more seconds.
Add a pinch of salt, black pepper and oregano, stir and take off heat.
Cut a pocket in each chicken breast and stuff with spinach mixture.
Arrange stuffed chicken breasts in your slow cooker, add stock, cover and cook on Low for 6 hours.
Divide on plates, sprinkle parsley on top, drizzle the lemon juice and serve.

Nutrition:

calories 245, fat 4, fiber 3, carbs 8, protein 15

Flavored Turkey Wings

Preparation time: 10 minutes
Cooking time: 8 hours
Servings: 4

Ingredients:

4 turkey wings	Salt and black pepper to the taste
1 yellow onion, chopped	2 tablespoons olive oil
1 carrot, chopped	A pinch of rosemary, dried
3 garlic cloves, minced	2 bay leaves
1 celery stalk, chopped	A pinch of sage, dried
1 cup chicken stock	A pinch of thyme, dried

Directions:

In your slow cooker, mix turkey with onion, carrot, garlic, celery, stock, salt, pepper, oil, rosemary, sage, thyme and bay leaves, toss, cover and cook on Low for 8 hours.
Divide between plates and serve hot.

Nutrition:

calories 223, fat 5, fiber 7, carbs 18, protein 14

Tasty Kimchi Chicken

Preparation time: 10 minutes
Cooking time: 5 hours and 20 minutes
Servings: 6

Ingredients:

6 garlic cloves, minced	1 teaspoon ginger, minced
4 scallions, sliced	2 pounds chicken thighs, skinless and boneless
1 cup veggie stock	
1 tablespoon sesame oil	
2 teaspoons palm sugar	2 cups cabbage Kimchi
1 tablespoon coconut aminos	

Directions:

In your slow cooker, mix stock with oil, scallions, garlic, sugar, aminos and ginger and whisk really well.
Add chicken, stir, cover and cook on Low for 5 hours.
Transfer chicken to plates, add Kimchi to your slow cooker, cover and cook on High for 20 minutes more.
Add Kimchi mix to plates next to the chicken and serve.
Enjoy!

Nutrition:

Calories 240, fat 3, fiber 4, carbs 7, protein 10

Wonderful Chicken

Preparation time: 10 minutes
Cooking time: 6 hours
Servings: 6

Ingredients:

1 whole chicken	2 carrots, chopped
5 thyme springs, chopped	1 yellow onion, chopped
2 celery stalks, chopped	A pinch of white pepper
3 garlic cloves, minced	Juice of 1 lemon

Directions:

Put half of the thyme, garlic, celery, onion and carrots in your slow cooker.
Add the chicken on top and season with a pinch of white pepper.
Add the rest of the thyme, onion, garlic, celery and carrots on top, drizzle the lemon juice, cover and cook on Low for 6 hours.
Divide chicken between plates and serve.
Enjoy!

Nutrition:

calories 230, fat 4, fiber 2, carbs 6, protein 6

Tasty Greek Chicken

Preparation time: 10 minutes
Cooking time: 4 hours
Servings: 4

Ingredients:

1 and ½ pounds chicken breast, skinless and boneless	A pinch of salt and black pepper
Juice from 2 lemons	1 cucumber, chopped
1 rosemary spring, chopped	1 cup kalamata olives, pitted and sliced
¼ cup olive oil	¼ cup red onions, chopped
3 garlic cloves, minced	2 tablespoons red vinegar

Directions:

In your slow cooker, mix chicken with lemon juice, rosemary, oil, garlic, salt and pepper, stir, cover and cook on High for 4 hours.
Transfer chicken to a cutting board, shred with 2 forks, and transfer to a bowl, add cucumber, olives, onion and vinegar, toss, divide between plates and serve.
Enjoy!

Nutrition:

calories 200, fat 3, fiber 3, carbs 12, protein 3

Mexican Chicken

Preparation time: 10 minutes
Cooking time: 4 hours
Servings: 8

Ingredients:

4 pounds chicken breast, skinless and boneless	2 teaspoons cumin, ground
1 cup chicken stock	A pinch of salt and black pepper
1 yellow onion, chopped	1 teaspoon chili powder
1 tablespoon chipotle powder	Lime wedges, for serving
4 garlic cloves, minced	

Directions:

In your slow cooker, mix chicken with stock, onion, chipotle powder, garlic, cumin, salt, pepper and chili, stir, cover and cook on High for 4 hours.
Transfer chicken to a cutting board, cool down, slice, divide between plates and serve with cooking juices on top, with a side salad and lemon wedges.
Enjoy!

Nutrition:

calories 271, fat 3, fiber 6, carbs 9, protein 8

Chicken Chowder

Preparation time: 10 minutes
Cooking time: 6 hours
Servings: 4

Ingredients:

3 chicken breasts, skinless and boneless and cubed	15 ounces coconut cream
4 cups chicken stock	1 teaspoon garlic powder
1 sweet potato, cubed	4 bacon strips, cooked and crumbled
8 ounces canned green chilies, chopped	A pinch of salt and black pepper
1 yellow onion, chopped	1 tablespoon parsley, chopped

Directions:

In your slow cooker, mix chicken with stock, sweet potato, green chilies, onion, garlic powder, salt and pepper, stir, cover and cook on Low for 5 hours and 40 minutes.
Add coconut cream and parsley, stir, cover and cook on Low for 20 minutes more.
Ladle chowder into bowls, sprinkle bacon on top and serve.
Enjoy!

Nutrition:

calories 232, fat 3, fiber 7, carbs 14, protein 7

Flavored Chicken Soup

Preparation time: 10 minutes
Cooking time: 4 hours
Servings: 4

Ingredients:

1 pound chicken breast, skinless, boneless and cubed	1 chipotle chili in adobo sauce
15 ounces canned tomatoes and chilies, chopped	½ teaspoon oregano, dried
2 teaspoons cumin, ground	1 red bell pepper, chopped
A pinch of salt and black pepper	2 cup chicken stock
1 yellow onion, chopped	1 avocado, pitted, peeled and chopped
	½ cup cilantro, chopped

Directions:

In your slow cooker, mix chicken with tomatoes and chilies, cumin, salt, pepper, onion, chipotle chili, oregano, bell pepper and stock, stir, cover and cook on Low for 4 hours.
Add cilantro, stir, ladle into bowls and serve with avocado on top.
Enjoy!

Nutrition:

calories 300, fat 3, fiber 7, carbs 16, protein 4

Chicken and Olives

Preparation time: 10 minutes
Cooking time: 6 hours
Servings: 6

Ingredients:

2 pounds chicken thighs, boneless and skinless
1 yellow onion, chopped
3 carrots, chopped
1/3 cup prunes, dried and halved
3 garlic cloves, minced
½ cup green olives, pitted
2 teaspoon sweet paprika
1 teaspoon cinnamon, ground
2 teaspoons cumin, ground
2 teaspoons ginger, grated
1 cup chicken stock
A pinch of salt and black pepper
1 tablespoon cilantro, chopped

Directions:

In your slow cooker, mix chicken with onion, carrots, prunes, garlic, olives, paprika, cinnamon, cumin, ginger, stock, salt and pepper, stir, cover and cook on Low for 6 hours. Divide on plates, sprinkle cilantro on top and serve.
Enjoy!

Nutrition:

calories 384, fat 12, fiber 4, carbs 20, protein 34

Italian Chicken

Preparation time: 10 minutes
Cooking time: 6 hours
Servings: 4

Ingredients:

4 chicken thighs, skinless and boneless
15 ounces canned tomatoes, chopped
½ cup mushrooms, sliced
½ cup kalamata olives, pitted
2 teaspoons Italian seasoning
3 garlic cloves, minced
A pinch of salt and black pepper
2 cups chicken stock
2 cups baby spinach
12 ounces tomato paste
Cooking spray

Directions:

Grease your slow cooker with cooking spray and add chicken, tomatoes, mushrooms, olives, Italian seasoning, garlic, salt, pepper, and stock and tomato paste.
Stir, cover, cook on Low for 6 hours, add spinach, stir, leave everything aside for 10 minutes, divide between plates and serve.
Enjoy!

Nutrition:

calories 321, fat 4, fiber 7, carbs 16, protein 14

Pineapple Chicken

Preparation time: 10 minutes
Cooking time: 7 hours
Servings: 8

Ingredients:

8 chicken thighs, bone in
A pinch of salt and black pepper
2 tablespoon ghee
1 cup pineapple juice
½ cup chicken stock
2 tablespoons coconut sugar
3 tablespoons coconut aminos
2 tablespoon apple cider vinegar
½ teaspoon ginger, grated
1 teaspoon garlic powder
8 ounces canned pineapple chunks
8 ounces canned pineapple, crushed
1 red bell pepper, chopped
1 red onion, chopped
2 tablespoons parsley, chopped
½ teaspoon sesame seeds

Directions:

In your slow cooker, mix chicken with salt, pepper, ghee, pineapple juice, stock, coconut sugar, aminos, vinegar, ginger, garlic powder, pineapple chunks and crushed pineapple, red bell pepper and onion, stir, cover and cook on Low for 7 hours.
Add parsley and sesame seeds, toss, divide between plates and serve.
Enjoy!

Nutrition:

calories 321, fat 5, fiber 7, carbs 15, protein 4

Lemon and Garlic Chicken

Preparation time: 10 minutes
Cooking time: 4 hours
Servings: 6

Ingredients:

1 yellow onion, cut into quarters
¼ cup olive oil
1 pound carrots, sliced
6 chicken thighs, bone in
3 tablespoons lemon juice
4 garlic cloves, minced
1 lemon, sliced
3 rosemary sprigs, chopped
6 thyme sprigs, chopped
A pinch of salt and black pepper

Directions:

In your slow cooker, mix onion with oil, carrots, chicken, lemon juice, garlic, lemon slices, rosemary, thyme, salt and pepper, stir, cover and cook on High for 4 hours.
Divide between plates and serve.
Enjoy!

Nutrition:

calories 300, fat 6, fiber 5, carbs 15, protein 5

Creamy Chicken

Preparation time: 10 minutes
Cooking time: 4 hours
Servings: 8

Ingredients:

2 pounds chicken breasts, skinless and boneless
2 tablespoons water
1 tablespoon olive oil
1 and ½ teaspoons cumin, ground
1 teaspoon chili powder
1 teaspoon garlic powder
1 teaspoon onion powder
½ teaspoon smoked paprika
½ teaspoon oregano, dried
A pinch of salt and black pepper to the taste
8 ounces coconut cream
Cooking spray

Directions:

Grease your slow cooker with cooking spray and add chicken, water, oil, cumin, chili, garlic powder, onion powder, paprika, oregano, salt and pepper, toss, cover and cook on High for 3 hours and 30 minutes.
Shred chicken using 2 forks, add coconut cream, toss, cover and cook on High for 30 minutes more.
Divide chicken mix between plates and serve.
Enjoy!

Nutrition:

calories 312, fat 4, fiber 6, carbs 20, protein 5

Chicken Breasts and Peach Sauce

Preparation time: 10 minutes
Cooking time: 6 hours
Servings: 8

Ingredients:

6 chicken breasts, skinless and boneless
12 ounces orange juice
2 tablespoons lemon juice
15 ounces canned peaches and their juice
1 teaspoon coconut aminos

Directions:

In your slow cooker, mix chicken with orange juice, lemon juice, peaches and coconut aminos, toss, cover and cook on Low for 6 hours.
Divide chicken breasts on plates, drizzle peach and orange sauce all over and serve.
Enjoy!

Nutrition:

calories 251, fat 4, fiber 6, carbs 18, protein 14

Turkey Gumbo

Preparation time: 10 minutes
Cooking time: 7 hours
Servings: 4

Ingredients:

1 pound turkey wings
Salt and black pepper to the taste
5 ounces water
1 yellow onion, chopped
1 yellow bell pepper, chopped
3 garlic cloves, chopped
2 tablespoons chili powder
1 and ½ teaspoons cumin, ground
A pinch of cayenne pepper
2 cups veggies stock

Directions:

In your slow cooker, mix turkey with salt, pepper, onion, bell pepper, garlic, chili powder, cumin, cayenne and stock, stir, cover and cook on Low for 7 hours.
Divide everything between plates and serve.
Enjoy!

Nutrition:

calories 232, fat 4, fiber 7, carbs 17, protein 20

Turkey and Orange Sauce

Preparation time: 10 minutes
Cooking time: 8 hours
Servings: 4

Ingredients:

4 turkey wings
2 tablespoons ghee, melted
2 tablespoons olive oil
1 and ½ cups cranberries, dried
Salt and black pepper to the taste
1 yellow onion, roughly chopped
1 cup walnuts
1 cup orange juice
1 bunch thyme, chopped

Directions:

In your slow cooker mix ghee with oil, turkey wings, cranberries, salt, pepper, onion, walnuts, orange juice and thyme, stir a bit, cover and cook on Low for 8 hours.
Divide turkey and orange sauce between plates and serve.
Enjoy!

Nutrition:

calories 300, fat 12, fiber 4, carbs 17, protein 1

Cinnamon Chicken

Preparation time: 10 minutes
Cooking time: 4 hours
Servings: 8

Ingredients:

1 whole chicken, cut into medium pieces
1 tablespoon olive oil
1 and ½ tablespoons lemon zest, grated
1 cup chicken stock
1 tablespoon thyme, chopped
1 teaspoon cinnamon powder
Salt and black pepper to the taste
1 tablespoon cumin, ground
2 teaspoons garlic powder

Directions:

In your slow cooker, mix chicken with oil, lemon zest, stock, thyme, cinnamon, salt, pepper, cumin and garlic, stir, cover and cook on High for 4 hours.
Divide everything between plates and serve.
Enjoy!

Nutrition:

calories 261, fat 4, fiber 6, carbs 12, protein 22

Chicken and Celery

Preparation time: 10 minutes
Cooking time: 4 hours
Servings: 4

Ingredients:

6 chicken thighs
1 teaspoon olive oil
Salt and black pepper to the taste
1 yellow onion, chopped
3 celery stalk, chopped
½ teaspoon thyme, dried
2 tablespoons tomato paste
15 ounces canned tomatoes, chopped
2 cups chicken stock

Directions:

In your slow cooker, mix chicken with oil, salt, pepper, onion, celery, thyme, tomato paste, tomatoes and stock, stir, cover and cook on High for 4 hours.
Divide between plates and serve hot.
Enjoy!

Nutrition:

calories 261, fat 10, fiber 6, carbs 17, protein 27

Chicken Stew

Preparation time: 10 minutes
Cooking time: 6 hours
Servings: 4

Ingredients:

1 pound smoked pork sausage, sliced
1 tablespoon olive oil
1 pound chicken thighs, halved
Salt and black pepper to the taste
1 teaspoon Cajun spice
1 bell pepper, chopped
1 yellow onion, chopped
1 celery stalk, chopped
4 garlic cloves, minced
2 quarts chicken stock
15 ounces canned tomatoes, chopped
½ cup parsley, chopped

Directions:

In your slow cooker, mix smoked sausage with oil, chicken, salt, pepper, Cajun spice, bell pepper, onion, celery, garlic, stock and tomatoes, stir, cover and cook on Low for 6 hours.
Add parsley, stir, divide stew into bowls and serve.
Enjoy!

Nutrition:

calories 223, fat 12, fiber 6, carbs 20, protein 10

French Chicken and Bacon

Preparation time: 10 minutes
Cooking time: 4 hours
Servings: 4

Ingredients:

2 pounds chicken thighs, skinless and boneless
4 ounces bacon, chopped
¼ cup olive oil
2 brown onions, sliced
2 garlic cloves, minced
14 ounces chicken stock
1 bay leaf
7 ounces white mushrooms, sliced
1 cup parsley, chopped
Salt and black pepper to the taste

Directions:

In your slow cooker, mix chicken with bacon, oil, onion, garlic, stock, bay leaf, mushrooms, salt, pepper and parsley, stir, cover and cook on High for 4 hours.
Divide chicken mix into plates and serve hot.
Enjoy!

Nutrition:

calories 300, fat 13, fiber 7, carbs 17, protein 18

Chicken and Sweet Potatoes

Preparation time: 10 minutes
Cooking time: 4 hours
Servings: 4

Ingredients:

2 sweet potatoes, cut into medium cubes
1 yellow onion, chopped
4 big tomatoes, cut into wedges
¼ cup chicken stock
8 chicken thighs, bone in
Salt and black pepper to the taste
2 bay leaves

Directions:

In your slow cooker, mix chicken thighs with sweet potatoes, onion, tomatoes, stock, salt, pepper and bay leaves, stir a bit, cover and cook on High for 4 hours.
Divide between plates and serve.
Enjoy!

Nutrition:

calories 300, fat 12, fiber 6, carbs 17, protein 12

Creole Chicken, Sausage and Shrimp

Preparation time: 10 minutes
Cooking time: 6 hours
Servings: 4

Ingredients:

8 ounces shrimp, peeled and deveined
8 ounces sausages, sliced
8 ounces chicken breasts, skinless, boneless and chopped
2 tablespoons olive oil
1 teaspoon Creole seasoning
2 teaspoons thyme, dried
A pinch of cayenne pepper
A pinch of salt and black pepper
2 cups canned tomatoes, chopped
3 garlic cloves, minced
1 yellow onion, chopped
1 green bell pepper, chopped
3 celery stalks, chopped
1 cup chicken stock
3 tablespoons parsley, chopped

Directions:

In your slow cooker, mix sausages with chicken, oil, Creole seasoning, thyme, cayenne, salt, pepper, tomatoes, garlic, onion, bell pepper, celery and stock, stir, cover and cook on Low for 5 hours and 30 minutes.
Add shrimp, stir a bit, cover and cook on Low for 30 minutes more.
Divide everything into bowls and serve.

Nutrition:

calories 261, fat 7, fiber 7, carbs 28, protein 17

Chicken and Apricot Sauce

Preparation time: 10 minutes
Cooking time: 4 hours
Servings: 4

Ingredients:

1 pound chicken thighs, skinless and boneless
Salt and black pepper to the taste
1 tablespoon olive oil
½ teaspoon sweet paprika
½ cup veggie stock
½ teaspoon marjoram, dried
2 tablespoons white vinegar
¼ cup apricot preserves
1 and ½ teaspoon ginger, grated
2 tablespoons stevia

Directions:

In your slow cooker, mix chicken with oil, salt, pepper, paprika, stock, marjoram, vinegar, apricot preserves, ginger and stevia, toss well, cover and cook on High for 4 hours.
Divide between plates and serve.
Enjoy!

Nutrition:

calories 251, fat 7, fiber 8, carbs 14, protein 17

Flavored Chicken Thighs

Preparation time: 10 minutes
Cooking time: 4 hours
Servings: 6

Ingredients:

10 chicken thighs, skinless and boneless
2 jalapeno peppers, chopped
28 ounces canned tomatoes and their juice, chopped
2 teaspoons cumin, ground
2 tablespoons ginger, chopped
½ cup ghee, melted
2 teaspoons garam masala
Salt and black pepper to the taste
1 cup coconut cream
¼ cup cilantro, chopped

Directions:

In your slow cooker, mix chicken thighs with jalapenos, tomatoes, cumin, ginger, ghee, garam masala, salt, pepper and coconut cream, stir, cover and cook on High for 4 hours.
Add cilantro, stir, divide into bowls and serve.
Enjoy!

Nutrition:

calories 300, fat 13, fiber 6, carbs 17, protein 20

Creamy Chicken and Broccoli

Preparation time: 10 minutes
Cooking time: 5 hours
Servings: 6

Ingredients:

2 chicken breasts, skinless and boneless
1 tablespoon ghee
1 tablespoon olive oil
½ cup yellow onion, chopped
14 ounces chicken stock
Salt and black pepper to the taste
A pinch of red pepper flakes
1 tablespoon parsley, chopped
3 cups broccoli florets
4 ounces coconut cream

Directions:

In your slow cooker, mix chicken with ghee, oil, onion, stock, salt, pepper, pepper flakes and broccoli, stir, cover and cook on High for 4 hours and 30 minutes.
Add parsley and coconut cream, toss, cover and cook on High for 30 minutes more.
Divide chicken and broccoli between plates and serve with the coconut sauce drizzled all over.
Enjoy!

Nutrition:

calories 300, fat 7, fiber 7, carbs 26, protein 27

Salsa Chicken Soup

Preparation time: 10 minutes
Cooking time: 4 hours
Servings: 4

Ingredients:

4 chicken breasts, skinless, boneless and cubed
2 tablespoons olive oil
1 onion, chopped
3 garlic cloves, minced
16 ounces Paleo salsa
Salt and black pepper to the taste
29 ounces canned tomatoes, peeled and chopped
29 ounces chicken stock
2 tablespoons parsley, chopped
1 teaspoon garlic powder
1 tablespoon onion powder
1 tablespoon chili powder

Directions:

In your slow cooker, mix chicken with oil, onion, garlic, salsa, salt, pepper, stock, tomatoes, garlic powder, onion powder and chili powder, stir, cover and cook on High for 4 hours.
Add parsley, stir, ladle soup into bowls and serve.

Nutrition:

calories 231, fat 6, fiber 7, carbs 18, protein 19

Hearty Pork Ribs

Preparation time: 12 hours and 10 minutes
Cooking time: 6 hours
Servings: 4

Ingredients:

4 cups vinegar
4 pounds pork ribs
2 tablespoons apple cider vinegar
2 cups water
3 tablespoons coconut aminos
Black pepper to the taste
A pinch of garlic powder
A pinch of Chinese 5 spice

Directions:

Put your ribs in a big bowl, add white vinegar and water, toss, cover and keep in the fridge for 12 hours.
Drain ribs, season with black pepper to the taste, garlic powder and Chinese 5 spice and rub well.
Place ribs in your slow cooker and add apple cider vinegar and aminos as well.
Toss to coat well, cover slow cooker and cook on High for 6 hours.
Divide ribs between plates and serve.

Nutrition:

calories 300, fat 6, fiber 3, carbs 8, protein 15

Simple And Easy Roast

Preparation time: 10 minutes
Cooking time: 8 hours and 30 minutes
Servings: 6

Ingredients:

4 pounds beef chuck roast
1 cup veggie stock
1 tablespoon coconut oil
1 bay leaf
10 thyme springs
4 garlic cloves, minced
1 carrot, roughly chopped
2 celery ribs, roughly chopped
1 cauliflower head, florets separated
A pinch of sea salt
Black pepper to the taste
1 onion, roughly chopped

Directions:

Season beef with a pinch of sea salt and some black pepper.
Heat up a pan with the oil over medium high heat, add beef roast, brown for 5 minutes on each side and then transfer to your slow cooker.
Add thyme springs, stock, bay leaf, garlic, celery, onion and carrot, cover and cook on Low for 8 hours.
Add cauliflower, cover slow cooker again and cook on High for 20 minutes more.
Divide roast and veggies between plates and serve.

Nutrition:

calories 340, fat 5, fiber 3, carbs 8, protein 22

Mexican Pork Delight

Preparation time: 10 minutes
Cooking time: 8 hours
Servings: 6

Ingredients:

1 yellow onion, chopped
2 tablespoons sweet paprika
15 ounces canned tomato, roasted and chopped
1 teaspoon cumin, ground
1 teaspoon coconut oil
A pinch of sea salt
Black pepper to the taste
A pinch of nutmeg, ground
5 pounds pork roast
Juice of 1 lemon
¼ cup apple cider vinegar

Directions:

Heat up a pan with the oil over medium high heat, add onions, stir and brown them for a couple of minutes.
Transfer onions to your slow cooker, add paprika, tomato, cumin, nutmeg, lemon juice, vinegar, a pinch of salt and black pepper and whisk really well.
Add pork, toss to coat and cook on Low for 8 hours.
Slice roast, arrange on plates and serve with tomatoes and onions mix.
Enjoy!

Nutrition:

calories 350, fat 5, fiber 2, carbs 8, protein 24

Hawaiian Pork

Preparation time: 10 minutes
Cooking time: 6 hours
Servings: 4

Ingredients:

2 pounds pork chops
1/3 cup coconut sugar
¼ cup sugar free ketchup
15 ounces pineapple, cubed
3 tablespoons apple cider vinegar
5 tablespoons coconut aminos
2 teaspoons garlic, minced
3 tablespoons tapioca flour
Cilantro, chopped for serving

Directions:

In a bowl, mix ketchup with sugar, vinegar, aminos and tapioca and whisk well.
Add pork chops, toss well and transfer everything to your slow cooker.
Add pineapple and garlic, toss again, cover and cook on Low for 6 hours.
Sprinkle cilantro, stir gently, divide everything between plates and serve.
Enjoy!

Nutrition:

calories 345, fat 5, fiber 6, carbs 7, protein 14

Incredible Pork Tenderloin

Preparation time: 10 minutes
Cooking time: 8 hours
Servings: 4

Ingredients:

A pinch of nutmeg, ground
2 pounds pork tenderloin
4 apples, cored and sliced
2 tablespoons maple syrup

Directions:

Place half of the apples in your Crockpot and sprinkle nutmeg over them.
Add pork tenderloin, top with the rest of the apples, sprinkle some more nutmeg and drizzle the maple syrup.
Cover and cook on Low for 8 hours.
Slice pork tenderloin, divide it between plates and serve with apple slices and cooking juices on top.
Enjoy!

Nutrition:

calories 400, fat 4, fiber 5, carbs 8, protein 20

Super Easy Pork Dinner

Preparation time: 10 minutes
Cooking time: 4 hours
Servings: 8

Ingredients:

1 pound chorizo, ground
1 pound pork, ground
3 tablespoons olive oil
1 tomato, chopped
1 avocado, pitted, peeled and chopped
Black pepper to the taste
1 small red onion, chopped
2 tablespoons Paleo enchilada sauce
Scrambled eggs for serving

Directions:

Heat up a pan with the oil over medium high heat, add pork meat, stir, brown for a couple of minutes and transfer to your slow cooker.
Add salt, pepper, chorizo, onion and enchilada sauce, stir, cover and cook on Low for 4 hours.
Divide between plates and serve with chopped tomato, avocado and maybe with some scrambled eggs on top.
Enjoy!

Nutrition:

calories 300, fat 12, fiber 3, carbs 7, protein 17

Simple Pork Stew

Preparation time: 10 minutes
Cooking time: 8 hours
Servings: 6

Ingredients:

1 tablespoon olive oil
2 pounds pork loin, cubed
1 cup tapioca flour
3 garlic cloves, minced
6 baby carrots, halved
2 onions, chopped
Black pepper to the taste
A pinch of sea salt
1 cabbage head, shredded
3 cups veggie stock
28 ounces canned tomatoes, chopped
3 big sweet potatoes, cubed

Directions:

Put pork in a bowl, add tapioca flour and toss well.
Heat up a pan with the oil over medium high heat, add meat, brown for a few minutes on each side and place in your slow cooker.
Add a pinch of salt, black pepper, carrots, garlic, onion, potatoes, cabbage, stock and tomatoes, stir well, cover and cook on Low for 8 hours.
Divide stew into bowls and serve right away.
Enjoy!

Nutrition:

calories 300, fat 5, fiber 4, carbs 8, protein 15

Simple Beef Stew

Preparation time: 10 minutes
Cooking time: 8 hours
Servings: 6

Ingredients:

2 pound beef, cubed
2 tablespoons Moroccan spices
2 big white onions, chopped
Black pepper to the taste
2 cups veggie stock
1/3 cup coconut oil, melted
1 lemon, sliced
3 garlic cloves, minced
Zest from 1 lemon, grated
Juice from 2 limes
1 bunch cilantro, chopped
1 butternut squash, peeled and cubed

Directions:

Put the stock in your slow cooker, add beef, spices, onions, black pepper, garlic, lemon slices, lemon zest, lime juice and oil.
Stir everything to coat well, cover and cook on Low for 7 hours.
Add cilantro and squash, stir, cover and cook for 1 more hour on Low.
Divide into serving bowls and serve right away.
Enjoy!

Nutrition:

calories 320, fat 10, fiber 3, carbs 5, protein 15

Lamb Stew

Preparation time: 10 minutes
Cooking time: 8 hours
Servings: 4

Ingredients:

1 and ½ pounds lamb meat, cubed
¼ cup tapioca flour
Black pepper to the taste
A pinch of sea salt
2 tablespoons olive oil
1 teaspoon rosemary, dried
1 onion, sliced
½ teaspoon thyme, dried
2 cups water
1 cup baby carrots
2 cups sweet potatoes, chopped

Directions:

In a bowl, mix lamb with tapioca and toss to coat.
Heat up a pan with the oil over medium high heat, add meat, brown it on all sides and transfer to your slow cooker.
Heat up the pan again over medium high heat, add onion, stir, cook for 3 minutes and add to your slow cooker as well.
Also add a pinch of salt, pepper, rosemary, thyme, water, carrots and sweet potatoes, stir, cover and cook on Low for 8 hours.
Divide lamb stew between plates and serve hot.
Enjoy!

Nutrition:

calories 350, fat 8, fiber 3, carbs 6, protein 16

Flavored Lamb Leg

Preparation time: 10 minutes
Cooking time: 8 hours
Servings: 4

Ingredients:

2 tablespoons olive oil
1 lamb leg, bone in
1 garlic head, peeled and cloves separated
5 sweet potatoes, cubed
5 rosemary springs
2 cups low sodium chicken stock
A pinch of sea salt
Black pepper to the taste

Directions:

Rub your lamb leg with the oil, a pinch of salt and some black pepper.
Place the potatoes and the garlic cloves on the bottom of your slow cooker.
Add lamb leg, rosemary springs and stock.
Cover the slow cooker and cook lamb on Low for 8 hours.
Divide lamb and potatoes between plates and serve.
Enjoy!

Nutrition:

calories 350, fat 6, fiber 5, carbs 8, protein 12

Exotic Lamb Curry

Preparation time: 10 minutes
Cooking time: 4 hours
Servings: 4

Ingredients:

1 and ½ tablespoons sweet paprika	3 carrots, chopped
3 tablespoons curry powder	4 celery stalks, chopped
Black pepper to the taste	1 onion, chopped
A pinch of sea salt	4 celery stalks, chopped
2 pounds lamb meat, cubed	1 cup low sodium chicken stock
2 tablespoons coconut oil	4 garlic cloves minced
	1 cup coconut milk

Directions:

Heat up a pan with the oil over medium high heat, add lamb meat, brown it on all sides and transfer to your slow cooker.
Heat up the pan again over medium high heat, add stock, stir, heat it up and add to the slow cooker as well.
Add onions, celery and carrots to the slow cooker and stir everything gently.
In a bowl, mix paprika with a pinch of salt, black pepper and curry powder and stir.
Add spice mix to the cooker and toss everything.
Add coconut milk, cover and cook on High for 4 hours.
Divide into bowls and serve.

Nutrition:

calories 300, fat 4, fiber 4, carbs 8, protein 13

Asian Style Ribs

Preparation time: 10 minutes
Cooking time: 6 hours
Servings: 6

Ingredients:

4 pounds beef short ribs	1 tablespoon ginger, grated
½ cup beef stock	4 garlic cloves, minced
½ cup coconut aminos	1 tablespoon green onions, chopped
2 tablespoons apple cider vinegar	1 teaspoon sesame seeds

Directions:

In your slow cooker, mix ribs with stock, aminos, vinegar, ginger, garlic and green onions, stir, cover and cook on Low for 6 hours.
Add sesame seeds, toss, divide between plates and serve with cooking juices from the Crockpot drizzled all over.
Enjoy!

Nutrition:

calories 349, fat 8, fiber 12, carbs 19, protein 4

Tasty Lamb Shanks

Preparation time: 10 minutes
Cooking time: 8 hours and 20 minutes
Servings: 4

Ingredients:

4 lamb shanks, trimmed	2 tablespoons tomato paste
3 tablespoons coconut oil	2 cups veggie stock
¼ cup arrowroot flour	1 tablespoon rosemary, dried
1 onion, chopped	1 tablespoon thyme, dried
2 carrots, chopped	1 tablespoon oregano, dried
15 ounces canned tomatoes, chopped	Black pepper to the taste
2 garlic cloves, minced	A pinch of sea salt
2 celery stalks, chopped	

Directions:

Heat up a pan with 2 tablespoons oil over medium high heat, add lamb shanks, brown them for 5 minutes on each side and transfer to your slow cooker.
Heat up the pan again with the rest of the oil over medium heat, add carrot, celery, garlic and onion, stir and cook for 8 minutes.
Add tomato paste, tomatoes, stock, a pinch of salt, black pepper, thyme, rosemary and oregano, stir, cook for 1 minute and pour over lamb shanks.
Cover your slow cooker and cook on Low for 7 hours.
Divide lamb shanks between plates, stir veggies and sauce left in the slow cooker, cover again and cook on High for 1 more hour.
Pour over lamb shanks and serve.

Nutrition:

calories 350, fat 5, fiber 4, carbs 9, protein 20

Greek Lamb

Preparation time: 15 minutes
Cooking time: 7 hours
Servings: 4

Ingredients:

6-pound lamb leg, boneless	1 teaspoon sage, dried
2 tablespoons olive oil	1 teaspoon ginger, grated
Salt and black pepper to the taste	3 garlic cloves, minced
1 bay leaf	1 teaspoon thyme, dried
1 teaspoon marjoram	2 cups veggie stock

Directions:

In your slow cooker, mix lamb with oil, salt, pepper, bay leaf, marjoram, sage, ginger, garlic, thyme and stock, stir, cover and cook on Low for 7 hours.
Divide between plates and serve.

Nutrition:

calories 263, fat 8, fiber 9, carbs 12, protein 4

Lamb And Bacon Stew

Preparation time: 10 minutes
Cooking time: 7 hours and 10 minutes
Servings: 6

Ingredients:

2 tablespoons tapioca flour
2 ounces bacon, cooked and crumbled
1 and ½ pounds lamb loin, chopped
Black pepper to the taste
A pinch of sea salt
1 garlic clove, minced
1 cup yellow onion, chopped
3 and ½ cups veggie stock
1 cup carrots, chopped
1 cup celery, chopped
2 cups sweet potatoes, chopped
1 tablespoon thyme, chopped
1 bay leaf
2 tablespoons coconut oil

Directions:

Put lamb meat in a bowl, add tapioca, a pinch of salt and pepper and toss to coat.
Heat up a pan with the oil over medium high heat, add lamb, brown for 5 minutes on each side and transfer to your slow cooker.
Heat up the pan again over medium heat, add onion and garlic, stir, sauté for 4 minutes and add to slow cooker.
Add bacon, carrots, potatoes, bay leaf, stock, thyme and celery to the slow cooker as well, stir gently, cover and cook on Low for 7 hours.
Discard bay leaf, stir your stew, divide into bowls and serve.
Enjoy!

Nutrition:

calories 360, fat 5, fiber 3, carbs 8, protein 16

French Lamb Chops

Preparation time: 10 minutes
Cooking time: 8 hours
Servings: 4

Ingredients:

4 lamb chops
1 cup onion, chopped
2 cups canned tomatoes, chopped
1 cup leek, chopped
2 tablespoons garlic, minced
1 teaspoon herbs de Provence
Salt and black pepper to the taste
3 cups water

Directions:

In your slow cooker mix, lamb chops with onion, tomatoes, leek, garlic, herbs de Provence, salt, pepper and water, stir, cover and cook on Low for 8 hours.
Divide lamb and veggies between plates and serve.
Enjoy!

Nutrition:

calories 430, fat 12, fiber 8, carbs 20, protein 18

Amazing Mediterranean Pork

Preparation time: 20 hours and 10 minutes
Cooking time: 8 hours
Servings: 6

Ingredients:

3 pounds pork shoulder, boneless
For the marinade:
¼ cup olive oil
2 teaspoons oregano, dried
¼ cup lemon juice
2 teaspoons mustard
2 teaspoons mint
6 garlic cloves, minced
2 teaspoons Paleo pesto sauce
Black pepper to the taste
A pinch of sea salt

Directions:

In a bowl, mix oil with lemon juice, oregano, mint, mustard, garlic, pesto, salt and pepper and stir very well.
Rub pork shoulder with the marinade, cover and keep in the fridge for 10 hours.
Flip pork shoulder and keep in the fridge for 10 more hours.
Transfer to your slow cooker along with the marinade, cover and cook on Low for 8 hours.
Slice roast and serve with a tasty side salad!
Enjoy!

Nutrition:

calories 300, fat 4, fiber 6, carbs 7, protein 10

Beef and Veggies

Preparation time: 10 minutes
Cooking time: 8 hours
Servings: 6

Ingredients:

4 pounds beef roast
2 cups beef stock
2 sweet potatoes, cubed
6 carrots, sliced
7 celery stalks, chopped
1 yellow onion, chopped
1 tablespoon onion powder
1 tablespoon garlic powder
1 tablespoon sweet paprika
A pinch of salt and black pepper

Directions:

In your slow cooker, beef with stock, sweet potatoes, carrots, celery, onion, onion powder, garlic powder, paprika, salt and pepper, stir, cover and cook on Low for 8 hours.
Slice roast, divide on plates, drizzle sauce from the pot all and serve with the veggies on the side.
Enjoy!

Nutrition:

calories 372, fat 6, fiber 12, carbs 19, protein 11

Special Roast

Preparation time: 10 minutes
Cooking time: 4 hours
Servings: 6

Ingredients:

1 pound sweet potatoes, chopped
3 and ½ pounds pork roast
8 medium carrots, chopped
15 ounces canned tomatoes, chopped
1 yellow onion, chopped
Grated zest and juice from 1 lemon
4 garlic cloves, minced
3 bay leaves
Black pepper to the taste
½ cup kalamata olives, pitted
A pinch of salt

Directions:

Put potatoes in your slow cooker and mix with carrots, tomatoes, onions, lemon juice and zest. Also add pork, bay leaves, a pinch of salt, black pepper and garlic, stir, cover and cook on High for 4 hours.
Transfer meat to a cutting board, slice it and divide among plates.
Discard bay leaves, transfer veggies to a bowl, mash them, mix with olives and add next to the meat.
Serve right away!

Nutrition:

calories 250, fat 4, fiber 3, carbs 8, protein 13

Delicious Beef And Pearl Onions

Preparation time: 10 minutes
Cooking time: 6 hours and 5 minutes
Servings: 6

Ingredients:

3 pounds beef roast, trimmed and boneless
1 tablespoon Italian seasoning
Black pepper to the taste
1 garlic clove, minced
1/3 cup sun-dried tomatoes, chopped
½ cup low sodium beef stock
½ cup kalamata olives pitted and halved
1 cup pearl onions
1 tablespoon olive oil

Directions:

Heat up a pan with the oil over medium high heat, add beef, brown for 5 minutes, take off heat and season with black pepper and Italian spices.
Transfer to your slow cooker, add tomatoes, onions and stock, cover and cook on Low for 6 hours.
Transfer to a cutting board, slice, divide between plates, add onions and tomatoes on the side and serve with cooking juices drizzled all over!

Nutrition:

calories 300, fat 5, fiber 5, carbs 8, protein 12

Light And Flavored Beef

Preparation time: 10 minutes
Cooking time: 4 hours and 10 minutes
Servings: 4

Ingredients:

2 tablespoons olive oil
8 ounces mushrooms, sliced
1 yellow onion, chopped
2 pounds beef meat, cubed
1 cup veggie stock
14 ounces canned tomatoes, chopped
½ cup tomato sauce
¼ cup balsamic vinegar
½ cup garlic cloves, minced
1 can black olives, pitted and sliced
2 tablespoons rosemary, chopped
2 tablespoon parsley, chopped
1 tablespoon capers
Black pepper to the taste

Directions:

Heat up a pan with half of the oil over medium high heat, add mushrooms, cook for 3-4 minutes stirring all the time and transfer them to your slow cooker.
Heat up the pan again over medium heat, add onion, stir, sauté for 3-4 minutes and add to slow cooker as well.
Heat up the pan once more over medium high heat, add meat, brown it for 10 minutes and add to slow cooker.
Add stock, tomatoes, tomato sauce, vinegar, garlic, olives, parsley, capers, black pepper and rosemary, stir gently, cover and cook on High for 4 hours.
Divide between plates and serve right away!

Nutrition:

calories 300, fat 4, fiber 3, carbs 6, protein 10

Beef Brisket Delight

Preparation time: 10 minutes
Cooking time: 8 hours
Servings: 6

Ingredients:

2 and ½ pounds beef brisket
4 cups veggie stock
2 bay leaves
3 garlic cloves, chopped
4 carrots, chopped
1 cabbage head cut into 6 wedges
Salt and black pepper to the taste
3 turnips, cut into quarters

Directions:

In your slow cooker, mix beef with stock, bay leaves, garlic, carrots, cabbage, salt, pepper and turnips, stir, cover and cook on Low for 8 hours.
Divide beef brisket on plates and serve.

Nutrition:

calories 321, fat 15, fiber 4, carbs 18, protein 19

Perfect Beef And Eggplants

Preparation time: 10 minutes
Cooking time: 8 hours and 10 minutes
Servings: 6

Ingredients:

2 pounds beef, cubed
2 garlic cloves, minced
2 yellow onions, chopped
8 medium eggplants, cubed
¼ cup olive oil
1 pound tomato sauce
1 cup veggie stock

1 tablespoon balsamic vinegar
1/8 teaspoon allspice
A pinch of cloves, ground
¼ cup parsley, chopped
Black pepper to the taste
A pinch of sea salt

Directions:

Heat up a pan with half of the oil over high heat, add meat, brown it for 5 minutes and transfer to your slow cooker.
Heat up the pan with the rest of the oil over medium heat, add eggplant pieces, garlic and onions, stir, cook for 4 minutes and add to slow cooker.
Also add stock, tomato sauce, vinegar, a pinch of salt, pepper, allspice and cloves, stir, cover and cook on Low for 8 hours.
Add parsley, stir gently, divide between plates and serve!
Enjoy!

Nutrition:

calories 353, fat 4, fiber 6, carbs 8, protein 10

Beef Cheeks

Preparation time: 10 minutes
Cooking time: 4 hours
Servings: 4

Ingredients:

4 beef cheeks, halved
2 tablespoons coconut oil
A pinch of salt and black pepper
1 white onion, chopped
4 garlic cloves, minced
2 cup beef stock
5 cardamom pods

1 tablespoon balsamic vinegar
3 bay leaves
7 cloves
2 vanilla beans, split
1 and ½ tablespoons tomato paste
1 carrot, sliced

Directions:

In your slow cooker, mix beef cheeks with melted coconut oil, salt, pepper, onion, garlic, stock, cardamom, vinegar, bay leaves, cloves, vanilla beans, tomato paste and carrot, toss, cover and cook on High for 4 hours.
Divide between plates and serve.
Enjoy!

Nutrition:

calories 321, fat 5, fiber 7, carbs 18, protein 12

Mediterranean Lamb

Preparation time: 10 minutes
Cooking time: 9 hours
Servings: 5

Ingredients:

1 pound lamb loin, cubed
2 garlic cloves, minced
1 teaspoon ginger, grated
1 red onion, chopped
1 teaspoon turmeric, ground
½ teaspoon cinnamon, ground
1 tablespoon honey
2 teaspoon cumin, ground
2 teaspoons coconut sugar

14 ounces canned tomatoes, crushed
1 cup low sodium chicken stock
1 cinnamon stick
Black pepper to the taste
10 prunes, pitted
¼ lemon, peeled and chopped
3 tablespoons tapioca flour
1 tablespoon parsley, chopped
1 tablespoon coriander, chopped

Directions:

Put lamb meat in your slow cooker.
Add garlic, ginger, onion, turmeric, cinnamon, cumin, honey, sugar, tomatoes, chicken stock, cinnamon stick, a pinch of salt and pepper, stir gently, cover and cook on Low for 8 hours and 30 minutes.
Add prunes, lemon, tapioca flour, parsley and coriander, stir, cover and cook on Low for 30 minutes more.
Divide into bowls and serve.

Nutrition:

calories 360, fat 4, fiber 6, carbs 8, protein 15

Lamb and Mushrooms

Preparation time: 10 minutes
Cooking time: 8 hours
Servings: 8

Ingredients:

1 and ½ pounds lamb leg, bone-in
2 carrots, sliced
½ pounds mushrooms, sliced
4 tomatoes, chopped
1 small yellow onion, chopped

6 garlic cloves, minced
2 tablespoons tomato paste
1 teaspoon olive oil
Salt and black pepper to the taste
A handful parsley, chopped

Directions:

In your slow cooker, mix lamb with carrots, mushrooms, tomatoes, onion, garlic, tomato paste, oil, salt, pepper and parsley, toss, cover and cook on Low for 8 hours.
Divide lamb mix between plates and serve.
Enjoy!

Nutrition:

calories 372, fat 12, fiber 7, carbs 18, protein 22

Rich Lamb Delight

Preparation time: 10 minutes
Cooking time: 8 hours and 10 minutes
Servings: 6

Ingredients:

3 pounds lamb shoulder, boneless
3 onions, roughly chopped
1 tablespoon olive oil
1 tablespoon oregano, chopped
6 garlic cloves, minced
1 tablespoon lemon zest, grated
A pinch of sea salt
Black pepper to the taste
½ teaspoon allspice
2 tablespoons tapioca flour
1 and ½ cups veggie stock
14 ounces canned artichoke hearts, chopped
¼ cup tomato paste
2 tablespoons parsley, chopped

Directions:

Heat up a pan with the oil over medium high heat, add lamb, brown for 5 minutes on each side and transfer to your slow cooker.
Heat up the pan again over medium high heat, add onion, lemon zest, garlic, a pinch of salt, pepper, oregano and allspice and cook for 5 minutes stirring often.
Add tapioca flour, stock and tomato paste, stir, bring to a boil over and pour over lamb.
Cover and cook on Low for 8 hours.
After 7 hours and 45 minutes add artichokes and parsley, stir gently, cover and cook on Low for 15 more minutes.
Divide into bowls and serve hot.

Nutrition:

calories 370, fat 4, fiber 5, carbs 7, protein 16

Slow Cooked Sausages and Sauce

Preparation time: 15 minutes
Cooking time: 3 hours
Servings: 6

Ingredients:

6 pork sausages
2 tablespoons olive oil
½ cup onion jam
3 ounces beef stock
3 ounces water
Salt and black pepper to the taste
1 tablespoon tapioca flour

Directions:

In your slow cooker, mix sausages with oil, onion jam, stock, water, salt, pepper and tapioca flour, toss, cover and cook on High for 3 hours.
Divide sausage and sauce between plates and serve.

Nutrition:

calories 431, fat 15, fiber 4, carbs 29, protein 13

Pork Shoulder

Preparation time: 10 minutes
Cooking time: 7 hours
Servings: 4

Ingredients:

2 and ½ pounds pork shoulder
4 cups chicken stock
½ cup coconut aminos
¼ cup white vinegar
2 tablespoons chili sauce
Juice from 1 lime
1 tablespoon ginger, grated
1 tablespoon Chinese 5 spice
2 cup by portabella mushrooms, sliced
A pinch of salt and black pepper
1 zucchini, sliced

Directions:

In your slow cooker, mix pork shoulder with stock, aminos, vinegar, chili sauce, lime juice, ginger, 5 spice, mushrooms, zucchini, salt and pepper, toss a bit, cover and cook on Low for 7 hours.
Transfer pork shoulder to a cutting board, shred using 2 forks, return to Crockpot and toss with the rest of the ingredients.
Divide pork between plates and serve.
Enjoy!

Nutrition:

calories 342, fat 6, fiber 8, carbs 27, protein 18

Flavored Beef

Preparation time: 10 minutes
Cooking time: 6 hours
Servings: 4

Ingredients:

4 cups cauliflower rice, steamed
2 pound beef chuck roast
1 poblano pepper, chopped
6 ounces tomato paste
1 white onion, chopped
1 cup beef stock
2 tablespoons cumin, ground
2 tablespoons olive oil
1 tablespoon garlic, minced
1 tablespoon oregano, chopped
1 tablespoon smoked paprika
½ cup cilantro, chopped
Lime wedges for serving

Directions:

In your slow cooker, mix oil with a beef roast, poblano pepper, tomato paste, onion, stock, cumin, garlic, oregano and smoked paprika, toss well, cover and cook on Low for 6 hours.
Slice meat, divide between plates and serve with cauliflower rice on the side, cilantro, sprinkled on top and lime wedges.
Enjoy!

Nutrition:

calories 345, fat 7, fiber 8, carbs 18, protein 20

Beef Chili

Preparation time: 10 minutes
Cooking time: 6 hours
Servings: 6

Ingredients:

2 pounds beef, ground
4 garlic cloves, minced
1 yellow onion, chopped
1 red bell pepper, chopped
1 green bell pepper, chopped
2 celery stalks, chopped
¼ cup green chilies, chopped
1 tomato, chopped
28 ounces canned tomatoes, crushed
14 ounces tomato sauce
2 tablespoons chili powder
1 tablespoons oregano, chopped
½ tablespoon basil, chopped
½ tablespoons cumin, ground
½ tablespoon adobo sauce
A pinch of salt and black pepper
A pinch of cayenne pepper

Directions:

In your instant pot, mix beef with garlic, onion, red bell pepper, green bell pepper, celery, chilies, tomato, crushed tomatoes, tomato sauce, chili powder, oregano, basil, cumin, adobo sauce, salt, pepper and cayenne, stir, cover and cook on Low for 6 hours.
Divide into bowls and serve.

Nutrition:

calories 372, fat 7, fiber 8, carbs 17, protein 16

Beef Stew

Preparation time: 10 minutes
Cooking time: 8 hours
Servings: 4

Ingredients:

2 cups beef stock
2 pounds beef stew meat
1 tablespoon balsamic vinegar
1 yellow onion, chopped
2 celery stalks, chopped
2 carrots, chopped
3 garlic cloves, minced
3 bay leaves
1 tablespoon sweet paprika
A pinch of salt and black pepper
1 teaspoon rosemary, dried
1 teaspoon basil, dried
1 teaspoon oregano, dried
1/8 cup arrowroot powder

Directions:

In your slow cooker, mix beef stock with beef meat, vinegar, onion, celery, carrots, garlic, bay leaves, paprika, salt, pepper, rosemary, basil oregano and arrowroot powder, stir, cover and cook on Low for 8 hours.
Divide into bowls and serve hot.

Nutrition:

calories 327, fat 4, fiber 7, carbs 18, protein 8

Lamb Stew

Preparation time: 10 minutes
Cooking time: 8 hours
Servings: 6

Ingredients:

1 and ½ pound lamb steak, cubed
1 yellow onion, chopped
1 tablespoon olive oil
1 carrot, sliced
A pinch of salt and black pepper
1 teaspoon lemon zest, grated
1 teaspoon cinnamon powder
1 and ½ teaspoon coriander seed powder
1 and ½ teaspoon cumin powder
½ teaspoon allspice
2 tablespoons lemon juice
1 teaspoon onion powder
2 garlic cloves, minced
7 apricots, dried and sliced
1 tablespoon tomato paste
2 bay leaves
1 and ½ cups water
¼ cup almonds, toasted
1 tablespoon parsley, chopped

Directions:

In your slow cooker, mix lamb with onion, oil, carrot, salt, pepper, lemon zest, cinnamon, coriander, cumin, allspice, lemon juice, onion powder, garlic, apricots, tomato paste, bay leaves and water, toss well, cover and cook on Low for 8 hours.
Add almonds and parsley, toss, divide into bowls and serve.

Nutrition:

calories 300, fat 4, fiber 8, carbs 17, protein 15

Beef Soup

Preparation time: 10 minutes
Cooking time: 6 hours
Servings: 4

Ingredients:

1 pound beef, ground
2 cups cauliflower, chopped
1 cup yellow onion, chopped
2 red bell peppers, chopped
15 ounces tomato sauce
15 ounces tomatoes, chopped
3 cups beef stock
½ teaspoon basil, dried
½ teaspoon oregano, dried
3 garlic cloves, minced
A pinch of salt and black pepper

Directions:

In your slow cooker, mix beef with cauliflower, onion, bell peppers, tomato sauce, tomatoes, stock, basil, oregano, garlic, salt and pepper, stir, cover and cook on Low for 6 hours.
Stir soup one more time, ladle into bowls and serve.

Nutrition:

calories 214, fat 6, fiber 6, carbs 18, protein 7

Tasty Ham Soup

Preparation time: 10 minutes
Cooking time: 7 hours
Servings: 6

Ingredients:

1 ham bone with meat
10 cups water
2 tablespoons apple cider vinegar
3 bay leaves
1 Serrano pepper, chopped
2 tablespoons avocado oil
2 leeks, chopped
1 yellow onion, chopped
4 garlic cloves, minced
1 sweet potato, cubed
2 celery stalks, chopped
2 carrots, chopped
2 turnips, chopped
½ Savoy cabbage head, cut into medium strips
1 tablespoon thyme, chopped
1 handful parsley, chopped
1 teaspoon cumin, ground
A pinch of salt and black pepper

Directions:

In your slow cooker, mix ham bone with water, vinegar, bay leaves, Serrano pepper, oil, leeks, onion, garlic, sweet potato, celery, carrots, turnips, cabbage, thyme, parsley, cumin, salt and pepper, stir, cover and cook on High for 5 hours.
Discard bone, return meat to pot, cover and cook on High for 2 more hours.
Divide soup into bowls and serve.
Enjoy!

Nutrition:

calories 333, fat 8, fiber 12, carbs 19, protein 12

Beef and Dill

Preparation time: 10 minutes
Cooking time: 5 hours
Servings: 6

Ingredients:

4 pounds beef brisket
2 oranges, sliced
2 garlic cloves, minced
2 yellow onions, thinly sliced
11 ounces celery, thinly sliced
1 tablespoon dill, dried
3 bay leaves
4 cinnamon sticks, cut into halves
Salt and black pepper to the taste
17 ounces veggie stock

Directions:

In your slow cooker, mix beef with orange slices, garlic, onion, celery, dill, bay leaves, cinnamon, salt, pepper and stock, stir, cover and cook on High for 5 hours.
Divide beef mix between plates and serve.
Enjoy!

Nutrition:

calories 300, fat 5, fiber 7, carbs 12, protein 4

Thai Pork Stew

Preparation time: 10 minutes
Cooking time: 7 hours
Servings: 4

Ingredients:

2 tablespoons olive oil
2 pounds pork butt, boneless and cubed
A pinch of salt and black pepper to the taste
6 eggs, hard boiled, peeled and sliced
1 tablespoon cilantro, chopped
1 tablespoon coriander seeds
1 tablespoon ginger, grated
1 tablespoon black peppercorns
2 tablespoons garlic, chopped
2 tablespoons 5 spice powder
1 and ½ cup coconut aminos
2 tablespoons cocoa powder
1 yellow onion, chopped
8 cups water

Directions:

In your slow cooker, mix oil with pork cubes, salt, pepper, cilantro, coriander, ginger, peppercorns, garlic, 5 spice, aminos, cocoa, onion and water, toss, cover and cook on Low for 7 hours.
Divide stew into bowls, add egg slices on top and serve.
Enjoy!

Nutrition:

calories 400, fat 10, fiber 9, carbs 28, protein 22

Beef Curry

Preparation time: 10 minutes
Cooking time: 4 hours
Servings: 4

Ingredients:

2 pounds beef steak, cubed
2 tablespoons olive oil
1 tablespoon mustard
2 and ½ tablespoons curry powder
2 yellow onions, chopped
2 garlic cloves, minced
10 ounces canned coconut milk
2 tablespoons tomato sauce
Salt and black pepper to the taste

Directions:

In your slow cooker, mix beef with oil, mustard, curry powder, onion, garlic, tomato paste, salt and pepper, stir, cover and cook on High for 3 hours and 40 minutes.
Add coconut milk, stir, cook on High for 20 minutes more, divide into bowls and serve.
Enjoy!

Nutrition:

calories 400, fat 18, fiber 7, carbs 18, protein 22

Creamy Beef

Preparation time: 10 minutes
Cooking time: 5 hours
Servings: 4

Ingredients:

10 pounds beef, cubed
1 yellow onion, chopped
2 and ½ tablespoons olive oil
2 garlic cloves, minced
4 ounces mushrooms, sliced
1 and ½ tablespoon tomato paste
Salt and black pepper to the taste
13 ounces beef stock
8 ounces coconut cream

Directions:

In your slow cooker, mix beef with onion, oil, garlic, mushrooms, tomato paste, salt, pepper, beef stock and coconut cream, stir, cover and cook on High for 5 hours.
Divide everything between plates and serve.
Enjoy!

Nutrition:

calories 383, fat 7, fiber 6, carbs 22, protein 16

Winter Beef and Mushrooms

Preparation time: 10 minutes
Cooking time: 7 hours
Servings: 4

Ingredients:

3.5 ounces button mushrooms, sliced
3.5 ounces shiitake mushrooms, sliced
2 pounds beef shoulder, cut into medium cubes
16 ounces shallots, chopped
9 ounces beef stock
2 garlic cloves, minced
2 tablespoons chives, chopped
1 teaspoon sage, dried
1/8 teaspoon thyme, dried
Salt and black pepper to the taste
3 and ½ tablespoons olive oil

Directions:

In your slow cooker, mix button mushrooms with shiitake mushrooms, beef, shallots, stock, garlic, chives, sage, thyme, salt, pepper and oil, toss, cover and cook on Low for 7 hours.
Divide beef and mushroom mix into plates and serve hot.
Enjoy!

Nutrition:

calories 362, fat 7, fiber 4, carbs 17, protein 37

Tender Lamb Shanks

Preparation time: 10 minutes
Cooking time: 7 hours
Servings: 4

Ingredients:

4 lamb shanks
2 tablespoons olive oil
1 yellow onion, finely chopped
3 carrots, roughly chopped
2 garlic cloves, minced
2 tablespoons tomato paste
1 teaspoon oregano, dried
1 tomato, roughly chopped
4 ounces chicken stock
Salt an black pepper to the taste

Directions:

In your slow cooker, mix lamb with oil, onion, garlic, carrots, tomato paste, tomato, oregano, stock, salt and pepper, stir, cover and cook on Low for 7 hours.
Divide into bowls and serve hot.
Enjoy!

Nutrition:

calories 400, fat 13, fiber 4, carbs 17, protein 24

Smoked Lamb Chops

Preparation time: 10 minutes
Cooking time: 7 hours
Servings: 4

Ingredients:

4 lamb chops
1 teaspoon liquid smoke
1 cup green onions, chopped
2 cups canned tomatoes, chopped
1 teaspoon smoked paprika
2 tablespoons garlic, minced
Salt and black pepper to the taste
3 cups beef stock

Directions:

In your slow cooker, mix lamb with liquid smoke, green onions, tomatoes, paprika, garlic, salt, pepper and stock, stir, cover and cook on Low for 7 hours.
Divide everything between plates and serve.
Enjoy!

Nutrition:

calorie 364, fat 12, fiber 7, carbs 29, protein 28

Creamy Pork Chops and Onion Sauce

Preparation time: 10 minutes
Cooking time: 5 hours
Servings: 4

Ingredients:

4 pork chops
2 tablespoons parsley, chopped
1 garlic clove, minced
2 tablespoons lime juice
2 tablespoons olive oil
1 pound onions, sliced
½ cup coconut milk
Salt and black pepper to the taste

Directions:

In your slow cooker, mix pork chops with garlic, lime juice, oil, onions, salt and pepper, stir, cover and cook on Low for 4 hours and 40 minutes.
Add parsley and coconut milk, stir, cover and cook on High for 20 minutes more.
Divide pork chops between plates and serve them with the creamy onion sauce on the side.
Enjoy!

Nutrition:

calories 243, fat 7, fiber 9, carbs 12, protein 22

Ribs and Apple Sauce

Preparation time: 10 minutes
Cooking time: 6 hours
Servings: 4

Ingredients:

2 and ½ pounds baby back ribs
1 teaspoon onion powder
1 teaspoon paprika
½ teaspoon dry mustard
½ teaspoon chili powder
½ teaspoon garlic powder
1 small yellow onion, chopped
2 bacon slices, chopped
6 ounces tomato paste
¾ cup tomato sauce
2 garlic cloves, minced
Salt and black pepper to the taste
¼ cup coconut aminos
1/3 cup apple cider vinegar
1 tablespoon olive oil
½ cup apple juice

Directions:

In your slow cooker, mix baby back ribs with onion powder, paprika, mustard powder, chili powder and garlic powder and rub well.
Add onion, bacon, tomato paste and sauce, garlic, salt, pepper, aminos, vinegar, oil and apple juice, toss well, cover and cook on Low for 6 hours.
Divide ribs and sauce between plates and serve them hot.
Enjoy!

Nutrition:

calories 300, fat 12, fiber 4, carbs 10, protein 14

Paleo Slow Cooker Dessert Recipes

Sweet Cookies

Preparation time: 10 minutes
Cooking time: 2 hours and 30 minutes
Servings: 12

Ingredients:

1 egg white
¼ cup coconut oil, melted
1 cup coconut sugar
½ teaspoon vanilla extract

1 teaspoon baking powder
1 and ½ cups almond meal
½ cup dark chocolate chips

Directions:

In a bowl, mix coconut oil with sugar, vanilla extract and egg white and beat well using your mixer.
Add baking powder and almond meal and stir well.
Fold in chocolate chips and stir gently.
Line your slow cooker with parchment paper and grease it a bit.
Transfer cookie mix to the slow cooker and press it well on the bottom.
Cover and cook on low for 2 hours and 30 minutes.
Take cookie sheet put of the slow cooker using the parchment paper as a handle.
Cut into 12 bars and serve cold.
Enjoy!

Nutrition:

calories 220, fat 2, fiber 1, carbs 3, protein 6

Glazed Pecans

Preparation time: 10 minutes
Cooking time: 2 hours
Servings: 5

Ingredients:

2 teaspoons vanilla extract
3 cups pecans

¼ cup maple syrup
1 tablespoon coconut oil

Directions:

Put your pecans in the slow cooker.
Add vanilla extract, oil and maple syrup, toss to coat and cook on Low for 2 hours.
Divide into small cups and serve.
Enjoy!

Nutrition:

calories 120, fat 2, fiber 2, carbs 4, protein 7

Simple Poached Pears

Preparation time: 10 minutes
Cooking time: 4 hours
Servings: 4

Ingredients:

4 pears, peeled and tops cut off and cored
5 cardamom pods
2 cups orange juice

¼ cup maple syrup
1 cinnamon stick
1 inch ginger, grated

Directions:

Put the pears in your slow cooker.
Add cardamom pods, orange juice, maple syrup, cinnamon and ginger, cover and cook on Low for 4 hours.
Divide pears between plates and serve with the orange sauce on top.
Enjoy!

Nutrition:

calories 200, fat 0, fiber 2, carbs 3, protein 4

Spiced Pears

Preparation time: 10 minutes
Cooking time: 4 hours
Servings: 6

Ingredients:

6 pears, cored and peeled
2 cups orange juice
¼ cup maple syrup

1 teaspoon cinnamon powder
4 cardamom pods
1-inch ginger, grated

Directions:

In your slow cooker, combine the pears with the orange juice, maple syrup, cinnamon, cardamom and ginger, cover, cook on Low for 4 hours, divide between plates and serve.
Enjoy!

Nutrition:

calories 200, fat 4, fiber 6, carbs 14, protein 8

Chocolate Cake

Preparation time: 10 minutes
Cooking time: 3 hours
Servings: 10

Ingredients:

1 cup almond flour
½ cup coconut sugar
½ cup cocoa powder
1 and ½ teaspoons baking powder
3 eggs
2 tablespoons coconut oil, melted
2/3 cup almond milk
1 teaspoon vanilla extract
Cooking spray

Directions:

In a bowl, combine the almond flour with the coconut sugar, cocoa powder, baking powder, eggs, coconut milk, vanilla extract and almond milk and stir well.
Grease your slow cooker with the cooking spray, add the cake batter, spread, cover, cook on Low for 3 hours, leave aside to cool down a bit, slice and serve.
Enjoy!

Nutrition:

calories 201, fat 11, fiber 5, carbs 9, protein 6

Simple Apples Stew

Preparation time: 10 minutes
Cooking time: 1 hour and 30 minutes
Servings: 4

Ingredients:

5 apples, cored and cut into wedges
1/3 cup coconut sugar
1 teaspoon ginger powder
¼ cup walnuts, chopped
½ teaspoon cinnamon powder
¼ teaspoon nutmeg, ground
1 teaspoon lemon zest, grated
1 teaspoon orange zest, grated
1 tablespoon coconut oil, melted
1 tablespoon lemon juice
½ cup water

Directions:

In your slow cooker, combine the apples with the sugar, ginger, walnuts, cinnamon, nutmeg, lemon zest, orange zest, oil, lemon juice and water, cover, cook on High for 1 hour and 30 minutes, divide into bowls and serve.
Enjoy!

Nutrition:

calories 171, fat 6, fiber 7, carbs 14, protein 4

Cinnamon Almonds Mix

Preparation time: 10 minutes
Cooking time: 2 hours
Servings: 10

Ingredients:

1 cup coconut sugar
3 tablespoons cinnamon powder
1 egg white
2 teaspoons vanilla extract
1/8 cup water
3 cups almonds

Directions:

In a bowl, combine the almonds with the vanilla, egg white, cinnamon and sugar and toss.
Transfer this to your slow cooker, add the water, toss, cover, cook on High for 2 hours, divide into bowls and serve.
Enjoy!

Nutrition:

calories 188, fat 6, fiber 8, carbs 12, protein 8

Lemony Apples

Preparation time: 10 minutes
Cooking time: 3 hours
Servings: 8

Ingredients:

8 apples, cored, peeled and sliced
3 tablespoons coconut sugar
1 tablespoons lemon juice
1 teaspoon cinnamon powder
2 tablespoons coconut oil, melted

Directions:

In your slow cooker, combine the apples with the coconut sugar, lemon juice, cinnamon and oil, toss, cover, cook on High for 3 hours, divide between plates and serve.
Enjoy!

Nutrition:

calories 200, fat 4, fiber 7, carbs 12, protein 9

Berry Cobbler

Preparation time: 10 minutes
Cooking time: 4 hours
Servings: 4

Ingredients:

16 ounces blueberries
12 ounces raspberries
¼ cup coconut sugar
2 teaspoons tapioca flour
2 teaspoons baking powder
¼ cup coconut milk
1 teaspoon vanilla extract
½ tablespoon cinnamon powder
Cooking spray

Directions:

In a bowl, combine the sugar with flour, baking powder, milk, vanilla and cinnamon, stir and pour into your slow cooker greased with the cooking spray.
Spread the raspberries and the blueberries all over, cover and cook on Low for 4 hours.
Slice, divide between plates and serve.
Enjoy!

Nutrition:

calories 199, fat 4, fiber 8, carbs 15, protein 6

Vanilla Apple Butter

Preparation time: 10 minutes
Cooking time: 5 hours
Servings: 12

Ingredients:

5 pounds apples, cored, peeled and roughly chopped
¼ cup coconut sugar
2 teaspoons vanilla extract

Directions:

In your slow cooker, combine the apples with the sugar and vanilla, cover, cook on Low for 5 hours, blend using an immersion blender, divide into small jars and serve.
Enjoy!

Nutrition:

calories 200, fat 7, fiber 6, carbs 10, protein 6

Simple Baked Apples

Preparation time: 10 minutes
Cooking time: 2 hours and 30 minutes
Servings: 4

Ingredients:

4 apples, cored
4 tablespoons rose water
3 tablespoons coconut sugar

Directions:

Put the apples in your slow cooker, add rose water and sugar, cover, cook on High for 2 hours and 30 minutes, divide into bowls and serve.
Enjoy!

Nutrition:

calories 200, fat 4, fiber 6, carbs 15, protein 7

Raspberry Cake

Preparation time: 10 minutes
Cooking time: 2 hours
Servings: 8

Ingredients:

2 cups coconut sugar
2 cups almond flour
4 teaspoons baking powder
1 cup coconut milk
2 tablespoons avocado oil
1 teaspoon vanilla extract
12 ounces raspberries
1 teaspoon vanilla extract
Cooking spray

Directions:

In a bowl, combine the sugar with the flour, baking powder, milk, oil, vanilla extract, raspberries and vanilla extract and stir well.
Grease your slow cooker with the cooking spray, add the cake batter, spread, cover, cook on High for 2 hours, leave aside to cool down, slice and serve.
Enjoy!

Nutrition:

calories 212, fat 2, fiber 4, carbs 12, protein 8

Rich Stuffed Apples

Preparation time: 10 minutes
Cooking time: 1 hour and 30 minutes
Servings: 5

Ingredients:

5 apples, tops cut off and cored	2 teaspoons lemon zest, grated
5 figs	¼ teaspoon nutmeg
1/3 cup coconut sugar	½ teaspoon cinnamon
1 teaspoon dried ginger	1 tablespoon lemon juice
¼ cup pecans, chopped	1 tablespoon coconut oil
	½ cup water

Directions:

In a bowl, mix figs with sugar, ginger, pecans, lemon zest, nutmeg, cinnamon, oil and lemon juice, whisk really well and stuff your apples with this mix.
Put the water in your slow cooker, arrange apples inside, cover and cook on High for 1 hour and 30 minutes.
Divide onto dessert plates and serve.
Enjoy!

Nutrition:

calories 200, fat 1, fiber 2, carbs 4, protein 7

Chocolate Cake

Preparation time: 10 minutes
Cooking time: 3 hours
Servings: 10

Ingredients:

1 cup almond flour	4 tablespoons coconut oil, melted
3 tablespoons egg white protein powder	¾ teaspoon vanilla extract
½ cup cocoa powder	2/3 cup almond milk
½ cup swerve	1/3 cup dark chocolate chips
1 and ½ teaspoons baking powder	
3 eggs	

Directions:

In a bowl, mix swerve with almond flour, egg white protein, cocoa powder and baking powder and stir.
Add almond milk, oil, eggs, chocolate chips and vanilla extract and whisk really well.
Pour this into your lined and greased slow cooker and cook on Low for 2 hours.
Leave cake aside to cool down, slice and serve it.
Enjoy!

Nutrition:

calories 200, fat 12, fiber 4, carbs 8, protein 6

Pumpkin Cake

Preparation time: 10 minutes
Cooking time: 2 hours and 15 minutes
Servings: 12

Ingredients:

1 and ½ teaspoons baking powder	1 tablespoon coconut oil, melted
2 cups almond flour	1 egg white
½ teaspoon baking soda	1 tablespoon vanilla extract
¼ teaspoon nutmeg, ground	1 cup pumpkin puree
1 and ½ teaspoons cinnamon, ground	1/3 cup maple syrup
¼ teaspoon ginger, ground	1 teaspoon lemon juice
	Cooking spray

Directions:

In a bowl, flour with baking powder, baking soda, cinnamon, ginger and nutmeg and stir.
In another bowl, mix oil with egg white, vanilla extract, pumpkin puree, maple syrup and lemon juice and stir well.
Combine flour mixture with butter mixture and stir well again.
Spray your slow cooker with cooking spray and line it with tin foil.
Pour cake mix into your slow cooker, spread, cover and cook on Low for 2 hours and 15 minutes.
Leave your cake to cool down, before slicing and serve it.
Enjoy!

Nutrition:

calories 200, fat 3, fiber 2, carbs 6, protein 6

Pear Dessert

Preparation time: 10 minutes
Cooking time: 4 hours
Servings: 10

Ingredients:

10 pears, cored and chopped	1 teaspoon ginger powder
½ cup raisins	¼ cup coconut sugar
¼ cup coconut milk	1 teaspoon lemon zest, grated

Directions:

In your slow cooker, combine the pars with the raisins, milk, ginger, sugar and lemon zest, toss, cover, cook on Low for 4 hours, divide into bowls and serve cold.
Enjoy!

Nutrition:

calories 200, fat 3, fiber 4, carbs 13, protein 7

Orange Pudding

Preparation time: 10 minutes
Cooking time: 5 hours and 3 minutes
Servings: 4

Ingredients:

Cooking spray
1 teaspoon baking powder
1 cup almond flour
1 cup palm sugar
½ teaspoon cinnamon, ground
3 tablespoons coconut oil, melted
½ cup almond milk
½ cup pecans, chopped
¾ cup water
½ cup raisins
½ cup orange peel, grated
¾ cup orange juice
Chopped pecans for serving

Directions:

Spray your slow cooker with cooking spray.
In a bowl, mix flour with half of the sugar, baking powder and cinnamon and stir.
Add 2 tablespoons oil and milk and stir again well.
Add pecans and raisins, stir and pour this into slow cooker.
Heat up a small pan over medium high heat, add water, orange juice, orange peel, the rest of the oil and the remaining sugar, stir, bring to a boil, pour over the mix in the slow cooker, cover and cook on Low for 5 hours.
Divide into dessert bowls and serve with chopped pecans on top.
Enjoy!

Nutrition:

calories 222, fat 3, fiber 1, carbs 8, protein 6

Brownies

Preparation time: 10 minutes
Cooking time: 2 hours
Servings: 12

Ingredients:

1 cup almond meal
3 eggs, whisked
½ cup tapioca flour
½ cup cocoa powder
2 tablespoons dark chocolate, unsweetened
1/3 cup honey
½ cup coconut oil, melted
1 teaspoon baking powder

Directions:

In a bowl, combine the almond meal with the eggs, tapioca flour, cocoa powder, chocolate, honey, baking powder and oil, stir well, pour this into your lined slow cooker, spread, cover, cook on Low for 2 hours, slice and serve cold.
Enjoy!

Nutrition:

calories 200, fat 4, fiber 6, carbs 15, protein 8

Apple Crisp

Preparation time: 10 minutes
Cooking time: 4 hours
Servings: 8

Ingredients:

Cooking spray
2 teaspoons lemon juice
3 tablespoons coconut sugar
¼ teaspoon ginger, grated
1 and ½ teaspoons arrowroot powder
6 big apples, roughly chopped
½ cup almond flour
½ cup palm sugar
1/8 teaspoon nutmeg, ground
¼ teaspoon cinnamon powder
¼ cup coconut oil, melted
½ cup walnuts, chopped

Directions:

Spray your slow cooker with cooking spray.
In a bowl, mix coconut sugar with lemon juice, ginger, arrowroot powder, apples and cinnamon, stir and pour into your slow cooker.
In another bowl, mix flour with palm sugar, nutmeg, walnuts and oil and stir well.
Pour this over apple mix in the slow cooker, cover and cook on Low for 4 hours. Divide into bowls and serve!
Enjoy!

Nutrition:

calories 180, fat 3, fiber 2, carbs 6, protein 5

Lemon Cookies

Preparation time: 10 minutes
Cooking time: 2 hours and 30 minutes
Servings: 8

Ingredients:

12 tablespoons ghee, soft
1 teaspoon vanilla extract
1 cup coconut sugar
1 egg
2 cups coconut flour
10 ounces Paleo lemon curd
Cooking spray

Directions:

In a bowl, combine the ghee with the vanilla, sugar, egg, flour and lemon curd and stir really well.
Grease your slow cooker with cooking spray, add the cookie batter, spread, cover, cook on High for 2 hours and 30 minutes, cut into bars and serve cold.
Enjoy!

Nutrition:

calories 244, fat 12, fiber 5, carbs 12, protein 5

Berry Cobbler

Preparation time: 10 minutes
Cooking time: 2 hours
Servings: 6

Ingredients:

1 pound fresh blackberries
1 pound fresh blueberries
¾ cup water
¾ cup coconut sugar
¾ cup almond flour
¼ cup tapioca flour
½ cup arrowroot powder
1 teaspoon baking powder
2 tablespoons palm sugar
1/3 cup almond milk
1 egg, whisked
1 teaspoon lemon zest, grated
3 tablespoons coconut oil, melted

Directions:

Put blueberries, blackberries, coconut sugar, water and tapioca in your slow cooker, cover and cook on High for 1 hour.
Meanwhile, in a bowl, mix flour with arrowroot, palm sugar and baking powder and stir well.
In a second bowl, mix the egg with milk, oil and lemon zest.
Combine egg mixture with flour mixture, stir well and drop tablespoons of this mix over the berries from the slow cooker.
Cover and cook on High for 1 more hour.
Leave cobbler aside to cool down, divide into dessert bowls and serve.
Enjoy!

Nutrition:

calories 240, fat 4, fiber 3, carbs 6, protein 6

Berry Crumble

Preparation time: 10 minutes
Cooking time: 2 hours
Servings: 8

Ingredients:

4 cups mixed berries
1 cup coconut flour
4 tablespoons coconut oil, melted
1 tablespoon honey

Directions:

In a bowl, combine the flour with half of the coconut oil and the honey and stir until you obtain a crumble.
Put the berries in your slow cooker, add the rest of the oil and toss them gently.
Sprinkle the crumble over the berries, cover the pot, cook on Low for 2 hours, divide into bowls and serve.
Enjoy!

Nutrition:

calories 214, fat 12, fiber 7, carbs 16, protein 6

Easy Apples Dessert

Preparation time: 10 minutes
Cooking time: 2 hours
Servings: 8

Ingredients:

8 apples, cored, peeled and sliced
2 tablespoons lemon juice
¾ cup coconut sugar
1 teaspoon nutmeg, ground
2 teaspoons lemon zest, grated
2 tablespoons cinnamon powder
¼ cup coconut flour
1 teaspoon vanilla extract
½ cup almond flour
¼ cup ghee, melted

Directions:

Put the apples in your slow cooker, add half of the sugar, nutmeg, lemon juice and half of the cinnamon and toss.
In a bowl, combine the rest of the sugar with the rest of the cinnamon, lemon zest, almond flour, coconut flour, vanilla and ghee and stir well.
Top the apples with this mix, cover, cook on Low for 2 hours, divide between dessert plates and serve.
Enjoy!

Nutrition:

calories 214, fat 4, fiber 6, carbs 15, protein 7

Apple Bread

Preparation time: 10 minutes
Cooking time: 2 hours and 20 minutes
Servings: 6

Ingredients:

3 cups apples, cored and cubed
1 cup coconut sugar
1 tablespoon vanilla
2 eggs
1 tablespoon apple pie spice
2 cups almond flour
1 tablespoon baking powder
1 tablespoon ghee

Directions:

In a bowl, mix apples with coconut sugar, vanilla, eggs, apple pie spice, almond flour, baking powder and ghee, whisk well, pour into your slow cooker, cover and cook on High for 2 hours and 20 minutes.
Leave sweet bread to cool down, slice and serve.
Enjoy!

Nutrition:

calories 100, fat 2, fiber 4, carbs 12, protein 4

Easy Peach Pie

Preparation time: 10 minutes
Cooking time: 4 hours
Servings: 8

Ingredients:

6 cups peaches, chopped
½ tablespoon cinnamon powder
A pinch of nutmeg, ground
1 and 1/3 cup coconut flour
1 teaspoon baking powder
¼ cup coconut oil, melted
4 eggs, whisked
3 and ½ tablespoons maple syrup
¼ teaspoon almond extract
2 tablespoons almond milk

Directions:

In a bowl, combine the coconut flour with the baking powder, eggs, coconut oil, almond extract, 2 and ½ tablespoons maple syrup and almond milk and stir well.
In another bowl, combine the peaches with 1 tablespoon maple syrup, cinnamon and nutmeg, stir and spread them in your slow cooker.
Drop spoonfuls of the coconut mix over the peaches, cover, cook on Low for 4 hours, divide into bowls and serve.
Enjoy!

Nutrition:

calories 261, fat 6, fiber 6, carbs 16, protein 6

Banana Dessert

Preparation time: 10 minutes
Cooking time: 2 hours
Servings: 5

Ingredients:

10 bananas, peeled and cut into quarters
1 cup coconut flakes
½ cup walnuts, chopped
1 teaspoon cinnamon powder
¼ cup honey
½ cup coconut oil, melted
1 teaspoon vanilla extract
¼ cup lemon juice
2 teaspoons lemon zest, grated

Directions:

In your slow cooker, combine the bananas with the coconut flakes, walnuts, cinnamon, honey, oil, vanilla, lemon juice and lemon zest, toss, cover, cook on Low for 2 hours, divide into bowls and serve cold.
Enjoy!

Nutrition:

calories 199, fat 4, fiber 7, carbs 16, protein 5

Coffee Cookies

Preparation time: 10 minutes
Cooking time: 4 hours
Servings: 10

Ingredients:

2 cups almond flour
1 cup coconut sugar
¾ cup cocoa powder
2 teaspoons baking powder
2 eggs, whisked
2 teaspoons baking soda
½ cup coconut milk
½ cup coconut oil, melted
2 teaspoons vanilla extract
1/3 cup brewed coffee

Directions:

In a bowl, combine the flour with the sugar, cocoa powder, baking powder, baking soda, eggs, milk, vanilla and coffee and stir well.
Add the oil to your slow cooker, add the cookie mix, spread, cover, cook on Low for 4 hours, take spoonfuls of this mix, shape medium balls, arrange them on a platter and serve cold.
Enjoy!

Nutrition:

calories 261, fat 6, fiber 6, carbs 17, protein 6

Peanut Cake

Preparation time: 10 minutes
Cooking time: 2 hours and 30 minutes
Servings: 8

Ingredients:

1 cup coconut sugar
1 cup coconut flour
3 tablespoons cocoa powder+ ½ cup
1 and ½ teaspoons baking powder
½ cup almond milk
2 tablespoons coconut oil
2 cups hot water
1 teaspoon vanilla extract
½ cup peanut butter
Cooking spray

Directions:

In a bowl, mix half of the sugar with 3 tablespoons cocoa, flour, baking powder, coconut oil, vanilla and milk, stir well and pour into your slow cooker greased with cooking spray.
In another bowl, mix the rest of the sugar with the rest of the cocoa, peanut butter and hot water, stir well, pour over the batter in the slow cooker, cover, cook on High for 2 hours and 30 minutes, leave aside to cool down, slice and serve.
Enjoy!

Nutrition:

calories 222, fat 4, fiber 7, carbs 12, protein 8

Blackberry Cake

Preparation time: 10 minutes
Cooking time: 1 hour and 30 minutes
Servings: 6

Ingredients:

½ cup coconut flour
¼ teaspoon baking powder
¼ teaspoon coconut sugar
¼ cup blackberries
1/3 cup coconut milk
1 teaspoon coconut oil, melted
1 teaspoon flaxseed, ground
½ teaspoon lemon zest, grated
¼ teaspoon vanilla extract
Cooking spray

Directions:

In a bowl, combine the flour with the baking powder, sugar, blackberries, milk, oil, flaxseed, lemon zest and vanilla and stir really well. Grease your slow cooker with cooking spray, pour cake batter, cover pot and cook on High for 1 hour and 30 minutes, cool down, slice and serve.
Enjoy!

Nutrition:

calories 200, fat 6, fiber 4, carbs 16, protein 4

Special Dessert

Preparation time: 10 minutes
Cooking time: 1 hour and 30 minutes
Servings: 8

Ingredients:

1/3 cup coconut flour
½ teaspoon baking soda
3 eggs
For the topping:
4 tablespoons coconut oil, melted
5 tablespoons coconut oil
2 tablespoons honey

1 tablespoon cinnamon powder
1 cup honey

Directions:

In a bowl, mix flour with baking soda, eggs, 5 tablespoons coconut oil and 2 tablespoons honey, stir well until you obtain a dough and shape 8 balls out of it.
In a bowl, mix 4 tablespoons melted oil with cinnamon and 1 cup honey and whisk really well.
Dip balls into this mix and arrange them in your slow cooker.
Cover and cook on Low for 1 hour and 30 minutes.
Leave this Paleo dessert to cool down before serving it.
Enjoy!

Nutrition:

calories 230, fat 2, fiber 4, carbs 6, protein 7

Apple Stew

Preparation time: 10 minutes
Cooking time: 4 hours
Servings: 10

Ingredients:

2 tablespoons lemon juice
2 pounds apples, cored, peeled and cubed
4 cups coconut sugar
1 teaspoon cinnamon powder
1 teaspoon vanilla extract

Directions:

In your slow cooker, combine the apples with the lemon juice, sugar, cinnamon and vanilla, toss, cover, cook on Low for 4 hours, divide into bowls and serve cold.
Enjoy!

Nutrition:

calories 210, fat 4, fiber 6, carbs 14, protein 7

Strawberry Pudding

Preparation time: 10 minutes
Cooking time: 5 hours
Servings: 4

Ingredients:

Cooking spray
1 teaspoon baking powder
1 cup almond flour
1 cup coconut sugar
½ teaspoon cinnamon powder
3 tablespoons coconut oil, melted
1 pound strawberries, chopped
1 cup almond milk
½ cup pecans, chopped
½ cup raisins
½ cup orange peel, grated
¾ cup orange juice

Directions:

In a bowl, combine the baking powder with the flour, sugar, cinnamon, oil, strawberries, milk, pecans, raisins, orange peel and orange juice, stir, pour into the slow cooker greased with cooking spray, cover, cook on Low for 5 hours, divide into bowls and serve cold.
Enjoy!

Nutrition:

calories 212, fat 5, fiber 4, carbs 15, protein 6

Almond Bars

Preparation time: 10 minutes
Cooking time: 3 hours
Servings: 12

Ingredients:

3 eggs, whisked
¼ cup coconut oil, melted
1 cup coconut sugar
½ teaspoon vanilla extract
1 teaspoon baking powder
2 cups almond meal
½ cup almonds, chopped

Directions:

In a bowl, combine the eggs with the oil, sugar, vanilla, baking powder, almond meal and almonds, stir well, spread on the bottom of your lined slow cooker, cover, cook on Low for 3 hours, leave cookie sheet to cool down, cut into medium bars and serve cold.
Enjoy!

Nutrition:

calories 220, fat 6, fiber 7, carbs 14, protein 6

Pumpkin Pudding Cake

Preparation time: 10 minutes
Cooking time: 2 hours and 30 minutes
Servings: 10

Ingredients:

Cooking spray
1 cup pumpkin puree
2 cups almond flour
1 teaspoon baking powder
½ teaspoon baking soda
2 teaspoons cinnamon powder
¼ teaspoon ginger powder
1 tablespoon coconut oil, melted
2 eggs, whisked
1 tablespoon vanilla extract
1/3 cup maple syrup
1 teaspoon lemon juice

Directions:

In a bowl, combine the pumpkin puree with the almond flour, baking powder, baking soda, cinnamon, ginger, oil, eggs, vanilla extract, maple syrup and lemon juice, stir well, pour into your slow cooker greased with cooking spray, spread, cover, cook on Low for 2 hours and 30 minutes, divide into bowls and serve.
Enjoy!

Nutrition:

calories 212, fat 5, fiber 2, carbs 14, protein 6

Coconut Lemon Jam

Preparation time: 10 minutes
Cooking time: 3 hours
Servings: 10

Ingredients:

2 pounds lemons, washed, peeled and roughly chopped
1 cup coconut flakes
2 pounds coconut sugar
1 tablespoon vinegar

Directions:

In your slow cooker, combine the lemons with coconut sugar, vinegar and coconut flakes, toss, cover, cook on High for 3 hours, divide into bowls and serve cold.
Enjoy!

Nutrition:

calories 190, fat 2, fiber 4, carbs 14, protein 5

Cherry Cream

Preparation time: 10 minutes
Cooking time: 3 hours
Servings: 6

Ingredients:

2 tablespoons lemon juice
3 tablespoons coconut cream
4 cups cherries, pitted
1 and ½ cups coconut sugar

Directions:

In your slow cooker, combine the cherries, cream, lemon juice and sugar, cover, cook on High for 3 hours, blend using an immersion blender, divide into bowls and serve cold.
Enjoy!

Nutrition:

calories 211, fat 6, fiber 4, carbs 14, protein 6

Coconut Cauliflower Pudding

Preparation time: 10 minutes
Cooking time: 5 hours
Servings: 4

Ingredients:

4 cups coconut milk
1 cup coconut sugar
2 cups cauliflower rice

2 tablespoons
cinnamon powder
½ cup coconut,
shredded

Directions:

In your slow cooker, combine milk with the sugar, cauliflower rice, cinnamon and coconut, stir, cover, cook on Low for 5 hours, stir well again, divide into cups and serve cold
Enjoy!

Nutrition:

calories 233, fat 4, fiber 6, carbs 13, protein 4

Strawberry Stew

Preparation time: 10 minutes
Cooking time: 6 hours
Servings: 4

Ingredients:

5 cups strawberries,
roughly chopped
2 tablespoons ghee,
melted

1/3 cup water
2/3 cup coconut sugar
1 teaspoon vanilla
extract

Directions:

In your slow cooker, combine the strawberries with the ghee, water, sugar and vanilla, cover, cook on Low for 6 hours, divide into bowls and serve cold.
Enjoy!

Nutrition:

calories 180, fat 4, fiber 5, carbs 14, protein 6

Banana Cake

Preparation time: 10 minutes
Cooking time: 2 hours
Servings: 6

Ingredients:

¾ cup coconut sugar
1/3 cup ghee, soft
1 teaspoon vanilla
1 egg
3 bananas, mashed
1 teaspoon baking
powder

1 and ½ cups coconut
flour
½ teaspoons baking
soda
1/3 cup cashew milk
Cooking spray

Directions:

In a bowl, mix ghee with coconut sugar, vanilla extract, eggs, mashed bananas, baking powder, coconut flour, baking soda and cashew milk and stir really well.
Grease your slow cooker with cooking spray, add cake batter, spread, cover and cook on High for 2 hours.
Leave cake to cool down, slice and serve.
Enjoy!

Nutrition:

calories 300, fat 4, fiber 4, carbs 27, protein 4

Carrot Pudding

Preparation time: 10 minutes
Cooking time: 5 hours
Servings: 3

Ingredients:

2 cups coconut milk
2 eggs, whisked
1 cup carrots, chopped

2 tablespoons coconut
sugar
1 teaspoon cardamom,
ground

Directions:

In your slow cooker, combine the milk with the eggs, carrots, sugar and cardamom, toss, cover, cook on Low for 5 hours, divide into bowls and serve cold.
Enjoy!

Nutrition:

calories 210, fat 4, fiber 4, carbs 14, protein 4

Cauliflower Rice And Plums Pudding

Preparation time: 10 minutes
Cooking time: 5 hours
Servings: 4

Ingredients:

3 cups coconut milk
½ cup coconut sugar
2 cups cauliflower rice
1 tablespoon
cinnamon powder
1 cup plums, pitted
and chopped
½ cup coconut, grated

Directions:

In your slow cooker, combine the milk with the sugar, rice, cinnamon, plums and coconut, toss, cover, cook on Low for 5 hours, divide into bowls and serve cold.
Enjoy!

Nutrition:

calories 210, fat 5, fiber 5, carbs 16, protein 4

Apple Cauliflower Rice

Preparation time: 10 minutes
Cooking time: 5 hours
Servings: 4

Ingredients:

2 cups cauliflower rice
1 teaspoon cinnamon
powder
1/3 cup coconut sugar
2 tablespoons coconut
oil, melted
2 apples, peeled,
cored and sliced
3 cups almond milk

Directions:

In your slow cooker, combine the cauliflower rice with the cinnamon, sugar, coconut oil, apples and milk, toss, cover, cook on Low for 5 hours, divide into bowls and serve.
Enjoy!

Nutrition:

calories 210, fat 3, fiber 4, carbs 15, protein 5

Peach Compote

Preparation time: 10 minutes
Cooking time: 5 hours
Servings: 6

Ingredients:

8 peaches, stones
removed and chopped
1 cup water
4 tablespoons coconut
sugar
1 teaspoon cinnamon
powder
1 teaspoon vanilla
extract

Directions:

In your slow cooker, combine the peaches with the water, sugar, cinnamon and vanilla, stir, cover, cook on Low for 5 hours, divide into bowls and serve.
Enjoy!

Nutrition:

calories 210, fat 2, fiber 4, carbs 4, protein 12, protein 6

Baby Carrots Bowls

Preparation time: 10 minutes
Cooking time: 5 hours
Servings: 4

Ingredients:

1 tablespoon coconut
sugar
4 cups baby carrots
½ cup water
½ tablespoon ghee,
melted

Directions:

In your slow cooker, combine the carrots with the sugar, water and ghee, toss, cover, cook on Low for 5 hours, divide into bowls and serve cold.
Enjoy!

Nutrition:

calories 146, fat 3, fiber 4, carbs 10, protein 4

Figs Compote

Preparation time: 10 minutes
Cooking time: 2 hours and 30 minutes
Servings: 4

Ingredients:

1 cup apple juice
¼ cup water
1 pound figs

2 tablespoons coconut sugar

Directions:

In your slow cooker, combine the apple juice with the water, figs and coconut sugar, toss, cover, cook on Low for 2 hours and 30 minutes, divide into bowls and serve cold
Enjoy!

Nutrition:

calories 153, fat 2, fiber 4, carbs 11, protein 4

Dates Pudding

Preparation time: 15 minutes
Cooking time: 4 hours
Servings: 8

Ingredients:

2 eggs, whisked
2 cups dates, chopped
¾ cup hot water
1 teaspoon baking powder
1 and ¼ cups coconut flour

2 tablespoons coconut sugar
1/3 cup ghee, melted
1 teaspoon vanilla extract

Directions:

Grease your slow cooker with cooking spray. In a bowl, combine the eggs with dates, water, baking powder, flour, sugar, ghee and vanilla, whisk well, pour into the slow cooker, cover, cook on Low for 4 hours, divide into cups and serve cold.
Enjoy!

Nutrition:

calories 214, fat 4, fiber 4, carbs 15, protein 5

Blueberries And Strawberries Cream

Preparation time: 10 minutes
Cooking time: 2 hours
Servings: 4

Ingredients:

2 cup blueberries
1 and ½ cups almond milk

2 cup strawberries, halved
3 medjol dates, chopped

Directions:

In your slow cooker, combine the blueberries with the strawberries, dates and milk, cover, cook on Low for 2 hours, stir really well, divide into bowls and serve the cream cold.
Enjoy!

Nutrition:

calories 178, fat 4, fiber 3, carbs 11, protein 5

Almond Banana Cream

Preparation time: 10 minutes
Cooking time: 2 hours
Servings: 2

Ingredients:

4 bananas, peeled and mashed
½ cup almond milk
1 teaspoon cinnamon powder

2 tablespoons almond butter
2 tablespoons honey
1 teaspoon vanilla extract

Directions:

In your slow cooker, combine the bananas with the milk, cinnamon, almond butter, honey and vanilla, stir, cover, cook on Low for 2 hours, stir well, divide into bowls and serve cold.
Enjoy!

Nutrition:

calories 216, fat 4, fiber 6, carbs 15, protein 7

Carrots, Walnuts And Raisins Dessert

Preparation time: 10 minutes
Cooking time: 4 hours
Servings: 6

Ingredients:

1 and ½ teaspoons cinnamon powder
1 and ½ teaspoon baking powder
1 and ½ cups carrots, shredded
1/3 cup pure maple syrup
3 cups coconut milk
1 teaspoons ginger, grated
2 teaspoons vanilla extract
1 cup walnuts, chopped
1 cup raisins

Directions:

In your slow cooker, combine the carrots with the baking powder, cinnamon, carrots, maple syrup, milk, ginger, vanilla, raisins and walnuts, toss, cover, cook on Low for 4 hours, divide into bowls and serve cold.
Enjoy!

Nutrition:

calories 210, fat 3, fiber 7, carbs 10, protein 4

Papaya And Banana Dessert

Preparation time: 5 minutes
Cooking time: 3 hours
Servings: 2

Ingredients:

1 cup papaya, peeled and roughly cubed
2 small bananas, peeled and roughly cubed
1 cup coconut milk
1 tablespoon cinnamon powder

Directions:

In your slow cooker, combine the papaya with the bananas, cinnamon and milk, toss, cover, cook on Low for 3 hours, divide into bowls and serve cold.
Enjoy!

Nutrition:

calories 210, fat 3, fiber 2, carbs 12, protein 6

Pineapple And Kiwi Bowls

Preparation time: 10 minutes
Cooking time: 2 hours
Servings: 8

Ingredients:

1 cup coconut milk
4 pineapples, peeled and cubed
4 kiwi, peeled and cubed

Directions:

In your slow cooker, combine the pineapples with the kiwi and milk, toss, cover, cook on Low for 2 hours, divide into bowls and serve.
Enjoy!

Nutrition:

calories 150, fat 2, fiber 4, carbs 10, protein 4

Avocado Cake

Preparation time: 10 minutes
Cooking time: 1 hour and 30 minutes
Servings: 4

Ingredients:

12 ounces apricots, chopped
2 tablespoons chia seeds
1 tablespoon cocoa nibs
1 and ½ tablespoon coconut oil, melted
2 tablespoons almond butter

For the filling:

4 avocados pitted and peeled
5 ounces coconut oil
5 ounces cocoa powder
3 ounces maple syrup
2 tablespoons coconut sugar
1 tablespoon vanilla extract

Directions:

In your food processor mix apricots with chia seeds, cocoa nibs, 1 and ½ tablespoon oil and almond butter, blend well, transfer everything to your lined slow cooker and press well on the bottom.
In your clean food processor, mix avocados with 5 ounces coconut oil, cocoa, maple syrup, sugar and vanilla extract, blend well, spread over the cake crust, cover the slow cooker, cook on Low for 1 hour and 30 minutes, leave aside to cool down and serve really cold.
Enjoy!

Nutrition:

calories 210, fat 4, fiber 2, carbs 15, protein 4

Coconut And Green Tea Cream

Preparation time: 10 minutes
Cooking time: 1 hour and 30 minutes
Servings: 6

Ingredients:

14 ounces coconut milk
2 tablespoons green tea powder

14 ounces coconut cream
3 tablespoons coconut sugar

Directions:

In your slow cooker, combine the milk with the tea powder, coconut cream and sugar, whisk, cover, cook on Low for 1 hour and 30 minutes, divide into bowls and keep in the fridge until you serve it.
Enjoy!

Nutrition:

calories 180, fat 4, fiber 3, carbs 15, protein 6

Chocolate Pudding

Preparation time: 10 minutes
Cooking time: 1 hour
Servings: 4

Ingredients:

4 ounces coconut cream
4 ounces dark chocolate, cut into chunks

1 teaspoon coconut sugar

Directions:

In a bowl, mix coconut cream with chocolate and sugar, whisk really well, pour into your slow cooker, cover and cook on High for 1 hour. Divide into bowls and serve cold.
Enjoy!

Nutrition:

calories 232, fat 12, fiber 6, carbs 9, protein 4

Rose Cauliflower Rice Pudding

Preparation time: 10 minutes
Cooking time: 4 hours
Servings: 4

Ingredients:

1 and ½ cups cauliflower rice
4 tablespoons rose water
2 cups natural apple juice

3 tablespoons coconut butter, melted
¼ cup almonds, chopped
½ cup coconut sugar
1 tablespoon cinnamon powder

Directions:

In your slow cooker, combine the cauliflower rice with the rose water, apple juice, coconut butter, almonds, sugar and cinnamon, toss, cover, cook on Low for 4 hours, divide into bowls and serve cold.
Enjoy!

Nutrition:

calories 216, fat 4, fiber 5, carbs 15, protein 11

Cauliflower Rice Pudding

Preparation time: 5 minutes
Cooking time: 2 hours
Servings: 6

Ingredients:

1 tablespoon ghee, melted
7 ounces cauliflower rice
4 ounces water
16 ounces coconut milk

3 ounces coconut sugar
1 egg
1 teaspoon cinnamon powder
1 teaspoon vanilla extract

Directions:

In your slow cooker, mix ghee with cauliflower rice, water, coconut milk, coconut sugar, egg, cinnamon and vanilla extract, stir, cover and cook on High for 2 hours.
Divide pudding into bowls and serve cold.
Enjoy!

Nutrition:

calories 162, fat 2, fiber 6, carbs 18, protein 4

Avocado and Green Tea Dessert

Preparation time: 6 minutes
Cooking time: 1 hour
Servings: 4

Ingredients:

½ cup coconut water
1 and ½ cup avocado, chopped
2 tablespoons green tea powder
2 teaspoons lime zest, grated
1 tablespoon coconut sugar

Directions:

In your slow cooker, mix coconut water with avocado, green tea powder, lime zest and coconut sugar, stir, cover and cook on Low for 1 hour.
Divide into bowls and serve.
Enjoy!

Nutrition:

calories 307, fat 4, fiber 8, carbs 11, protein 7

Pumpkin and Chia Pudding

Preparation time: 10 minutes
Cooking time: 1 hour
Servings: 4

Ingredients:

1 cup almond milk
½ cup pumpkin puree
2 tablespoons maple syrup
½ cup coconut milk
¼ cup chia seeds
½ teaspoon cinnamon powder
¼ teaspoon ginger, grated

Directions:

In your slow cooker, mix almond milk with coconut milk, pumpkin puree, maple syrup, chia, cinnamon and ginger, stir, cover and cook on High for 1 hour.
Divide pudding into bowls and serve.
Enjoy!

Nutrition:

calories 105, fat 2, fiber 7, carbs 11, protein 4

Figs and Coconut Butter Dessert

Preparation time: 10 minutes
Cooking time: 1 hour
Servings: 4

Ingredients:

2 tablespoons coconut butter
12 figs, halved
1 cup almonds, chopped
¼ cup maple syrup

Directions:

In your slow cooker, mix coconut butter with maple syrup and whisk well.
Add figs and almonds, toss, cover and cook on Low for 1 hour.
Divide into bowls and serve warm.
Enjoy!

Nutrition:

calories 200, fat 6, fiber 8, carbs 9, protein 12

Apples and Sweet Sauce

Preparation time: 10 minutes
Cooking time: 1 hour
Servings: 4

Ingredients:

4 green apples cored and cut into medium cubes
1 tablespoon pure maple syrup
A pinch of cardamom
½ teaspoon cinnamon powder
½ teaspoon vanilla extract

Directions:

In your slow cooker, mix apples with maple syrup, cardamom, cinnamon and vanilla, stir, cover and cook on Low for 1 hour.
Divide into bowls and serve.
Enjoy!

Nutrition:

calories 135, fat 1, fiber 3, carbs 4, protein 2

Grapefruit Compote

Preparation time: 10 minutes
Cooking time: 2 hours
Servings: 6

Ingredients:

1 cup water
1 cup maple syrup
½ cup mint, chopped
64 ounces red grapefruit juice
2 grapefruits, peeled and chopped

Directions:

In your slow cooker, mix grapefruit with water, maple syrup, mint and grapefruit juice, stir, cover and cook on High for 2 hours.
Divide into bowls and serve cold.
Enjoy!

Nutrition:

120, fat 1, fiber, 2, carbs 2, protein 1

Cherry Compote

Preparation time: 10 minutes
Cooking time: 2 hours
Servings: 6

Ingredients:

½ cup dark cocoa powder
¾ cup red cherry juice
¼ cup maple syrup
1 pound cherries, pitted and halved
2 tablespoons stevia
2 cups water

Directions:

In your slow cooker, mix cocoa powder with cherry juice, maple syrup, cherries, water and stevia, stir, cover and cook on High for 2 hours.
Divide into bowls and serve cold.
Enjoy!

Nutrition:

calories 197, fat 1, fiber 4, carbs 5, protein 2

Apricots Jam

Preparation time: 10 minutes
Cooking time: 6 hours
Servings: 10

Ingredients:

4 pounds apricots, chopped
1 cup water
1 teaspoon cinnamon powder
½ teaspoon cardamom powder
1 cup coconut sugar

Directions:

In your slow cooker, combine the apricots with the water, cinnamon, cardamom and sugar, stir, cover, cook on Low for 6 hours, stir well again, divide into cups and serve cold.
Enjoy!

Nutrition:

calories 170, fat 2, fiber 5, carbs 3, protein 6

Plum Bowls

Preparation time: 10 minutes
Cooking time: 3 hours
Servings: 4

Ingredients:

2 pounds plums, pitted and halved
½ cup honey
1 teaspoon cinnamon powder
2 tablespoons lemon zest, grated
2 teaspoons balsamic vinegar
1 cup hot water

Directions:

In your slow cooker, combine the plums with the honey, cinnamon, lemon zest, vinegar and water, toss, cover, cook on Low for 3 hours, divide into bowls and serve cold.
Enjoy!

Nutrition:

calories 180, fat 4, fiber 4, carbs 11, protein 6

Pineapple And Cherries Mix

Preparation time: 10 minutes
Cooking time: 4 hours
Servings: 4

Ingredients:

30 ounces canned pineapple chunks, drained
31 ounces canned cherries, drained
25 ounces apple juice
¼ cup coconut sugar
1 teaspoon cinnamon powder

Directions:

In your slow cooker, combine the pineapple chunks with the cherries, apple juice, sugar and cinnamon, toss, cover, cook on Low for 4 hours, divide into bowls and serve cold.
Enjoy!

Nutrition:

calories 210, fat 4, fiber 2, carbs 10, protein 5

Almond Chia Pudding

Preparation time: 10 minutes
Cooking time: 1 hour and 30 minutes
Servings: 4

Ingredients:

½ cup chia seeds
4 teaspoons coconut sugar
2 cups almond milk
¼ cup almonds
¼ cup coconut, shredded

Directions:

In your slow cooker, combine the chia seeds with the sugar, almonds, almond milk and coconut, stir, cover, cook on Low for 1 hour and 30 minutes, divide into bowls and serve cold.
Enjoy!

Nutrition:

calories 150, fat 1, fiber 4, carbs 8, protein 6

Apple Cobbler

Preparation time: 10 minutes
Cooking time: 4 hours
Servings: 4

Ingredients:

3 apples, cored and chopped
2 tablespoons honey
½ teaspoon cinnamon powder
3 tablespoons coconut oil
¼ cup coconut, shredded
2 tablespoons sunflower seeds
2 tablespoons walnuts, chopped

Directions:

Grease your slow cooker with the oil, add apples, honey and cinnamon and stir.
In a bowl, combine the coconut with walnuts and sunflower seeds, stir, spread over the apples mix, cover, cook on Low for 4 hours, divide into bowls and serve.
Enjoy!

Nutrition:

calories 214, fat 3, fiber 2, carbs 11, protein 5

Cinnamon Blueberries Cream

Preparation time: 10 minutes
Cooking time: 2 hours and 30 minutes
Servings: 12

Ingredients:

5 cups blueberries, pureed
2 teaspoons cinnamon powder
Zest of 1 lemon, grated
1 cup coconut sugar
1 teaspoon nutmeg, ground

Directions:

In your slow cooker, combine the blueberries with the cinnamon, lemon zest, sugar and nutmeg, cover, cook on Low for 2 hours and 30 minutes, divide into bowls and serve cold.
Enjoy!

Nutrition:

calories 213, fat 4, fiber 3, carbs 14, protein 6

Strawberry Maple Cookies

Preparation time: 10 minutes
Cooking time: 4 hours
Servings: 10

Ingredients:

½ teaspoon baking soda
2 and ½ cups coconut flour
1 tablespoon vanilla extract
¼ cup coconut oil, melted
¼ cup coconut milk
2 eggs
¼ cup maple syrup
3 tablespoons cinnamon powder
1 cup strawberries, chopped

Directions:

In a bowl, mix, the flour with baking soda, vanilla, oil, milk, eggs, maple syrup, cinnamon and strawberries, stir well, pour into your lined slow cooker, spread, cover, cook on Low for 4 hours, leave aside to cool down, slice and serve.
Enjoy!

Nutrition:

calories 210, fat 4, fiber 4, carbs 15, protein 5

Cherry Bowls

Preparation time: 10 minutes
Cooking time: 4 hours
Servings: 4

Ingredients:

2 cups coconut milk
2 tablespoons flax seed
2 tablespoons cocoa powder
1/3 cup cherries, pitted
3 tablespoons honey
½ teaspoon almond extract

Directions:

In your slow cooker, combine the milk with the flaxseed, cocoa powder, cherries, honey and almond extract, stir, cover, cook on Low for 4 hours, divide into bowls and serve cold.
Enjoy!

Nutrition:

calories 213, fat 4, fiber 4, carbs 11, protein 4

Passion Fruit Pudding

Preparation time: 10 minutes
Cooking time: 2 hours
Servings: 6

Ingredients:

1 cup passion fruit curd
4 passion fruits, pulp and seeds separated
3 and ½ ounces maple syrup
3 eggs
2 ounces ghee, melted
3 and ½ ounces almond milk
½ cup almond flour
½ teaspoon baking powder

Directions:

In your slow cooker, mix curd with passion fruits pulp and seeds, maple syrup, eggs, ghee, almond milk, almond flour and baking powder, whisk really well, cover and cook on High for 2 hours.
Divide into bowls and serve cold.
Enjoy!

Nutrition:

calories 230, fat 12, fiber 3, carbs 7, protein 8

Cashew Cake

Preparation time: 10 minutes
Cooking time: 2 hours
Servings: 6

Ingredients:
For the crust:

½ cup dates, pitted
1 tablespoon water
For the cake:
2 and ½ cups cashews, soaked for 8 hours
1 cup blueberries
½ teaspoon vanilla
½ cup almonds

¾ cup maple syrup
1 tablespoon coconut oil

Directions:

In your food processor, mix dates with water, vanilla, almonds, and pulse well.
Transfer dough to a working surface, flatten it and arrange on the bottom of your slow cooker.
In your blender, mix maple syrup with coconut oil, cashews and blueberries, blend well, spread over crust, cover and cook on High for 2 hours.
Leave cake to cool down, slice and serve.
Enjoy!

Nutrition:

calories 200, fat 3, fiber 5, carbs 12, protein 3

Lemon Pudding

Preparation time: 10 minutes
Cooking time: 1 hour
Servings: 4

Ingredients:

1/3 cup natural cashew butter
1 and ½ tablespoons coconut oil
2 tablespoons coconut butter
5 tablespoons lemon juice
½ teaspoon lemon zest
1 tablespoons maple syrup

Directions:

In a bowl, mix cashew butter with coconut butter, coconut oil, lemon juice, lemon zest and maple syrup and stir until you obtain a creamy mix.
Pour into your slow cooker, cook on High for 1 hour, divide into bowls and serve.
Enjoy!

Nutrition:

calories 102, fat 4, fiber 0, carbs 4, protein 1

Pumpkin Cake

Preparation time: 10 minutes
Cooking time: 2 hours
Servings: 10

Ingredients:

1 and ½ teaspoons baking powder
2 cups coconut flour
½ teaspoon baking soda
¼ teaspoon nutmeg, ground
1 teaspoons cinnamon powder
¼ teaspoon ginger, grated
1 tablespoon coconut oil, melted
1 egg white
1 tablespoon vanilla extract
1 cup pumpkin puree
2 tablespoons stevia
1 teaspoon lemon juice

Directions:

In a bowl, flour with baking powder, baking soda, cinnamon, ginger, nutmeg, oil, egg white, ghee, vanilla extract, pumpkin puree, stevia and lemon juice, stir well and transfer this your slow cooker.
Cover, cook on High for 2 hours, leave aside to cool down, slice and serve.
Enjoy!

Nutrition:

calories 180, fat 3, fiber 2, carbs 3, protein 4

Orange Pudding

Preparation time: 10 minutes
Cooking time: 1 hour
Servings: 4

Ingredients:

1 teaspoon baking powder
1 cup coconut flour
2 tablespoons stevia
½ teaspoon cinnamon powder
3 tablespoons coconut oil, melted
½ cup coconut milk
½ cup pecans, chopped
½ cup raisins
½ cup orange peel, grated
¾ cup orange juice

Directions:

In a bowl, mix flour with stevia, baking powder, cinnamon, 2 tablespoons oil, milk, pecans and raisins, stir and pour into your slow cooker
In a pan, mix orange juice, orange peel and the rest of the oil, stir, bring to a boil over medium heat and pour over the pecans mix.
Cover, cook on High for 1 hour, leave aside to cool down, slice and serve.
Enjoy!

Nutrition:

calories 142, fat 3, fiber 1, carbs 3, protein 3

Fruits Mix

Preparation time: 10 minutes
Cooking time: 1 hour
Servings: 6

Ingredients:

1-quart water
2 tablespoons stevia
1 pound mixed apples and pears
5-star anise
2 cinnamon sticks
Zest from 1 orange, grated
Zest from 1 lemon, grated

Directions:

Put the water, stevia, apples, pears, star anise, cinnamon, orange and lemon zest in your slow cooker, cover and cook on High for 1 hour
Divide into bowls and serve cold.
Enjoy!

Nutrition:

calories 98, fat 0, fiber 0, carbs 0, protein 2

Delicious Flavored Apples

Preparation time: 10 minutes
Cooking time: 1 hour
Servings: 8

Ingredients:

1 teaspoon cinnamon powder
12 ounces apples, cored and chopped
2 tablespoons flax seed meal mixed with 1 tablespoon water
½ cup coconut cream
3 tablespoons stevia
½ teaspoon nutmeg
2 teaspoons vanilla extract
1/3 cup pecans, chopped

Directions:

In your slow cooker, mix flax seed meal with coconut cream, vanilla, nutmeg, stevia, apples and cinnamon, stir a bit, cover and cook on High for 1 hour.
Divide into bowls, sprinkle pecans on top and serve cold
Enjoy!

Nutrition:

calories 120, fat 3, fiber 2, carbs 4, protein 3

Plum Compote

Preparation time: 10 minutes
Cooking time: 1 hour
Servings: 10

Ingredients:

4 pounds plums, stones removed and chopped
1 cup water
2 tablespoons stevia
1 teaspoon cinnamon powder

Directions:

Put plums, water, stevia and cinnamon in your slow cooker, cover and cook on High for 1 hour.
Divide bowls and serve cold.
Enjoy!

Nutrition:

calories 103, fat 0, fiber 1, carbs 2, protein 4

Lemon Jam

Preparation time: 10 minutes
Cooking time: 2 hours
Servings: 8

Ingredients:

2 pounds lemons, sliced
2 cups dates
1 cup water
1 tablespoon vinegar
2 tablespoons coconut sugar

Directions:

Put dates in your blender, add water and pulse really well.
Put lemon slices in your slow cooker, add dates paste, sugar and vinegar, stir, cover and cook on Low for 2 hours
Divide into small jars and serve cold.
Enjoy!

Nutrition:

calories 102, fat 2, fiber 1, carbs 2, protein 4

Apple Cake

Preparation time: 10 minutes
Cooking time: 2 hours and 30 minutes
Servings: 6

Ingredients:

3 cups apples, cored and cubed
3 tablespoons stevia
1 tablespoon vanilla extract
2 eggs
1 tablespoon apple pie spice
2 cups coconut flour
1 tablespoon baking powder
1 tablespoon ghee

Directions:

In a bowl mix eggs with ghee, apple pie spice, vanilla, apples and stevia and stir using your mixer.
In another bowl, mix baking powder with flour, stir, add to apple mix, stir again well and transfer to your slow cooker.
Cover, cook on High for 2 hours and 30 minutes, and leave cake aside to cool down, slice and serve.
Enjoy!

Nutrition:

calories 130, fat 2, fiber 1, carbs 2, protein 4

Conclusion

The book you are holding in your hands is an ultimate guide to tasty and healthy Paleo slow cooking. Making the meals of your own is a piece of cake now. If you already tried some of these recipes and even picked some new must-haves then you know for sure that the Paleo diet can be tasty! Create fuss-free Paleo-friendly meals every day, because it's easy and this cookbook knows how to do it.

Quick and nutritive recipes for weekdays, yummy and crave-worthy ideas for weekends – this cookbook is an essential collection of all the Paleo and Slow Cooker recipes you might ever need. From the best home breakfasts through hearty main dishes to Paleo-friendly desserts this cookbook will take you on a cooking journey to the best diet you have ever tried.

Become one step closer to the cooking perfection you dream about. Cook your best wholesome dishes without being involved in the process, make your prep and cleanup a breeze and finally enjoy your Paleo diet with all the creative meals this cookbook has to offer.

Printed in Great Britain
by Amazon

27264809R00079